Cram101 Textbook Outlines to accompany:

Business Law: Text

Kenneth W. Clarkson, 11th Edition

A Cram101 Inc. publication (c) 2010.

Learning System

Cram101 Textbook Outlines is a learning system. The notes in this book are the highlights of your textbook, you will never have to highlight a book again.

How to use this book. Take this book to class, it is your notebook for the lecture. The notes and highlights on the left hand side of the pages follow the outline and order of the textbook. All you have to do is follow along while your instructor presents the lecture. Circle the items emphasized in class and add other important information on the right side. With Cram101 Textbook Outlines you'll spend less time writing and more time listening. Learning becomes more efficient.

Cram101.com Online

Increase your studying efficiency by using Cram101.com's practice tests and online reference material. It is the perfect complement to Cram101 Textbook Outlines. Use self-teaching matching tests or simulate in-class testing with comprehensive multiple choice tests, or simply use Cram's true and false tests for quick review. Cram101.com even allows you to enter your in-class notes for an integrated studying format combining the textbook notes with your class notes.

Visit **www.Cram101.com**, click Sign Up at the top of the screen, and enter **DK73DW7995** in the promo code box on the registration screen. Access to www.Cram101.com is normally $9.95 per month, but because you have purchased this book, your access fee is only $4.95 per month. Sign up and stop highlighting textbooks forever.

 ISBN(s): 9781616544188. EDR-2.20091229

Business Law: Text
Kenneth W. Clarkson, 11th

CONTENTS

Business Law: Text
Kenneth W. Clarkson, 11th

CONTENTS (continued)

Chapter 1. Introduction to Law and Legal Reasoning

Contract

Agreement is said to be reached when an offer capable of immediate acceptance is met with a "mirror image" acceptance (ie, an unqualified acceptance). The parties must have the necessary capacity to Contract and the Contract must not be either trifling, indeterminate, impossible or illegal. Contract law is based on the principle expressed in the Latin phrase pacta sunt servanda .

Statute

A statute is a formal written enactment of a legislative authority that governs a country, state, city, or county. Typically, statute s command or prohibit something, or declare policy. The word is often used to distinguish law made by legislative bodies from case law and the regulations issued by Government agencies.

Uniform Commercial Code

The Uniform Commercial Code is one of a number of uniform acts that have been promulgated in conjunction with efforts to harmonize the law of sales and other commercial transactions in all 50 states within the United States of America. This objective is deemed important because of the prevalence today of commercial transactions that extend beyond one state (for example, where the goods are manufactured in state A, warehoused in state B, sold from state C and delivered in state D.) The Uniform Commercial Code deals primarily with transactions involving personal property (movable property), not real property (immovable property.)

Supreme Court

A supreme court is in some jurisdictions the highest judicial body within that jurisdiction"s court system, whose rulings are not subject to further review by another court. The designations for such courts differ among jurisdictions. Courts of last resort typically function primarily as appellate courts, hearing appeals from the lower trial courts or intermediate-level appellate courts.

United States

- History of competition law
- Monopoly
    - Coercive monopoly
    - Natural monopoly
    - Barriers to entry
    - Market power
    - SSNIP test
    - Relevant market
    - Merger control

Anti-competitive practices

- Monopolization
- Collusion

- Formation of cartels
- Price fixing
- Bid rigging
- Product bundling and tying
- Refusal to deal

· Group boycott
· Exclusive dealing
· Dividing territories
· Conscious parallelism
· Predatory pricing
· Misuse of patents and copyrights

Laws and doctrines

United States

· Sherman Antitrust Act
· Clayton Antitrust Act
· Robinson-Patman Act
· FTC Act
· Hart-Scott-Rodino Act
· Merger guidelines
· Essential facilities doctrine
· Noerr-Pennington doctrine
· Parker immunity doctrine
· Rule of reason

Europe

· UK competition law
· Irish competition law

Australia

· Trade Practices Act 1974

Enforcement authorities and organizations

Competition law history refers to attempts by governments to regulate competitive markets for goods and services, leading up to the modern competition or antitrust laws around the world today. The earliest records traces back to the efforts of Roman legislators to control price fluctuations and unfair trade practices. Through the Middle Ages in Europe, Kings and Queens repeatedly cracked down on monopolies, including those created through state legislation.

· International Competition Network
· List of competition regulators

Business

There are many ways in which a business may be owned under the legal system of England and Wales. Different types of ownership are suitable for organisations depending on the degree of control the owners wish to have over the business. The choice of ownership methor also relates to the organisations ability to raise funds for the business activities.

Lease	A Lease is a contract conferring a right on one person to possess property belonging to another person (called a landlord or lessor) to the exclusion of the owner landlord, and all others except with the invitation of the tenant. It is a rental agreement between landlord and tenant. The relationship between the tenant and the landlord is called a tenancy, and the right to possession by the tenant is sometimes called a Leasehold interest.
Arbitration	Arbitration, a form of alternative dispute resolution (ADR), is a legal technique for the resolution of disputes outside the courts, wherein the parties to a dispute refer it to one or more persons (the "arbitrators", "arbiters" or "arbitral tribunal"), by whose decision (the "award") they agree to be bound. It is a settlement technique in which a third party reviews the case and imposes a decision that is legally binding for both sides. Other forms of ADR include mediation (a form of settlement negotiation facilitated by a neutral third party) and non-binding resolution by experts.
Constitution	· Apostolic Constitution (a class of Roman Catholic Church documents) · Constitution of the Roman Republic · Constitutional court · Constitutionalism · Corporate Constitution · Judicial activism · Judicial restraint · Judicial review Judicial philosophies of Constitutional interpretation (note: generally specific to United States Constitutional law) · List of national Constitutions · Originalism · Strict constructionism · Textualism · Proposed European Union Constitution · Treaty of Lisbon (adopts same changes, but without Constitutional name) · United Nations Charter
Negotiable Instrument	A Negotiable instrument is a specialized type of "contract" for the payment of money that is unconditional and capable of transfer by negotiation. Common examples include cheques, banknotes (paper money), and commercial paper. A Negotiable instrument is not a contract, as contract formation requires an offer, acceptance, and consideration, none of which is an element of a Negotiable instrument.
Restatements of the Law	The Restatements of the Law are treatises on U.S. legal topics published by the American Law Institute, an organization of legal academics and practitioners, as scholarly refinements of black-letter law, to "address uncertainty in the law through a restatement of basic legal subjects that would tell judges and lawyers what the law was."

As Harvard Law School describes the Restatements:

> The ALI"s aim is to distill the "black letter law" from cases, to indicate a trend in common law, and, occasionally, to recommend what a rule of law should be. In essence, they restate existing common law into a series of principles or rules.

While considered secondary authority (compare to primary authority), the authoritativeness of the Restatements of the Law is evidenced by their acceptance by courts throughout the United States.

Statutory law

Statutory law or statute law is written law (as opposed to oral or customary law) set down by a legislature (as opposed to regulatory law promulgated by the executive branch or common law of the judiciary.) Statutes are enacted in response to a perceived need to clarify the functioning of government, improve civil order, to codify existing law, or for an individual or company to obtain special treatment. Examples of statutory law comprehend traditional civil law and modern civil code systems in contrast to common law.

Tort

Tort law is a body of law that addresses, and provides remedies for, civil wrongs not arising out of contractual obligations. A person who suffers legal damages may be able to use Tort law to receive compensation from someone who is legally responsible, or "liable," for those injuries. Generally speaking, Tort law defines what constitutes a legal injury and establishes the circumstances under which one person may be held liable for another"s injury.

Chief brand officer

A Chief brand officer is a relatively new executive level position at a corporation, company, organization typically reporting directly to the CEO or board of directors. The Chief brand officer is responsible for a brand"s image, experience, and promise, and propagating it throughout all aspects of the company. The brand officer oversees marketing, advertising, design, public relations and customer service departments.

Bankruptcy

Bankruptcy is a legally declared inability or impairment of ability of an individual or organization to pay its creditors. Creditors may file a Bankruptcy petition against a debtor ("involuntary Bankruptcy") in an effort to recoup a portion of what they are owed or initiate a restructuring. In the majority of cases, however, Bankruptcy is initiated by the debtor (a "voluntary Bankruptcy" that is filed by the insolvent individual or organization).

United Nations Convention on Contracts for the International Sale of Goods

The United Nations Convention on Contracts for the International Sale of Goods is a treaty offering a uniform international sales law that, as of July 2008, had been ratified by 71 countries that account for a significant proportion of world trade, making it one of the most successful international uniform laws. Japan is the most recent State to have ratified the Convention.

It allows exporters to avoid choice of law issues as it offers "accepted substantive rules on which contracting parties, courts, and arbitrators may rely".

Federal Trade Commission	The Federal Trade Commission is an independent agency of the United States government, established in 1914 by the Federal Trade Commission Act. Its principal mission is the promotion of "consumer protection" and the elimination and prevention of what regulators perceive to be harmfully "anti-competitive" business practices, such as coercive monopoly. The Federal Trade Commission Act was one of President Wilson"s major acts against trusts.
Liquidation	In law, Liquidation refers to the process by which a company (or part of a company) is brought to an end, and the assets and property of the company redistributed. Liquidation can also be referred to as winding-up or dissolution, although dissolution technically refers to the last stage of Liquidation. The process of Liquidation also arises when customs, an authority or agency in a country responsible for collecting and safeguarding customs duties, determines the final computation or ascertainment of the duties or drawback accruing on an entry.
Securities and Exchange Commission	The U.S. Securities and Exchange Commission is an independent agency of the United States government which holds primary responsibility for enforcing the federal securities laws and regulating the securities industry, the nation"s stock and options exchanges, and other electronic securities markets. The SEC was created by section 4 of the Securities Exchange Act of 1934 (now codified as 15 U.S.C. Â§ 78d and commonly referred to as the 1934 Act.)
Regulatory	Regulation refers to "controlling human or societal behaviour by rules or restrictions." Regulation can take many forms: legal restrictions promulgated by a government authority, self-regulation, social regulation (e.g. norms), co-regulation and market regulation. One can consider regulation as actions of conduct imposing sanctions (such as a fine.) This action of administrative law, or implementing regulatory law, may be contrasted with statutory or case law.
Damages	Damages for breach of contract is a common law remedy, available as of right. It is designed to compensate the victim for their actual loss as a result of the wrongdoer"s breach rather than to punish the wrongdoer. If no loss has been occasioned by the plaintiff, only nominal Damages will be awarded.
Rescission	In contract law, rescission has been defined as the unmaking of a contract between parties. rescission is the unwinding of a transaction. This is done to bring the parties, as far as possible, back to the position in which they were before they entered into a contract (the "status quo ante".)
Specific performance	In the law of Remedy, an order of specific performance is an order of the court which requires a party to perform a specific act, usually what is stated in a contract. While specific performance can be in the form of any type of forced action, it is usually used to complete a previously established transaction, thus being the most effective remedy in protecting the expectation interest of the innocent party to a contract. It is usually the opposite of a prohibitory injunction but there are mandatory injunctions which have a similar effect to specific performance.
Petition	A petition is a request to change something, most commonly made to a government official or public entity. petition s to a deity are a form of prayer.

In the colloquial sense, a petition is a document addressed to some official and signed by numerous individuals.

Petitioner

A Petitioner is a person who pleads with a governmental institution for a legal remedy or a redress of grievances.
The Petitioner may seek a legal remedy if the state or another private person has acted unlawfully. In this case, the Petitioner, often called a plaintiff, will submit a plea to a court to resolve the dispute.

Plaintiff

A plaintiff is the party who initiates a lawsuit before a court. By doing so, the plaintiff seeks a legal remedy, and if successful, the court will issue judgment in favor of the plaintiff and make the appropriate court order
In some jurisdictions the commencement of a lawsuit is done by filing a summons, claim form and/or a complaint -- these documents are known as pleadings -- that set forth the alleged wrongs committed by the defendant or defendants with a demand for relief.

Star

The STAR (Situation, Task, Action, Result) format is a job interview technique used by interviewers to gather all the relevant information about a specific capability that the job requires. This interview format is said to have a higher degree of predictability of future on-the-job performance than the traditional interview.

· Situation: The interviewer wants you to present a recent challenge and situation in which you found yourself.
· Task: What did you have to achieve? The interviewer will be looking to see what you were trying to achieve from the situation.
· Action: What did you do? The interviewer will be looking for information on what you did, why you did it and what were the alternatives.
· Results: What was the outcome of your actions? What did you achieve through your actions and did you meet your objectives. What did you learn from this experience and have you used this learning since? .

Stare decisis

Stare decisis is the legal principle under which judges are obligated to follow the precedents established in prior decisions.
In the United States, which uses a common law system in its federal courts and most of its state courts, the Ninth Circuit Court of Appeals has stated:
Stare decisis is the policy of the court to stand by precedent; the term is but an abbreviation of Stare decisis et quieta non movere -- "to stand by and adhere to decisions and not disturb what is settled." Consider the word "decisis." The word means, literally and legally, the decision. Nor is the doctrine stare dictis; it is not "to stand by or keep to what was said." Nor is the doctrine stare rationibus decidendi -- "to keep to the rationes decidendi of past cases." Rather, under the doctrine of Stare decisis a case is important only for what it decides -- for the "what," not for the "why," and not for the "how." Insofar as precedent is concerned, Stare decisis is important only for the decision, for the detailed legal consequence following a detailed set of facts.

Statute of limitations	A statute of limitations is a statute in a common law legal system that sets forth the maximum period of time, after certain events, that legal proceedings based on those events may be initiated. In civil law systems, similar provisions are usually part of the civil code or criminal code and are often known collectively as "periods of prescription" or "prescriptive periods." A common law legal system might have a statute limiting the time for prosecution of crimes called misdemeanors to two years after the offense occurred. In that statute, if a person is discovered to have committed a misdemeanor three years ago, the time has expired for the prosecution of the misdemeanor.
Precedent	In common law legal systems, a Precedent or authority is a legal case establishing a principle or rule that a court or other judicial body utilizes when deciding subsequent cases with similar issues or facts. The Precedent on an issue is the collective body of judicially announced principles that a court should consider when interpreting the law. When a Precedent establishes an important legal principle, or represents a new or changed law on a particular issue, that Precedent is often known as a landmark decision.
Public policy	Public policy can be generally defined as the course of action or inaction taken by governmental entities with regard to a particular issue or set of issues. Other scholars define it as a system of "courses of action, regulatory measures, laws, and funding priorities concerning a given topic promulgated by a governmental entity or its representatives." public policy is commonly embodied "in constitutions, legislative acts, and judicial decisions." In the United States, this concept refers not only to the end result of policies, but more broadly to the decision-making and analysis of governmental decisions. public policy is also considered an academic discipline, as it is studied by professors and students at public policy schools of major universities throughout the country.
Terrorism	Terrorism is a policy or ideology of violence intended to intimidate or cause terror for the purpose of "exerting pressure on decision making by state bodies." The term "terror" is largely used to indicate clandestine, low-intensity violence that targets civilians and generates public fear. Thus "terror" is distinct from asymmetric warfare, and violates the concept of a common law of war in which civilian life is regarded. The term "-ism" is used to indicate an ideology --typically one that claims its attacks are in the domain of a "just war" concept, though most condemn such as crimes against humanity.
State court	In the United States, a state court has jurisdiction over disputes with some connection to a U.S. state. Cases are heard before and evidence is presented in a trial court, which is usually located in a courthouse in the county seat. Territory outside of any state in the United States, such as the District of Columbia or American Samoa, often have courts established under federal or territorial law which substitute for a state court system, distinct from the ordinary federal court system.
Trial	In law, a trial is when parties come together to a dispute present information (in the form of evidence) in a formal setting, usually a court, before a judge, jury in order to achieve a resolution to their dispute.

· Where the trial is held before a group of members of the community, it is called a jury trial
· Where the trial is held solely before a judge, it is called a bench trial Bench trial s involve fewer formalities, and are typically resolved faster. Furthermore, a favorable ruling for one party in a bench trial will frequently lead the other party to offer a settlement.

Hearings before administrative bodies may have many of the features of a trial before a court, but are typically not referred to as trial s.

An appellate proceeding is also generally not deemed a trial because such proceedings are usually restricted to review of the evidence presented before the trial court, and do not permit the introduction of new evidences.

trial s can also be divided by the type of dispute at issue.

Trial court

A Trial court or court of first instance is a court in which trials take place.

A Trial court of general jurisdiction is authorized to hear any type of civil or criminal case that is not committed exclusively to another court. In the United States, the United States district courts are the Trial court s of general jurisdiction of the federal judiciary; each U.S. state has a state court systems establishing Trial court s of general jurisdiction, such as the Florida Circuit Courts in Florida, the Superior Courts of California in California, and the New York Supreme Court in New York.

United States Code

The United States Code is a compilation and codification of the general and permanent federal law of the United States. It contains 50 titles and is published every six years by the Office of the Law Revision Counsel of the US House of Representatives.

The official text of an Act of Congress is that of the "enrolled bill" (traditionally printed on parchment) presented to the President for his signature or disapproval.

United States Statutes at Large

The United States Statutes at Large, commonly referred to as the Statutes at Large and abbreviated Stat., is the official source for the laws and resolutions passed by United States Congress.

The Statutes at Large are generically referred to as the "session laws" of the Congress. They are part of a three-part model for publication of Federal statutes consisting of (1) slip laws, (2) session laws, and (3) codification.

United States Reports

The United States Reports are the official record of the rulings, orders, case tables, and other proceedings of the Supreme Court of the United States. Opinions of the court in each case, prepended with a headnote prepared by the Reporter of Decisions, and any concurring or dissenting opinions are published sequentially. The Court"s Publication Office oversees the binding and publication of the volumes of United States Reports, although the actual printing, binding, and publication is performed by private firms under contract with the United States Government Printing Office.

Constitution

- Apostolic Constitution (a class of Roman Catholic Church documents)
- Constitution of the Roman Republic
- Constitutional court
- Constitutionalism
- Corporate Constitution
- Judicial activism
- Judicial restraint
- Judicial review

Judicial philosophies of Constitutional interpretation (note: generally specific to United States Constitutional law)

- List of national Constitutions
- Originalism
- Strict constructionism
- Textualism
- Proposed European Union Constitution

- Treaty of Lisbon (adopts same changes, but without Constitutional name)
- United Nations Charter

Supreme Court

A supreme court is in some jurisdictions the highest judicial body within that jurisdiction"s court system, whose rulings are not subject to further review by another court. The designations for such courts differ among jurisdictions. Courts of last resort typically function primarily as appellate courts, hearing appeals from the lower trial courts or intermediate-level appellate courts.

United States

- History of competition law
- Monopoly
  - Coercive monopoly
  - Natural monopoly
  - Barriers to entry
  - Market power
  - SSNIP test
  - Relevant market
  - Merger control

Anti-competitive practices

- Monopolization
- Collusion

· Formation of cartels
· Price fixing
· Bid rigging
· Product bundling and tying
· Refusal to deal

· Group boycott
· Exclusive dealing
· Dividing territories
· Conscious parallelism
· Predatory pricing
· Misuse of patents and copyrights

Laws and doctrines

United States

· Sherman Antitrust Act
· Clayton Antitrust Act
· Robinson-Patman Act
· FTC Act
· Hart-Scott-Rodino Act
· Merger guidelines
· Essential facilities doctrine
· Noerr-Pennington doctrine
· Parker immunity doctrine
· Rule of reason

Europe

· UK competition law
· Irish competition law

Australia

· Trade Practices Act 1974

Enforcement authorities and organizations

Competition law history refers to attempts by governments to regulate competitive markets for goods and services, leading up to the modern competition or antitrust laws around the world today. The earliest records traces back to the efforts of Roman legislators to control price fluctuations and unfair trade practices. Through the Middle Ages in Europe, Kings and Queens repeatedly cracked down on monopolies, including those created through state legislation.

· International Competition Network
· List of competition regulators

Business | There are many ways in which a business may be owned under the legal system of England and Wales.

Different types of ownership are suitable for organisations depending on the degree of control the owners wish to have over the business. The choice of ownership methor also relates to the organisations ability to raise funds for the business activities.

State court

In the United States, a state court has jurisdiction over disputes with some connection to a U.S. state. Cases are heard before and evidence is presented in a trial court, which is usually located in a courthouse in the county seat. Territory outside of any state in the United States, such as the District of Columbia or American Samoa, often have courts established under federal or territorial law which substitute for a state court system, distinct from the ordinary federal court system.

Statute

A statute is a formal written enactment of a legislative authority that governs a country, state, city, or county. Typically, statute s command or prohibit something, or declare policy. The word is often used to distinguish law made by legislative bodies from case law and the regulations issued by Government agencies.

Arbitration

Arbitration, a form of alternative dispute resolution (ADR), is a legal technique for the resolution of disputes outside the courts, wherein the parties to a dispute refer it to one or more persons (the "arbitrators", "arbiters" or "arbitral tribunal"), by whose decision (the "award") they agree to be bound. It is a settlement technique in which a third party reviews the case and imposes a decision that is legally binding for both sides. Other forms of ADR include mediation (a form of settlement negotiation facilitated by a neutral third party) and non-binding resolution by experts.

Bankruptcy

Bankruptcy is a legally declared inability or impairment of ability of an individual or organization to pay its creditors. Creditors may file a Bankruptcy petition against a debtor ("involuntary Bankruptcy") in an effort to recoup a portion of what they are owed or initiate a restructuring. In the majority of cases, however, Bankruptcy is initiated by the debtor (a "voluntary Bankruptcy" that is filed by the insolvent individual or organization).

Original

Original ity is the aspect of created or invented works by as being new or novel, and thus can be distinguished from reproductions, clones, forgeries, or derivative works. An original work is one not received from others nor one copied based on the work of others. The term " original ity" is often applied as a compliment to the creativity of artists, writers, and thinkers.

Probate

Probate is the legal process of administering the estate of a deceased person by resolving all claims and distributing the deceased person"s property under the valid will. A surrogate court decides the validity of a testator"s will. A probate interprets the instructions of the deceased, decides the executor as the personal representative of the estate, and adjudicates the interests of heirs and other parties who may have claims against the estate.

Probate Court

A surrogate court, sometimes referred to as probate Court, is a specialized court which deals with matters of probate and the administration of estates. It adjudicates in cases to do with the distribution of deceased persons" estates. The surrogate court issues the grant of probate or, if a person dies intestate, a grant of administration, thereby giving judicial approval to the personal representative to administer matters of the estate.

Question of fact	In law, a Question of fact is a question which must be answered by reference to facts and evidence, and inferences arising from those facts. Such a question is distinct from a question of law, which must be answered by applying relevant legal principles. The answer to a Question of fact is usually dependent on particular circumstances or factual situations.
Trial	In law, a trial is when parties come together to a dispute present information (in the form of evidence) in a formal setting, usually a court, before a judge, jury in order to achieve a resolution to their dispute. · Where the trial is held before a group of members of the community, it is called a jury trial · Where the trial is held solely before a judge, it is called a bench trial Bench trial s involve fewer formalities, and are typically resolved faster. Furthermore, a favorable ruling for one party in a bench trial will frequently lead the other party to offer a settlement. Hearings before administrative bodies may have many of the features of a trial before a court, but are typically not referred to as trial s. An appellate proceeding is also generally not deemed a trial because such proceedings are usually restricted to review of the evidence presented before the trial court, and do not permit the introduction of new evidences. trial s can also be divided by the type of dispute at issue.
Trial court	A Trial court or court of first instance is a court in which trials take place. A Trial court of general jurisdiction is authorized to hear any type of civil or criminal case that is not committed exclusively to another court. In the United States, the United States district courts are the Trial court s of general jurisdiction of the federal judiciary; each U.S. state has a state court systems establishing Trial court s of general jurisdiction, such as the Florida Circuit Courts in Florida, the Superior Courts of California in California, and the New York Supreme Court in New York.
Precedent	In common law legal systems, a Precedent or authority is a legal case establishing a principle or rule that a court or other judicial body utilizes when deciding subsequent cases with similar issues or facts. The Precedent on an issue is the collective body of judicially announced principles that a court should consider when interpreting the law. When a Precedent establishes an important legal principle, or represents a new or changed law on a particular issue, that Precedent is often known as a landmark decision.
Contract	Agreement is said to be reached when an offer capable of immediate acceptance is met with a "mirror image" acceptance (ie, an unqualified acceptance). The parties must have the necessary capacity to Contract and the Contract must not be either trifling, indeterminate, impossible or illegal. Contract law is based on the principle expressed in the Latin phrase pacta sunt servanda .
Writ	In law, a writ is a formal writ ten order issued by a body with administrative or judicial jurisdiction; in modern usage, this public body is generally a court. Warrants, prerogative writ s and subpoenas are types of writ s; there are many others.

	Originally, a writ was a letter or command from the Sovereign, or from some person with appropriate jurisdiction.
Writ of attachment	A Writ of attachment is a court order to "attach" or seize an asset. It is issued by a court to a law enforcement officer or sheriff. The Writ of attachment is issued in order to satisfy a judgment issued by the court.
Petition	A petition is a request to change something, most commonly made to a government official or public entity. petition s to a deity are a form of prayer. In the colloquial sense, a petition is a document addressed to some official and signed by numerous individuals.
Rule of four	The rule of four is a Supreme Court of the United States practice that permits four of the nine justices to grant a writ of certiorari. This is done specifically to prevent a majority of the court from controlling all the cases it agrees to hear. The rule of four is not required by the Constitution, any law, or even the Supreme Court"s own published rules .
Federal Arbitration Act	In United States law, the Federal Arbitration Act is a statute that provides for judicial facilitation of private dispute resolution through arbitration. It applies in both state courts and federal courts, as was held in Southland v. Keating (although several Justices of the Supreme Court have admitted that Southland was wrongly decided and they would be willing to overrule it). It applies where the transaction contemplated by the parties "involves" interstate commerce and is predicated on an exercise of the "Commerce Clause" powers given to Congress in the U.S. Constitution.
Lease	A Lease is a contract conferring a right on one person to possess property belonging to another person (called a landlord or lessor) to the exclusion of the owner landlord, and all others except with the invitation of the tenant. It is a rental agreement between landlord and tenant. The relationship between the tenant and the landlord is called a tenancy, and the right to possession by the tenant is sometimes called a Leasehold interest.
Arbitration clause	An Arbitration clause is a commonly used clause in a contract that requires the parties to resolve their disputes through an arbitration process. Although such a clause may or may not specify that arbitration occur within a specific jurisdiction, it always binds the parties to a type of resolution outside of the courts, and is therefore considered a kind of forum selection clause. In the United States, the federal government has expressed a policy of support of Arbitration clauses, because they reduce the burden on court systems to resolve disputes.
Employment	Employment is a contract between two parties, one being the employer and the other being the employee. An employee may be defined as: "A person in the service of another under any contract of hire, express or implied, oral or written, where the employer has the power or right to control and direct the employee in the material details of how the work is to be performed." Black"s Law Dictionary page 471 (5th ed. 1979).

Mandatory arbitration	Mandatory arbitration is a contract term that prevents a conflict from receiving judicial attention. In a Mandatory arbitration, as mandated in the contract, liability for damages must be determined as a result of an arbitration process before a civil lawsuit can be filed in the court system. In arbitration, neutral arbitrators (often knowledgeable practicing attorneys) are selected and then evidence is presented.
Evaluation	Evaluation is systematic determination of merit, worth, and significance of something or someone using criteria against a set of standards. Evaluation often is used to characterize and appraise subjects of interest in a wide range of human enterprises, including the arts, criminal justice, foundations and non-profit organizations, government, health care, and other human services. Depending on the topic of interest, there are professional groups which look to the quality and rigor of the Evaluation process.
Service provider	A service provider is an entity that provides services to other entities. Usually this refers to a business that provides subscription or web service to other businesses or individuals. Examples of these services include Internet access, Mobile phone operator, and web application hosting.
Online dispute resolution	Online dispute resolution is a branch of dispute resolution which uses technology to facilitate the resolution of disputes between parties. It primarily involves negotiation, mediation or arbitration, or a combination of all three. In this respect it is often seen as being the online equivalent of alternative dispute resolution (ADR.)
Parol evidence	The Parol evidence rule is the legal application of a rule of substantive law in contract cases that prevents a party to a written contract from contradicting (or sometimes adding to) the terms of the contract by seeking the admission of evidence "extrinsic" (outside) to the contract. For example, Carl agrees in writing to sell Betty a car for $1,000. Betty argues that Carl told her that she would only need to pay Carl $800.
Parol evidence rule	The Parol evidence rule is the legal application of a rule of substantive law in contract cases that prevents a party to a written contract from contradicting (or sometimes adding to) the terms of the contract by seeking the admission of evidence "extrinsic" (outside) to the contract. For example, Carl agrees in writing to sell Betty a car for $1,000. Betty argues that Carl told her that she would only need to pay Carl $800.
Sale of Goods	The sale of goods Act 1979 (c.54) is an Act of the Parliament of the United Kingdom which regulates contracts in which goods are sold and bought. The Act consolidates the sale of goods Act 1893 and subsequent legislation, which in turn consolidated the previous common law. The sale of goods Act performs several functions.
Statute of Frauds	The Statute of Frauds refers to the requirement that certain kinds of contracts be made in writing and signed. Traditionally, the Statute of Frauds requires a writing signed by the defendant in the following circumstances:

· Contracts in consideration of marriage.
· Contracts which cannot be performed within one year.
· Contracts for the transfer of an interest in land.
· Contracts by the executor of a will to pay a debt of the estate with their own money.
· Contracts for the sale of goods above a certain value.
· Contracts in which one party becomes a surety (acts as guarantor) for another party"s debt or other obligation.

This can be remembered by the mnemonic "MY LEGS": Marriage, one year, land, executor, goods, surety.

The term Statute of Frauds comes from an English Act of Parliament passed in 1677 (authored by Sir Leoline Jenkins and passed by the Cavalier Parliament), and more properly called An Act for Prevention of Frauds and Perjuries. Many common law jurisdictions have made similar statutory provisions, while a number of civil law jurisdictions have equivalent legislation incorporated into their civil codes.

Consideration

Consideration is the legal concept of value in connection with contracts. It is anything of value in the common sense, promised to another when making a contract. It can take the form of money, physical objects, services, promised actions, or even abstinence from a future action.

International Arbitration

International arbitration is the established method for resolving disputes between parties to international commercial agreements. As with arbitration generally, it is a creature of contract, i.e., the parties" decision to submit any disputes to private adjudication by one or more arbitrators appointed in accordance with rules the parties themselves have agreed to adopt, usually by including a provision for the same in their contract. The practice of International arbitration has developed so as to allow parties from different legal and cultural backgrounds to resolve their disputes, generally without the formalities of their underlying legal systems.

Plaintiff

A plaintiff is the party who initiates a lawsuit before a court. By doing so, the plaintiff seeks a legal remedy, and if successful, the court will issue judgment in favor of the plaintiff and make the appropriate court order

In some jurisdictions the commencement of a lawsuit is done by filing a summons, claim form and/or a complaint -- these documents are known as pleadings -- that set forth the alleged wrongs committed by the defendant or defendants with a demand for relief.

Trial

In law, a trial is when parties come together to a dispute present information (in the form of evidence) in a formal setting, usually a court, before a judge, jury in order to achieve a resolution to their dispute.

· Where the trial is held before a group of members of the community, it is called a jury trial
· Where the trial is held solely before a judge, it is called a bench trial Bench trial s involve fewer formalities, and are typically resolved faster. Furthermore, a favorable ruling for one party in a bench trial will frequently lead the other party to offer a settlement.

Hearings before administrative bodies may have many of the features of a trial before a court, but are typically not referred to as trial s.

An appellate proceeding is also generally not deemed a trial because such proceedings are usually restricted to review of the evidence presented before the trial court, and do not permit the introduction of new evidences.

trial s can also be divided by the type of dispute at issue.

Service of process

Service of process is the procedure employed to give legal notice to a person (such as a defendant) of a court or administrative body"s exercise of its jurisdiction over that person so as to enable that person to respond to the proceeding before the court, body or other tribunal. Usually, notice is furnished by delivering a set of court documents (called "process") to the person to be served.

Each jurisdiction has rules regarding the means of Service of process.

Summons

A Summons is a legal document issued by a court (a judicial Summons) or by an administrative agency of government (an administrative Summons) for various purposes.

A judicial Summons is addressed to a defendant in a legal proceeding. Typically, the Summons will announce to the person to whom it is directed that a legal proceeding has been started against that person, and that a file has been started in the court records.

Registered agent

In the US, a Registered agent is a business or individual designated to receive service of process (SOP) when a business entity is a party in a legal action such as a lawsuit or summons. In some states the agent is also referred to as a resident agent or statutory agent, but most states have changed their statutes and now call this function "Registered agent". The Registered agent for a business entity may be an individual member of the company, or (more often) a third party, such as the organization"s lawyer or a service company.

Waiver

A waiver is the voluntary relinquishment or surrender of some known right or privilege.

While a waiver is often in writing, sometimes a person"s actions can act as a waiver. An example of a written waiver is a disclaimer, which becomes a waiver when accepted.

Real property

In the common law, real property refers to one of the three main classes of property, the other two classes being personal property and intellectual property. real property generally encompasses land, land improvements resulting from human effort including buildings and machinery sited on land, and various property rights over the preceding.

The concept is variously named and defined in other jurisdictions: heritable property in Scotland, immobilier in France, and immovable property in Canada, United States, India, Pakistan, Bangladesh, Malta, Cyprus, and in countries where civil law systems prevail, including most of Europe, Russia, and South America.

Statute

A statute is a formal written enactment of a legislative authority that governs a country, state, city, or county. Typically, statute s command or prohibit something, or declare policy. The word is often used to distinguish law made by legislative bodies from case law and the regulations issued by Government agencies.

Statute of Frauds

The Statute of Frauds refers to the requirement that certain kinds of contracts be made in writing and signed.

Traditionally, the Statute of Frauds requires a writing signed by the defendant in the following circumstances:

· Contracts in consideration of marriage.
· Contracts which cannot be performed within one year.
· Contracts for the transfer of an interest in land.
· Contracts by the executor of a will to pay a debt of the estate with their own money.
· Contracts for the sale of goods above a certain value.
· Contracts in which one party becomes a surety (acts as guarantor) for another party"s debt or other obligation.

This can be remembered by the mnemonic "MY LEGS": Marriage, one year, land, executor, goods, surety.

The term Statute of Frauds comes from an English Act of Parliament passed in 1677 (authored by Sir Leoline Jenkins and passed by the Cavalier Parliament), and more properly called An Act for Prevention of Frauds and Perjuries. Many common law jurisdictions have made similar statutory provisions, while a number of civil law jurisdictions have equivalent legislation incorporated into their civil codes.

Voir dire

Voir dire is a phrase in law which derives from Anglo-Norman.

· In origin it refers to an oath to tell the truth , in other words to give a true verdict. The word voir , in this context, is an old French word meaning "truth". It is unconnected with the modern French word voir, which derives from Latin vidÄ“re , though the expression is now often interpreted by false etymology to mean "to see [them] say".
· In the UK, Australia, New Zealand, Canada, and sometimes in the U.S. it refers to a "trial within a trial." It is a hearing to determine the admissibility of evidence, or the competency of a witness or juror.
· In the United States, it now generally refers to the process by which prospective jurors are questioned about their backgrounds and potential biases before being chosen to sit on a jury. It also refers to the process by which expert witnesses are questioned about their backgrounds and qualifications, in order to potentially give an expert opinion in court testimony. As defined by Gordon P. Cleary: "Voir dire is the process by which attorneys select, or perhaps more appropriately reject, certain jurors to hear a case." .

Rules of Evidence

Rules of evidence govern whether, when, how, and for what purpose proof of a case may be placed before a trier of fact for consideration.
In the legal systems of Canada and the United States, the trier of fact may be a judge or a jury, depending on the purpose of the trial and the choices of the parties.
The rules of evidence developed over several centuries and are based upon the rules from Anglo-American common Law brought to the New World by early settlers.

Opening Statement

An opening statement is generally the first occasion that the trier of fact (jury or judge) has to hear from a lawyer in a trial, aside possibly from questioning during voir dire. The opening statement is generally constructed to serve as a "road map" for the fact-finder. This is especially essential in jury trials, since jurors (at least theoretically) know nothing at all about the case before the trial, (or if they do, they are strictly instructed by the judge to put preconceived notions aside.)

Trial Court

A Trial court or court of first instance is a court in which trials take place.
A Trial court of general jurisdiction is authorized to hear any type of civil or criminal case that is not committed exclusively to another court. In the United States, the United States district courts are the Trial court s of general jurisdiction of the federal judiciary; each U.S. state has a state court systems establishing Trial court s of general jurisdiction, such as the Florida Circuit Courts in Florida, the Superior Courts of California in California, and the New York Supreme Court in New York.

Verdict

In law, a verdict is the formal finding of fact made by a jury on matters or questions submitted to the jury by a judge. (see Black"s Law Dictionary, p. 1398 (5th ed.

Parol evidence

The Parol evidence rule is the legal application of a rule of substantive law in contract cases that prevents a party to a written contract from contradicting (or sometimes adding to) the terms of the contract by seeking the admission of evidence "extrinsic" (outside) to the contract. For example, Carl agrees in writing to sell Betty a car for $1,000. Betty argues that Carl told her that she would only need to pay Carl $800.

Parol evidence rule	The Parol evidence rule is the legal application of a rule of substantive law in contract cases that prevents a party to a written contract from contradicting (or sometimes adding to) the terms of the contract by seeking the admission of evidence "extrinsic" (outside) to the contract. For example, Carl agrees in writing to sell Betty a car for $1,000. Betty argues that Carl told her that she would only need to pay Carl $800.
Arbitration	Arbitration, a form of alternative dispute resolution (ADR), is a legal technique for the resolution of disputes outside the courts, wherein the parties to a dispute refer it to one or more persons (the "arbitrators", "arbiters" or "arbitral tribunal"), by whose decision (the "award") they agree to be bound. It is a settlement technique in which a third party reviews the case and imposes a decision that is legally binding for both sides. Other forms of ADR include mediation (a form of settlement negotiation facilitated by a neutral third party) and non-binding resolution by experts.
Petition	A petition is a request to change something, most commonly made to a government official or public entity. petition s to a deity are a form of prayer. In the colloquial sense, a petition is a document addressed to some official and signed by numerous individuals.
Petitioner	A Petitioner is a person who pleads with a governmental institution for a legal remedy or a redress of grievances. The Petitioner may seek a legal remedy if the state or another private person has acted unlawfully. In this case, the Petitioner, often called a plaintiff, will submit a plea to a court to resolve the dispute.
State court	In the United States, a state court has jurisdiction over disputes with some connection to a U.S. state. Cases are heard before and evidence is presented in a trial court, which is usually located in a courthouse in the county seat. Territory outside of any state in the United States, such as the District of Columbia or American Samoa, often have courts established under federal or territorial law which substitute for a state court system, distinct from the ordinary federal court system.
Supreme Court	A supreme court is in some jurisdictions the highest judicial body within that jurisdiction"s court system, whose rulings are not subject to further review by another court. The designations for such courts differ among jurisdictions. Courts of last resort typically function primarily as appellate courts, hearing appeals from the lower trial courts or intermediate-level appellate courts.
United States	· History of competition law · Monopoly

- Coercive monopoly
- Natural monopoly
- Barriers to entry
- Market power
- SSNIP test
- Relevant market
- Merger control

Anti-competitive practices

- Monopolization
- Collusion

- Formation of cartels
- Price fixing
- Bid rigging
- Product bundling and tying
- Refusal to deal

- Group boycott
- Exclusive dealing
- Dividing territories
- Conscious parallelism
- Predatory pricing
- Misuse of patents and copyrights

Laws and doctrines

United States

- Sherman Antitrust Act
- Clayton Antitrust Act
- Robinson-Patman Act
- FTC Act
- Hart-Scott-Rodino Act
- Merger guidelines
- Essential facilities doctrine
- Noerr-Pennington doctrine
- Parker immunity doctrine
- Rule of reason

Europe

- UK competition law
- Irish competition law

Australia

· Trade Practices Act 1974

Enforcement authorities and organizations

Competition law history refers to attempts by governments to regulate competitive markets for goods and services, leading up to the modern competition or antitrust laws around the world today. The earliest records traces back to the efforts of Roman legislators to control price fluctuations and unfair trade practices. Through the Middle Ages in Europe, Kings and Queens repeatedly cracked down on monopolies, including those created through state legislation.

· International Competition Network
· List of competition regulators

Writ	In law, a writ is a formal writ ten order issued by a body with administrative or judicial jurisdiction; in modern usage, this public body is generally a court. Warrants, prerogative writ s and subpoenas are types of writ s; there are many others. Originally, a writ was a letter or command from the Sovereign, or from some person with appropriate jurisdiction.
Writ of attachment	A Writ of attachment is a court order to "attach" or seize an asset. It is issued by a court to a law enforcement officer or sheriff. The Writ of attachment is issued in order to satisfy a judgment issued by the court.

Constitution

· Apostolic Constitution (a class of Roman Catholic Church documents)
· Constitution of the Roman Republic
· Constitutional court
· Constitutionalism
· Corporate Constitution
· Judicial activism
· Judicial restraint
· Judicial review

Judicial philosophies of Constitutional interpretation (note: generally specific to United States Constitutional law)

· List of national Constitutions
· Originalism
· Strict constructionism
· Textualism
· Proposed European Union Constitution

· Treaty of Lisbon (adopts same changes, but without Constitutional name)
· United Nations Charter

Sexual harassment

Sexual harassment is unwelcome harassment of a sexual nature, or based upon the receiving party"s sex or gender. In some contexts or circumstances, Sexual harassment may be illegal. It includes a range of behavior from seemingly mild transgressions and annoyances to actual sexual abuse or sexual assault.

United States

· History of competition law
· Monopoly

  · Coercive monopoly
  · Natural monopoly
  · Barriers to entry
  · Market power
  · SSNIP test
  · Relevant market
  · Merger control

Anti-competitive practices

· Monopolization
· Collusion

Constitutional Authority to Regulate Business

Regulatory powers of the States -

State Regulatory powers - police powers

Delineating State + National powers

- Formation of cartels
- Price fixing
- Bid rigging
- Product bundling and tying
- Refusal to deal
  - Group boycott
  - Exclusive dealing
  - Dividing territories
  - Conscious parallelism
  - Predatory pricing
  - Misuse of patents and copyrights

Laws and doctrines

United States

- Sherman Antitrust Act
- Clayton Antitrust Act
- Robinson-Patman Act
- FTC Act
- Hart-Scott-Rodino Act
- Merger guidelines
- Essential facilities doctrine
- Noerr-Pennington doctrine
- Parker immunity doctrine
- Rule of reason

Europe

- UK competition law
- Irish competition law

Australia

- Trade Practices Act 1974

Enforcement authorities and organizations

Competition law history refers to attempts by governments to regulate competitive markets for goods and services, leading up to the modern competition or antitrust laws around the world today. The earliest records traces back to the efforts of Roman legislators to control price fluctuations and unfair trade practices. Through the Middle Ages in Europe, Kings and Queens repeatedly cracked down on monopolies, including those created through state legislation.

- International Competition Network
- List of competition regulators

Business | There are many ways in which a business may be owned under the legal system of England and Wales.

Different types of ownership are suitable for organisations depending on the degree of control the owners wish to have over the business. The choice of ownership methor also relates to the organisations ability to raise funds for the business activities.

Constitutional Court

The Constitutional Court of Belgium (Dutch: Â·), French: Cour constitutionelle, German: Verfassungsgerichtshof) plays a central role within the federal Belgian state. This is a judicial court founded in 1980. Its jurisdiction was augmented in 1988 and 2003.

Regulatory

Regulation refers to "controlling human or societal behaviour by rules or restrictions." Regulation can take many forms: legal restrictions promulgated by a government authority, self-regulation, social regulation (e.g. norms), co-regulation and market regulation. One can consider regulation as actions of conduct imposing sanctions (such as a fine.) This action of administrative law, or implementing regulatory law, may be contrasted with statutory or case law.

Privileges and immunities clause

The privileges and immunities clause (U.S The clause also embraces a right to travel, so that a citizen of one state can go and enjoy privileges and immunities in any other state. The text of the clause reads: The privileges and immunities clause is similar to a provision that was contained in the Articles of Confederation.

Chief brand officer

A Chief brand officer is a relatively new executive level position at a corporation, company, organization typically reporting directly to the CEO or board of directors. The Chief brand officer is responsible for a brand''s image, experience, and promise, and propagating it throughout all aspects of the company. The brand officer oversees marketing, advertising, design, public relations and customer service departments.

Supremacy clause

The Supremacy clause is a clause in the United States Constitution, article VI, paragraph 2. The clause establishes the Constitution, Federal Statutes, and U.S. treaties as "the supreme law of the land". The text establishes these as the highest form of law in the American legal system, mandating that state judges uphold them, even if state laws or constitutions conflict.

Freedom of contract

Freedom of contract or contractualism is the freedom of individuals to bargain among themselves the terms of their own contracts, without government interference. Anything more than minimal regulations and taxes may be seen as infringements. It is the underpinning of the theory of laissez-faire economics.

Misrepresentation

Misrepresentation is a contract law concept. It means a false statement of fact made by one party to another party, which has the effect of inducing that party into the contract. For example, under certain circumstances, false statements or promises made by a seller of goods regarding the quality or nature of the product that the seller has may constitute Misrepresentation.

Self-incrimination

Self-incrimination is the act of accusing oneself of a crime for which a person can then be prosecuted. self-incrimination can occur either directly or indirectly: directly, by means of interrogation where information of a self-incriminatory nature is disclosed; indirectly, when information of a self-incriminatory nature is disclosed voluntarily without pressure from another person.

The Fifth Amendment to the United States Constitution protects witnesses from being forced to incriminate themselves.

Guarantee

The act of becoming a surety is also called a Guarantee. Traditionally a Guarantee was distinguished from a surety in that the surety"s liability was joint and primary with the principal, whereas the guaranty"s liability was ancillary and derivative, but many jurisdictions have abolished this distinction

Trial

In law, a trial is when parties come together to a dispute present information (in the form of evidence) in a formal setting, usually a court, before a judge, jury in order to achieve a resolution to their dispute.

· Where the trial is held before a group of members of the community, it is called a jury trial

· Where the trial is held solely before a judge, it is called a bench trial Bench trial s involve fewer formalities, and are typically resolved faster. Furthermore, a favorable ruling for one party in a bench trial will frequently lead the other party to offer a settlement.

Hearings before administrative bodies may have many of the features of a trial before a court, but are typically not referred to as trial s.

An appellate proceeding is also generally not deemed a trial because such proceedings are usually restricted to review of the evidence presented before the trial court, and do not permit the introduction of new evidences.

trial s can also be divided by the type of dispute at issue.

License

The verb License or grant License means to give permission. The noun License refers to that permission as well as to the document memorializing that permission. License may be granted by a party to another party as an element of an agreement between those parties.

Statute

A statute is a formal written enactment of a legislative authority that governs a country, state, city, or county. Typically, statute s command or prohibit something, or declare policy. The word is often used to distinguish law made by legislative bodies from case law and the regulations issued by Government agencies.

Arbitration

Arbitration, a form of alternative dispute resolution (ADR), is a legal technique for the resolution of disputes outside the courts, wherein the parties to a dispute refer it to one or more persons (the "arbitrators", "arbiters" or "arbitral tribunal"), by whose decision (the "award") they agree to be bound. It is a settlement technique in which a third party reviews the case and imposes a decision that is legally binding for both sides. Other forms of ADR include mediation (a form of settlement negotiation facilitated by a neutral third party) and non-binding resolution by experts.

Pornography

Pornography or porn is the depiction of explicit sexual subject matter for the purpose of sexually exciting the viewer. Pornography makes no claim to artistic merit, unlike erotica which does.

Over the past few decades, an immense industry for the production and consumption of Pornography has grown, with the increasing use of the VCR, the DVD, and the Internet, as well as the emergence of social attitudes more tolerant of sexual portrayals.

Child labour	Child labour refers to the employment of children at regular and sustained labour. This practice is considered exploitative by many international organizations and is illegal in many countries. Child labour was utilized to varying extents through most of history, but entered public dispute with the advent of universal schooling, with changes in working conditions during the industrial revolution, and with the emergence of the concepts of workers" and children"s rights.
Probable cause	The right of the people to be secure in their persons, houses, papers, and effects, against unreasonable searches and seizures, shall not be violated, and no Warrants shall issue, but upon Probable cause, supported by Oath or affirmation, and particularly describing the place to be searched, and the persons or things to be seized. The most well-known definition of Probable cause is "a reasonable belief that a person has committed a crime". Another common definition is "a reasonable amount of suspicion, supported by circumstances sufficiently strong to justify a prudent and cautious person"s belief that certain facts are probably true".
Reasonable accommodation	Reasonable accommodation is a term used in Canada to refer to the theory that equality rights set out in section 15 of the Canadian Charter of Rights and Freedoms demand that accommodation be made to various ethnic minorities. The concept is especially applied with reference to the anti-discrimination laws in Québec"s Charter of Human Rights and Freedoms. (The origin of the term "Reasonable accommodation" is found in labour law jurisprudence, specifically Central Okanagan School District No.
Substantive Due process	Substantive due process is an aspect of American jurisprudence under the Due Process Clause, involving substantive unenumerated rights. Substantive due process is to be distinguished from procedural due process, which involves procedural unenumerated rights. The term "Substantive due process", is commonly used in two ways: first to identify a particular line of cases, and second to signify a particular attitude toward judicial review under the Due Process Clause.
Statute of limitations	A statute of limitations is a statute in a common law legal system that sets forth the maximum period of time, after certain events, that legal proceedings based on those events may be initiated. In civil law systems, similar provisions are usually part of the civil code or criminal code and are often known collectively as "periods of prescription" or "prescriptive periods." A common law legal system might have a statute limiting the time for prosecution of crimes called misdemeanors to two years after the offense occurred. In that statute, if a person is discovered to have committed a misdemeanor three years ago, the time has expired for the prosecution of the misdemeanor.

Strict scrutiny	Strict scrutiny is the most stringent standard of judicial review used by United States courts reviewing federal law. Along with the lower standards of rational basis review and intermediate scrutiny, Strict scrutiny is part of a hierarchy of standards courts employ to weigh an asserted government interest against a constitutional right or policy that conflicts with the manner in which the interest is being pursued. Strict scrutiny is applied based on the constitutional conflict at issue, regardless of whether a law or action of the U.S. federal government, a state government, or a local municipality is at issue.
Security Interest	A Security interest is a property interest created by agreement or by operation of law over assets to secure the performance of an obligation, usually the payment of a debt. It gives the beneficiary of the Security interest certain preferential rights in the disposition of secured assets. Such rights vary according to the type of Security interest, but in most cases, a holder of the Security interest is entitled to seize, and usually sell, the property to discharge the debt that the Security interest secures.
Privacy	Privacy is the ability of an individual or group to seclude themselves or information about themselves and thereby reveal themselves selectively. The boundaries and content of what is considered private differ among cultures and individuals, but share basic common themes. Privacy is sometimes related to anonymity, the wish to remain unnoticed or unidentified in the public realm.
Rational basis review	Rational basis review, in U.S. constitutional law, is the lowest level of scrutiny applied by courts deciding constitutional issues through judicial review. The higher levels are typically referred to as intermediate scrutiny and strict scrutiny. Although the default level of constitutional scrutiny, Rational basis review does not apply in situations where a suspect or quasi-suspect classification is involved, or a fundamental right is implicated.
USA Patriot Act	The USA Patriot Act, commonly known as the "Patriot Act", is a statute enacted by the United States Government that President George W. Bush signed into law on October 26, 2001. The contrived acronym stands for Uniting and Strengthening America by Providing Appropriate Tools Required to Intercept and Obstruct Terrorism Act of 2001 (Public Law Pub.L. 107-56.)
Terrorism	Terrorism is a policy or ideology of violence intended to intimidate or cause terror for the purpose of "exerting pressure on decision making by state bodies." The term "terror" is largely used to indicate clandestine, low-intensity violence that targets civilians and generates public fear. Thus "terror" is distinct from asymmetric warfare, and violates the concept of a common law of war in which civilian life is regarded. The term "-ism" is used to indicate an ideology --typically one that claims its attacks are in the domain of a "just war" concept, though most condemn such as crimes against humanity.
Federal Trade Commission	The Federal Trade Commission is an independent agency of the United States government, established in 1914 by the Federal Trade Commission Act. Its principal mission is the promotion of "consumer protection" and the elimination and prevention of what regulators perceive to be harmfully "anti-competitive" business practices, such as coercive monopoly. The Federal Trade Commission Act was one of President Wilson"s major acts against trusts.

Business	There are many ways in which a business may be owned under the legal system of England and Wales. Different types of ownership are suitable for organisations depending on the degree of control the owners wish to have over the business. The choice of ownership methor also relates to the organisations ability to raise funds for the business activities.
Sarbanes-Oxley Act	The Sarbanes-Oxley Act of 2002 (Pub.L. 107-204, 116 Stat. 745, enacted July 30, 2002), also known as the Public Company Accounting Reform and Investor Protection Act of 2002 and commonly called Sarbanes-Oxley, Sarbox or SOX, is a United States federal law enacted on July 30, 2002, as a reaction to a number of major corporate and accounting scandals including those affecting Enron, Tyco International, Adelphia, Peregrine Systems and WorldCom.
Tyco International	Tyco International Ltd. NYSE: TYC is a highly diversified global manufacturing company incorporated in Switzerland, with United States operational headquarters in Princeton, New Jersey (Tyco International (US) Inc).. Tyco International is composed of five major business segments: ADT Worldwide, Fire Protection Services, Safety Products, Flow Control and Electrical and Metal Products.
Arbitration	Arbitration, a form of alternative dispute resolution (ADR), is a legal technique for the resolution of disputes outside the courts, wherein the parties to a dispute refer it to one or more persons (the "arbitrators", "arbiters" or "arbitral tribunal"), by whose decision (the "award") they agree to be bound. It is a settlement technique in which a third party reviews the case and imposes a decision that is legally binding for both sides. Other forms of ADR include mediation (a form of settlement negotiation facilitated by a neutral third party) and non-binding resolution by experts.
Terrorism	Terrorism is a policy or ideology of violence intended to intimidate or cause terror for the purpose of "exerting pressure on decision making by state bodies." The term "terror" is largely used to indicate clandestine, low-intensity violence that targets civilians and generates public fear. Thus "terror" is distinct from asymmetric warfare, and violates the concept of a common law of war in which civilian life is regarded. The term "-ism" is used to indicate an ideology --typically one that claims its attacks are in the domain of a "just war" concept, though most condemn such as crimes against humanity.
Profit	A profit , in the law of real property, is a nonpossessory interest in land similar to the better-known easement, which gives the holder the right to take natural resources such as petroleum, minerals, timber, and wild game from the land of another. Indeed, because of the necessity of allowing access to the land so that resources may be gathered, every profit contains an implied easement for the owner of the profit to enter the other party"s land for the purpose of collecting the resources permitted by the profit. Like an easement, profits can be created expressly by an agreement between the property owner and the owner of the profit, or by prescription, where the owner of the profit has made "open and notorious" use of the land for a continuous and uninterrupted statutory period.
Statute	A statute is a formal written enactment of a legislative authority that governs a country, state, city, or county. Typically, statute s command or prohibit something, or declare policy. The word is often used to distinguish law made by legislative bodies from case law and the regulations issued by Government agencies.

Duty	Duty (from "due," that which is owing, O. Fr. deu, did, past participle of devoir; Lat. debere, debitum; cf.
Estoppel	Estoppel is a legal doctrine at common law, where a party is barred from claiming or denying an argument on an equitable ground. Estoppel complements the requirement of consideration in contract law. In general, Estoppel protects an aggrieved party, if the counter-party induced an expectation from the aggrieved party, and the aggrieved party reasonably relied on the expectation and would suffer detriment if the expectation is not met.
Obligation	An obligation is a requirement to take some course of action, whether legal or moral. There are also obligation s in other normative contexts, such as obligation s of etiquette, social obligation s, and possibly in terms of politics, where obligation s are requirements which must be fulfilled. These are generally legal obligation s, which can incur a penalty for unfulfilment, although certain people are obliged to carry out certain actions for other reasons as well, whether as a tradition or for social reasons.
Chief brand officer	A Chief brand officer is a relatively new executive level position at a corporation, company, organization typically reporting directly to the CEO or board of directors. The Chief brand officer is responsible for a brand"s image, experience, and promise, and propagating it throughout all aspects of the company. The brand officer oversees marketing, advertising, design, public relations and customer service departments.
Shareholder	A mutual shareholder or stockholder is an individual or company (including a corporation) that legally owns one or more shares of stock in a joint stock company. A company"s shareholder s collectively own that company. Thus, the typical goal of such companies is to enhance shareholder value.
Utilitarianism	Utilitarianism is the idea that the moral worth of an action is determined solely by its contribution to overall utility: that is, its contribution to happiness or pleasure as summed among all people. It is thus a form of consequentialism, meaning that the moral worth of an action is determined by its outcome. Utility, the good to be maximized, has been defined by various thinkers as happiness or pleasure (versus suffering or pain), although preference utilitarians like Peter Singer define it as the satisfaction of preferences.
Option	In finance, an option is a contract between a buyer and a seller that gives the buyer the right--but not the obligation--to buy or to sell a particular asset (the underlying asset) at a later day at an agreed price. In return for granting the option, the seller collects a payment (the premium) from the buyer. A call option gives the buyer the right to buy the underlying asset; a put option gives the buyer of the option the right to sell the underlying asset.
Business judgment rule	The Business judgment rule is an American case law-derived concept in corporations law whereby the "directors of a corporation .

Options backdating

Options backdating is the practice of granting an employee stock option that is dated prior to the date that the company actually granted the option. This practice raises a number of legal and accounting issues. The practice of backdating itself is not illegal, nor is granting of discounted stock options.

Federal Trade Commission

The Federal Trade Commission is an independent agency of the United States government, established in 1914 by the Federal Trade Commission Act. Its principal mission is the promotion of "consumer protection" and the elimination and prevention of what regulators perceive to be harmfully "anti-competitive" business practices, such as coercive monopoly.

The Federal Trade Commission Act was one of President Wilson"s major acts against trusts.

Securities and Exchange Commission

The U.S. Securities and Exchange Commission is an independent agency of the United States government which holds primary responsibility for enforcing the federal securities laws and regulating the securities industry, the nation"s stock and options exchanges, and other electronic securities markets. The SEC was created by section 4 of the Securities Exchange Act of 1934 (now codified as 15 U.S.C. Â§ 78d and commonly referred to as the 1934 Act.)

Arthur Andersen

Arthur Andersen LLP, based in Chicago, was once one of the "Big Five" accounting firms among PricewaterhouseCoopers, Deloitte Touche Tohmatsu, Ernst ' Young and KPMG, providing auditing, tax, and consulting services to large corporations. In 2002, the firm voluntarily surrendered its licenses to practice as Certified Public Accountants in the United States after being found guilty of criminal charges relating to the firm"s handling of the auditing of Enron, the energy corporation, resulting in the loss of 85,000 jobs. Although the verdict was subsequently overturned by the Supreme Court of the United States, it has not returned as a viable business.

Breach of contract

Breach of contract is a legal concept in which a binding agreement or bargained-for exchange is not honored by one or more of the parties to the contract by non-performance or interference with the other party"s performance.

A minor breach, a partial breach or an immaterial breach, occurs when the non-breaching party is unentitled to an order for performance of its obligations, but only to collect the actual amount of their damages. For example, suppose a homeowner hires a contractor to install new plumbing and insists that the pipes, which will ultimately be sealed behind the walls, be red.

Employment

Employment is a contract between two parties, one being the employer and the other being the employee. An employee may be defined as: "A person in the service of another under any contract of hire, express or implied, oral or written, where the employer has the power or right to control and direct the employee in the material details of how the work is to be performed." Black"s Law Dictionary page 471 (5th ed. 1979).

Employment discrimination

Employment discrimination (or workplace discrimination) is discrimination in hiring, promotion, job assignment, termination, and compensation. It includes various types of harassment.

Many jurisdictions prohibit some types of Employment discrimination, often by forbidding discrimination based on certain traits ("protected categories").

Damages	Damages for breach of contract is a common law remedy, available as of right. It is designed to compensate the victim for their actual loss as a result of the wrongdoer"s breach rather than to punish the wrongdoer. If no loss has been occasioned by the plaintiff, only nominal Damages will be awarded.
Tort	Tort law is a body of law that addresses, and provides remedies for, civil wrongs not arising out of contractual obligations. A person who suffers legal damages may be able to use Tort law to receive compensation from someone who is legally responsible, or "liable," for those injuries. Generally speaking, Tort law defines what constitutes a legal injury and establishes the circumstances under which one person may be held liable for another"s injury.
Guarantee	The act of becoming a surety is also called a Guarantee. Traditionally a Guarantee was distinguished from a surety in that the surety"s liability was joint and primary with the principal, whereas the guaranty"s liability was ancillary and derivative, but many jurisdictions have abolished this distinction
Punitive Damages	Punitive Damages are damages not awarded in order to compensate the plaintiff, but in order to reform or deter the defendant and similar persons from pursuing a course of action such as that which damaged the plaintiff. punitive Damages are often awarded where compensatory damages are deemed an inadequate remedy. The court may impose them to prevent under-compensation of plaintiffs, to allow redress for undetectable torts and taking some strain away from the criminal justice system.
Product liability	Product liability is the area of law in which manufacturers, distributors, suppliers, retailers, and others who make products available to the public are held responsible for the injuries those products cause. In the United States, the claims most commonly associated with Product liability are negligence, strict liability, breach of warranty, and various consumer protection claims. The majority of Product liability laws are determined at the state level and vary widely from state to state.
Reasonable person standard	The reasonable person is a legal fiction of the common law representing an objective standard against which any individual"s conduct can be measured. It is used to determine if a breach of the standard of care has occurred, provided a duty of care can be proven. The Reasonable person standard holds: each person owes a duty to behave as a reasonable person would under the same or similar circumstances.
Tort reform	Tort reform refers to proposed changes in the civil justice system that would reduce tort litigation or damages. Tort is a system for compensating wrongs and harm done by one party to another"s person, property or other protected interests (e.g. reputation, under libel and slander laws.) tort reform advocates focus on personal injury in particular.
Plaintiff	A plaintiff is the party who initiates a lawsuit before a court. By doing so, the plaintiff seeks a legal remedy, and if successful, the court will issue judgment in favor of the plaintiff and make the appropriate court order

In some jurisdictions the commencement of a lawsuit is done by filing a summons, claim form and/or a complaint -- these documents are known as pleadings -- that set forth the alleged wrongs committed by the defendant or defendants with a demand for relief.

Duty	Duty (from "due," that which is owing, O. Fr. deu, did, past participle of devoir; Lat. debere, debitum; cf.
Freedom of contract	Freedom of contract or contractualism is the freedom of individuals to bargain among themselves the terms of their own contracts, without government interference. Anything more than minimal regulations and taxes may be seen as infringements. It is the underpinning of the theory of laissez-faire economics.
Misrepresentation	Misrepresentation is a contract law concept. It means a false statement of fact made by one party to another party, which has the effect of inducing that party into the contract. For example, under certain circumstances, false statements or promises made by a seller of goods regarding the quality or nature of the product that the seller has may constitute Misrepresentation.
Obligation	An obligation is a requirement to take some course of action, whether legal or moral. There are also obligation s in other normative contexts, such as obligation s of etiquette, social obligation s, and possibly in terms of politics, where obligation s are requirements which must be fulfilled. These are generally legal obligation s, which can incur a penalty for unfulfilment, although certain people are obliged to carry out certain actions for other reasons as well, whether as a tradition or for social reasons.
Slander	In law, defamation, Slander, and vilification) is the communication of a statement that makes a claim, expressly stated or implied to be factual, that may give an individual, business, product, group, government or nation a negative image. It is usually, but not always, a requirement that this claim be false and that the publication is communicated to someone other than the person defamed In common law jurisdictions, Slander refers to a malicious, false and defamatory spoken statement or report, while libel refers to any other form of communication such as written words or images.
Estoppel	Estoppel is a legal doctrine at common law, where a party is barred from claiming or denying an argument on an equitable ground. Estoppel complements the requirement of consideration in contract law. In general, Estoppel protects an aggrieved party, if the counter-party induced an expectation from the aggrieved party, and the aggrieved party reasonably relied on the expectation and would suffer detriment if the expectation is not met.
Puffery	Puffery as a legal term refers to promotional statements and claims that express subjective rather than objective views, such that no reasonable person would take literally. Puffery is especially featured in testimonials. In a legal context, the term originated in the English Court of Appeal case Carlill v Carbolic Smoke Ball Company, which centred on whether a monetary reimbursement should be paid when an influenza preventative device failed to work.

Statute	A statute is a formal written enactment of a legislative authority that governs a country, state, city, or county. Typically, statute s command or prohibit something, or declare policy. The word is often used to distinguish law made by legislative bodies from case law and the regulations issued by Government agencies.
Statute of Frauds	The Statute of Frauds refers to the requirement that certain kinds of contracts be made in writing and signed. Traditionally, the Statute of Frauds requires a writing signed by the defendant in the following circumstances: · Contracts in consideration of marriage. · Contracts which cannot be performed within one year. · Contracts for the transfer of an interest in land. · Contracts by the executor of a will to pay a debt of the estate with their own money. · Contracts for the sale of goods above a certain value. · Contracts in which one party becomes a surety (acts as guarantor) for another party"s debt or other obligation. This can be remembered by the mnemonic "MY LEGS": Marriage, one year, land, executor, goods, surety. The term Statute of Frauds comes from an English Act of Parliament passed in 1677 (authored by Sir Leoline Jenkins and passed by the Cavalier Parliament), and more properly called An Act for Prevention of Frauds and Perjuries. Many common law jurisdictions have made similar statutory provisions, while a number of civil law jurisdictions have equivalent legislation incorporated into their civil codes.
Chief brand officer	A Chief brand officer is a relatively new executive level position at a corporation, company, organization typically reporting directly to the CEO or board of directors. The Chief brand officer is responsible for a brand"s image, experience, and promise, and propagating it throughout all aspects of the company. The brand officer oversees marketing, advertising, design, public relations and customer service departments.
Business	There are many ways in which a business may be owned under the legal system of England and Wales. Different types of ownership are suitable for organisations depending on the degree of control the owners wish to have over the business. The choice of ownership methor also relates to the organisations ability to raise funds for the business activities.
License	The verb License or grant License means to give permission. The noun License refers to that permission as well as to the document memorializing that permission. License may be granted by a party to another party as an element of an agreement between those parties.
Revocation	Revocation is the act of recall or annulment. It is the reversal of an act, the recalling of a grant, or the making void of some deed previously existing.

	In the law of contracts, revocation is a type of remedy for buyers when the buyer accepts a nonconforming good from the seller.
Trespass	Trespass is a legal concept, which refers to intrusion into another person''s property.
Personal property	Personal property is a type of property. In the common law systems Personal property may also be called chattels or personalty. It is distinguished from real property, or real estate. Personal property may be classified in a variety of ways. Tangible Personal property refers to any type of property that can generally be moved (i.e., it is not attached to real property or land), touched or felt. These generally include items such as furniture, clothing, jewelry, art, writings, or household goods. In some cases, there can be formal title documents that show the ownership and transfer rights of that property after a person''s death (for example, motor vehicles, boats, etc.) In many cases, however, tangible Personal property will not be "titled" in an owner''s name and is presumed to be whatever property he or she was in possession of at the time of his or her death. Intangible Personal property or "intangibles" refers to Personal property that cannot actually be moved, touched or felt, but instead represents something of value such as negotiable instruments, securities, goods, and intangible assets including chose in action.
Lien	In law, a Lien is a form of security interest granted over an item of property to secure the payment of a debt or performance of some other obligation. The owner of the property, who grants the Lien, is referred to as the Lienor and the person who has the benefit of the Lien is referred to as the Lienee. The etymological root is Anglo-French Lien, loyen bond, restraint, from Latin ligamen, from ligare to bind.
Personalty	Personal property is a type of property. In the common law systems personal property may also be called chattels or Personalty. It is distinguished from real property, or real estate.
Slander of Title	In law, Slander of title is normally a claim involving real estate in which one entity falsely claims to own another entity''s property. Alternatively, it is casting aspersion on someone else''s property, business or goods, e.g. claiming a house is infested with termites (when it is not), or falsely claiming you own someone else''s copyright (what allegedly occurred in the SCO v. Novell case.) Slander of title is a form of jactitation.
Service provider	A service provider is an entity that provides services to other entities. Usually this refers to a business that provides subscription or web service to other businesses or individuals. Examples of these services include Internet access, Mobile phone operator, and web application hosting.
Pornography	Pornography or porn is the depiction of explicit sexual subject matter for the purpose of sexually exciting the viewer. Pornography makes no claim to artistic merit, unlike erotica which does. Over the past few decades, an immense industry for the production and consumption of Pornography has grown, with the increasing use of the VCR, the DVD, and the Internet, as well as the emergence of social attitudes more tolerant of sexual portrayals.

Breach of contract	Breach of contract is a legal concept in which a binding agreement or bargained-for exchange is not honored by one or more of the parties to the contract by non-performance or interference with the other party"s performance. A minor breach, a partial breach or an immaterial breach, occurs when the non-breaching party is unentitled to an order for performance of its obligations, but only to collect the actual amount of their damages. For example, suppose a homeowner hires a contractor to install new plumbing and insists that the pipes, which will ultimately be sealed behind the walls, be red.
Strict liability	Strict liability makes a person responsible for the damage and loss caused by his/her acts and omissions regardless of culpability .) Strict liability is important in torts (especially product liability), corporations law, and criminal law. For analysis of the pros and cons of Strict liability as applied to product liability, the most important Strict liability regime, see product liability.
Business	There are many ways in which a business may be owned under the legal system of England and Wales. Different types of ownership are suitable for organisations depending on the degree of control the owners wish to have over the business. The choice of ownership methor also relates to the organisations ability to raise funds for the business activities.
Reasonable person standard	The reasonable person is a legal fiction of the common law representing an objective standard against which any individual"s conduct can be measured. It is used to determine if a breach of the standard of care has occurred, provided a duty of care can be proven. The Reasonable person standard holds: each person owes a duty to behave as a reasonable person would under the same or similar circumstances.
Duty	Duty (from "due," that which is owing, O. Fr. deu, did, past participle of devoir; Lat. debere, debitum; cf.
Damages	Damages for breach of contract is a common law remedy, available as of right. It is designed to compensate the victim for their actual loss as a result of the wrongdoer"s breach rather than to punish the wrongdoer. If no loss has been occasioned by the plaintiff, only nominal Damages will be awarded.
Proximate cause	In the law, a Proximate cause is an event sufficiently related to a legally recognizable injury to be held the cause of that injury. There are two types of causation in the law, cause-in-fact and proximate (or legal) cause. Cause-in-fact is determined by the "but-for" test: but for the action, the result would not have happened.
Arbitration	Arbitration, a form of alternative dispute resolution (ADR), is a legal technique for the resolution of disputes outside the courts, wherein the parties to a dispute refer it to one or more persons (the "arbitrators", "arbiters" or "arbitral tribunal"), by whose decision (the "award") they agree to be bound. It is a settlement technique in which a third party reviews the case and imposes a decision that is legally binding for both sides. Other forms of ADR include mediation (a form of settlement negotiation facilitated by a neutral third party) and non-binding resolution by experts.

Unilateralism

Unilateralism is any doctrine or agenda that supports one-sided action. Such action may be in disregard for other parties, or as an expression of a commitment toward a direction which other parties may find agreeable. Unilateralism is a neologism, (used in all countries) coined to be an antonym for multilateralism --the doctrine which asserts the benefits of participation from as many parties as possible.

Per se

Per se:

· A Latin phrase used in English arguments for "by itself" or "by themselves"
It also is used in law:

· Illegal per se, the legal usage of "per se" in criminal and anti-trust law
· Negligence per se, legal use in tort law
Other uses:

· per se (restaurant), a New York City restaurant run by Thomas Keller
"Gun ownership in Japan is not, per se, illegal; however, the restrictions are such that one could easily arrive at that conclusion."
"Data trustworthiness should be attributed primarily to data per se, rather than being merely a reï¬‚ection of the trust attributed to data-reporting entities."

Statute

A statute is a formal written enactment of a legislative authority that governs a country, state, city, or county. Typically, statute s command or prohibit something, or declare policy. The word is often used to distinguish law made by legislative bodies from case law and the regulations issued by Government agencies.

Product liability

Product liability is the area of law in which manufacturers, distributors, suppliers, retailers, and others who make products available to the public are held responsible for the injuries those products cause. In the United States, the claims most commonly associated with Product liability are negligence, strict liability, breach of warranty, and various consumer protection claims. The majority of Product liability laws are determined at the state level and vary widely from state to state.

Prima facie

Prima facie is a Latin expression meaning on its first appearance, or by first instance; at first sight. The literal translation would be "from first face", prima first, facie face, both in the ablative case. It is used in modern legal English to signify that on first examination, a matter appears to be self-evident from the facts.

Constitution

· Apostolic Constitution (a class of Roman Catholic Church documents)
· Constitution of the Roman Republic
· Constitutional court
· Constitutionalism
· Corporate Constitution
· Judicial activism
· Judicial restraint
· Judicial review

Judicial philosophies of Constitutional interpretation (note: generally specific to United States Constitutional law)

· List of national Constitutions
· Originalism
· Strict constructionism
· Textualism
· Proposed European Union Constitution

· Treaty of Lisbon (adopts same changes, but without Constitutional name)
· United Nations Charter

Patent

A patent is a set of exclusive rights granted by a state to an inventor or his assignee for a limited period of time in exchange for a disclosure of an invention.

The procedure for granting patent s, the requirements placed on the patent ee and the extent of the exclusive rights vary widely between countries according to national laws and international agreements. Typically, however, a patent application must include one or more claims defining the invention which must be new, inventive, and useful or industrially applicable.

Service mark

In some countries, notably the United States, a trademark used to identify a service rather than a product is called a Service mark or servicemark. When a Service mark is federally registered, the standard registration symbol Â® or "Reg U.S. Pat ' TM Off" may be used (the same symbol is used to mark registered trademarks.) Before it is registered, it is common practice (but has no legal standing) to use the Service mark symbol [Service mark] (a superscript Service mark.)

Trade secret

A trade secret is a formula, practice, process, design, instrument, pattern by which a business can obtain an economic advantage over competitors or customers. In some jurisdictions, such secrets are referred to as "confidential information" or "classified information".

Coke cola

The precise language by which a trade secret is defined varies by jurisdiction (as do the particular types of information that are subject to trade secret protection.)

Trademark

A trademark or trade mark is a distinctive sign or indicator used by an individual, business organization and to distinguish its products or services from those of other entities.

A trademark is designated by the following symbols:

· â„¢ (for an unregistered trademark that is, a mark used to promote or brand goods);
· â„ (for an unregistered service mark, that is, a mark used to promote or brand services); and
· Â® (for a registered trademark)

A trademark is a type of intellectual property, and typically a name, word, phrase, logo, symbol, design, image, or a combination of these elements. There is also a range of non-conventional trademark s comprising marks which do not fall into these standard categories.

The owner of a registered trademark may commence legal proceedings for trademark infringement to prevent unauthorized use of that trademark

United States

- History of competition law
- Monopoly
  - Coercive monopoly
  - Natural monopoly
  - Barriers to entry
  - Market power
  - SSNIP test
  - Relevant market
  - Merger control

Anti-competitive practices

- Monopolization
- Collusion

- Formation of cartels
- Price fixing
- Bid rigging
- Product bundling and tying
- Refusal to deal
  - Group boycott
  - Exclusive dealing
  - Dividing territories
  - Conscious parallelism
  - Predatory pricing
  - Misuse of patents and copyrights

Laws and doctrines

United States

- Sherman Antitrust Act
- Clayton Antitrust Act
- Robinson-Patman Act
- FTC Act
- Hart-Scott-Rodino Act
- Merger guidelines
- Essential facilities doctrine
- Noerr-Pennington doctrine
- Parker immunity doctrine
- Rule of reason

Europe

- UK competition law
- Irish competition law

Australia

- Trade Practices Act 1974

Enforcement authorities and organizations

Competition law history refers to attempts by governments to regulate competitive markets for goods and services, leading up to the modern competition or antitrust laws around the world today. The earliest records traces back to the efforts of Roman legislators to control price fluctuations and unfair trade practices. Through the Middle Ages in Europe, Kings and Queens repeatedly cracked down on monopolies, including those created through state legislation.

- International Competition Network
- List of competition regulators

Business	There are many ways in which a business may be owned under the legal system of England and Wales. Different types of ownership are suitable for organisations depending on the degree of control the owners wish to have over the business. The choice of ownership methor also relates to the organisations ability to raise funds for the business activities.
United States Patent and Trademark Office	The United States Patent and Trademark Office is an agency in the United States Department of Commerce that issues patents to inventors and businesses for their inventions, and trademark registration for product and intellectual property identification. The USPTO is currently based in Alexandria, Virginia, after a 2006 move from the Crystal City area of Arlington, Virginia. The offices under Patents and the Chief Information Officer that remained just outside the southern end of Crystal City completed moving to Randolph Square, a brand new building in Shirlington Village, on 27 April 2009.

Trade dress

Trade dress is a legal term of art that generally refers to characteristics of the visual appearance of a product or its packaging (or even the design of a building) that signify the source of the product to consumers. Trade dress is a form of intellectual property. In the U.S., like trademarks, a product"s Trade dress is legally protected by the Lanham Act, the federal statute which regulates trademarks and Trade dress.

Trademark Infringement

Trademark infringement is a violation of the exclusive rights attaching to a trademark without the authorization of the trademark owner or any licensees (provided that such authorization was within the scope of the license.) Infringement may occur when one party, the "infringer", uses a trademark which is identical or confusingly similar to a trademark owned by another party, in relation to products or services which are identical or similar to the products or services which the registration covers. An owner of a trademark may commence legal proceedings against a party which infringes its registration.

Counterfeit

A Counterfeit product is an imitation which infringes upon a production monopoly held by either a state or corporation. Goods are produced with the intent to bypass this monopoly and thus take advantage of the established worth of the previous product. The word Counterfeit frequently describes both the forgeries of currency and documents, as well as the imitations of clothing, software, pharmaceuticals, watches, electronics, and company logos and brands.

Counterfeit Goods

The spread of counterfeit goods has become global in recent years and the range of goods subject to infringement has increased significantly. According to the study of Counterfeiting Intelligence Bureau (CIB) of the International Chamber of Commerce (ICC) counterfeit goods make up 5 to 7% of World Trade, however, these figures cannot be substantiated. According to the International Anti-Counterfeiting Coalition if the knockoff economy were a business, it would be the world"s biggest.

Trade name

A Trade name is the name which a business trades under for commercial purposes, although its registered, legal name, used for contracts and other formal situations, may be another. Pharmaceuticals also have Trade name s, often dissimilar to their chemical names

Trading names are sometimes registered as trademarks or are regarded as brands.

Consumer Protection

Consumer protection laws are designed to ensure fair competition and the free flow of truthful information in the marketplace. The laws are designed to prevent businesses that engage in fraud or specified unfair practices from gaining an advantage over competitors and may provide additional protection for the weak and those unable to take care of themselves. Consumer protection laws are a form of government regulation which protects the interests of consumers.

License

The verb License or grant License means to give permission. The noun License refers to that permission as well as to the document memorializing that permission. License may be granted by a party to another party as an element of an agreement between those parties.

Patent Infringement

Patent infringement is the performance of a prohibited act with respect to a patented invention without permission from the patent holder. Permission may typically be granted in the form of a licence. The acts may vary by jurisdiction, but typically include using or selling the patented invention.

United States Copyright Office	The United States Copyright Office, a part of the Library of Congress, is the official U.S. government body that maintains records of copyright registration in the United States. It is used by copyright title searchers who are attempting to clear a chain of title for copyrighted works. The head of the Copyright Office is called the Register of Copyrights.
Service provider	A service provider is an entity that provides services to other entities. Usually this refers to a business that provides subscription or web service to other businesses or individuals. Examples of these services include Internet access, Mobile phone operator, and web application hosting.
Peer-to-peer	A Peer-to-peer computer network uses diverse connectivity between participants in a network and the cumulative bandwidth of network participants rather than conventional centralized resources where a relatively low number of servers provide the core value to a service or application. P2P networks are typically used for connecting nodes via largely ad hoc connections. Such networks are useful for many purposes.
Duty	Duty (from "due," that which is owing, O. Fr. deu, did, past participle of devoir; Lat. debere, debitum; cf.
Obligation	An obligation is a requirement to take some course of action, whether legal or moral. There are also obligation s in other normative contexts, such as obligation s of etiquette, social obligation s, and possibly in terms of politics, where obligation s are requirements which must be fulfilled. These are generally legal obligation s, which can incur a penalty for unfulfilment, although certain people are obliged to carry out certain actions for other reasons as well, whether as a tradition or for social reasons.
Vicarious Liability	Vicarious liability is a form of strict, secondary liability that arises under the common law doctrine of agency - respondeat superior - the responsibility of the superior for the acts of their subordinate, or, in a broader sense, the responsibility of any third party that had the "right, ability or duty to control" the activities of a violator. It can be distinguished from contributory liability, another form of secondary liability, which is rooted in the tort theory of enterprise liability. Employers are vicariously liable, under the respondeat superior doctrine, for negligent acts or omissions by their employees in the course of employment.
Uniform Trade Secrets Act	The Uniform Trade Secrets Act is a model law drafted by the National Conference of Commissioners on Uniform State Laws to better define rights and remedies of common law trade secret. It has been adopted by 46 states, the District of Columbia and the U.S. Virgin Islands. Massachusetts, New Jersey, New York and Texas have not adopted the Uniform Trade Secrets Act.
World Intellectual Property Organization	The World Intellectual Property Organization is one of the 16 specialized agencies of the United Nations. World Intellectual Property Organization was created in 1967 "to encourage creative activity, to promote the protection of intellectual property throughout the world". World Intellectual Property Organization currently has 184 member states, administers 24 international treaties, and is headquartered in Geneva, Switzerland.

World Intellectual Property Organization Copyright Treaty	The World Intellectual Property Organization Copyright Treaty, abbreviated as the WIPO Copyright Treaty, is an international treaty on copyright law adopted by the member states of the World Intellectual Property Organization (WIPO) in 1996. It provides additional protections for copyright deemed necessary due to advances in information technology since the formation of previous copyright treaties before it. There have been a variety of criticisms of this treaty, including that it is overbroad (for example in its prohibition of circumvention of technical protection measures, even where such circumvention is used in the pursuit of legal and fair use rights) and that it applies a "one size fits all" standard to all signatory countries despite widely differing stages of economic development and knowledge industry.

Parol evidence	The Parol evidence rule is the legal application of a rule of substantive law in contract cases that prevents a party to a written contract from contradicting (or sometimes adding to) the terms of the contract by seeking the admission of evidence "extrinsic" (outside) to the contract. For example, Carl agrees in writing to sell Betty a car for $1,000. Betty argues that Carl told her that she would only need to pay Carl $800.
Parol evidence rule	The Parol evidence rule is the legal application of a rule of substantive law in contract cases that prevents a party to a written contract from contradicting (or sometimes adding to) the terms of the contract by seeking the admission of evidence "extrinsic" (outside) to the contract. For example, Carl agrees in writing to sell Betty a car for $1,000. Betty argues that Carl told her that she would only need to pay Carl $800.
Trial	In law, a trial is when parties come together to a dispute present information (in the form of evidence) in a formal setting, usually a court, before a judge, jury in order to achieve a resolution to their dispute. · Where the trial is held before a group of members of the community, it is called a jury trial · Where the trial is held solely before a judge, it is called a bench trial Bench trial s involve fewer formalities, and are typically resolved faster. Furthermore, a favorable ruling for one party in a bench trial will frequently lead the other party to offer a settlement. Hearings before administrative bodies may have many of the features of a trial before a court, but are typically not referred to as trial s. An appellate proceeding is also generally not deemed a trial because such proceedings are usually restricted to review of the evidence presented before the trial court, and do not permit the introduction of new evidences. trial s can also be divided by the type of dispute at issue.
Verdict	In law, a verdict is the formal finding of fact made by a jury on matters or questions submitted to the jury by a judge. (see Black"s Law Dictionary, p. 1398 (5th ed.
Tort	Tort law is a body of law that addresses, and provides remedies for, civil wrongs not arising out of contractual obligations. A person who suffers legal damages may be able to use Tort law to receive compensation from someone who is legally responsible, or "liable," for those injuries. Generally speaking, Tort law defines what constitutes a legal injury and establishes the circumstances under which one person may be held liable for another"s injury.
Reasonable person standard	The reasonable person is a legal fiction of the common law representing an objective standard against which any individual"s conduct can be measured. It is used to determine if a breach of the standard of care has occurred, provided a duty of care can be proven. The Reasonable person standard holds: each person owes a duty to behave as a reasonable person would under the same or similar circumstances.
Standard of Care	In tort law, the standard of care is the degree of prudence and caution required of an individual who is under a duty of care. A breach of the standard is necessary for a successful action in negligence. The requirements of the standard are closely dependent on circumstances.

Trade secret

A trade secret is a formula, practice, process, design, instrument, pattern by which a business can obtain an economic advantage over competitors or customers. In some jurisdictions, such secrets are referred to as "confidential information" or "classified information".

The precise language by which a trade secret is defined varies by jurisdiction (as do the particular types of information that are subject to trade secret protection.)

Chief brand officer

A Chief brand officer is a relatively new executive level position at a corporation, company, organization typically reporting directly to the CEO or board of directors. The Chief brand officer is responsible for a brand"s image, experience, and promise, and propagating it throughout all aspects of the company. The brand officer oversees marketing, advertising, design, public relations and customer service departments.

Embezzlement

Embezzlement is the act of dishonestly appropriating or secreting assets, usually financial in nature, by one or more individuals to whom such assets have been entrusted. It is a kind of financial fraud. For instance, a clerk or cashier handling large sums of money can embezzle cash from his or her employer, a lawyer can embezzle funds from clients" trust accounts, a financial advisor can embezzle funds from investors, or a spouse can embezzle funds from his or her partner.

Misrepresentation

Misrepresentation is a contract law concept. It means a false statement of fact made by one party to another party, which has the effect of inducing that party into the contract. For example, under certain circumstances, false statements or promises made by a seller of goods regarding the quality or nature of the product that the seller has may constitute Misrepresentation.

Public order

In criminology public order crime is defined by Siegel (2004) as "...crime which involves acts that interfere with the operations of society and the ability of people to function efficiently", i.e. it is behaviour that has been labelled criminal because it is contrary to shared norms, social values, and customs. Robertson (1989:123) maintains that a crime is nothing more than "...an act that contravenes a law." Generally speaking, deviancy is criminalized when it is too disruptive and has proved uncontrollable through informal sanctions.

public order crime should be distinguished from political crime.

White-collar

The term white-collar worker refers to a salaried professional or an educated worker who performs semi-professional office, administrative, and sales coordination tasks, as opposed to a blue-collar worker, whose job requires manual labor. "white-collar work" is an informal term, defined in contrast to "blue-collar work".

The term "white collar" was first used by Upton Sinclair in relation to modern clerical, administrative and management workers during the 1930s.

White-collar Crime

Within the field of criminology, White-collar crime has been defined by Edwin Sutherland as "a crime committed by a person of respectability and high social status in the course of his occupation" (1949.) Sutherland was a proponent of Symbolic Interactionism, and believed that criminal behavior was learned from interpersonal interaction with others. White-collar crime therefore overlaps with corporate crime because the opportunity for fraud, bribery, insider trading, embezzlement, computer crime, and forgery is more available to white-collar employees.

Wire Fraud	Wire fraud is a legal concept in the United States Code which provides for enhanced penalty of any criminally fraudulent activity if it is determined that the activity involved electronic communications of any kind, at any phase of the event. As in the case of mail fraud, this statute is often used as a basis for a separate federal prosecution of what would otherwise have been only a violation of a state law. The crime of Wire fraud is codified in Title 18 of the United States Code at 18 U.S.C.
Breach of contract	Breach of contract is a legal concept in which a binding agreement or bargained-for exchange is not honored by one or more of the parties to the contract by non-performance or interference with the other party"s performance. A minor breach, a partial breach or an immaterial breach, occurs when the non-breaching party is unentitled to an order for performance of its obligations, but only to collect the actual amount of their damages. For example, suppose a homeowner hires a contractor to install new plumbing and insists that the pipes, which will ultimately be sealed behind the walls, be red.
Warranty	In commercial and consumer transactions, a warranty is an obligation or guarantee that an article or service sold is as factually stated or legally implied by the seller, and that often provides for a specific remedy such as repair or replacement in the event the article or service fails to meet the warranty. A breach of warranty occurs when the promise is broken, i.e., a product is defective or not as should be expected by a reasonable buyer. In business and legal transactions, a warranty is an assurance by one party to the other party that certain facts or conditions are true or will happen; the other party is permitted to rely on that assurance and seek some type of remedy if it is not true or followed.
Bank Secrecy Act	The Bank Secrecy Act of 1970 (or Bank Secrecy Act, or otherwise known as the Currency and Foreign Transactions Reporting Act) requires financial institutions in the United States to assist U.S. government agencies to detect and prevent money laundering. Specifically, the act requires financial institutions to keep records of [cash purchases of negotiable instruments, and file reports of cash purchases of these negotiable instruments of $3,000 or more (daily aggregate amount), and to report suspicious activity that might signify money laundering, tax evasion, or other criminal activities. Many banks will no longer sell negotiable instruments when purchased with cash, requiring the purchase to be withdrawn from an account at that institution.
Bankruptcy	Bankruptcy is a legally declared inability or impairment of ability of an individual or organization to pay its creditors. Creditors may file a Bankruptcy petition against a debtor ("involuntary Bankruptcy") in an effort to recoup a portion of what they are owed or initiate a restructuring. In the majority of cases, however, Bankruptcy is initiated by the debtor (a "voluntary Bankruptcy" that is filed by the insolvent individual or organization).
RICO	The Racketeer Influenced and Corrupt Organizations Act (commonly referred to as RICO Act or RICO) is a United States federal law that provides for extended criminal penalties and a civil cause of action for acts performed as part of an ongoing criminal organization. RICO was enacted by section 901(a) of the Organized Crime Control Act of 1970 (Pub.L. 91-452, 84 Stat.

Damages

Damages for breach of contract is a common law remedy, available as of right. It is designed to compensate the victim for their actual loss as a result of the wrongdoer"s breach rather than to punish the wrongdoer. If no loss has been occasioned by the plaintiff, only nominal Damages will be awarded.

Treble Damages

Treble damages, in law, is a term that indicates that a statute permits a court to triple the amount of the actual/compensatory damages to be awarded to a prevailing plaintiff, generally in order to punish the losing party for willful conduct. Treble damages are a multiple of, and not an addition to, actual damages. Thus, where a person received an award of $100 for an injury, a court applying Treble damages would raise the award to $300.

Duress

Duress or coercion (as a term of jurisprudence) is a possible legal defense, one of four of the most important justification defenses, by which defendants argue that they should not be held liable because the actions that broke the law were only performed out of an immediate fear of injury. Black"s Law Dictionary (6th ed). defines Duress as "any unlawful threat or coercion used...

Constitution

· Apostolic Constitution (a class of Roman Catholic Church documents)
· Constitution of the Roman Republic
· Constitutional court
· Constitutionalism
· Corporate Constitution
· Judicial activism
· Judicial restraint
· Judicial review

Judicial philosophies of Constitutional interpretation (note: generally specific to United States Constitutional law)

· List of national Constitutions
· Originalism
· Strict constructionism
· Textualism
· Proposed European Union Constitution

· Treaty of Lisbon (adopts same changes, but without Constitutional name)
· United Nations Charter

Self-incrimination

Self-incrimination is the act of accusing oneself of a crime for which a person can then be prosecuted. self-incrimination can occur either directly or indirectly: directly, by means of interrogation where information of a self-incriminatory nature is disclosed; indirectly, when information of a self-incriminatory nature is disclosed voluntarily without pressure from another person.

The Fifth Amendment to the United States Constitution protects witnesses from being forced to incriminate themselves.

Statute

A statute is a formal written enactment of a legislative authority that governs a country, state, city, or county. Typically, statute s command or prohibit something, or declare policy. The word is often used to distinguish law made by legislative bodies from case law and the regulations issued by Government agencies.

Statute of limitations

A statute of limitations is a statute in a common law legal system that sets forth the maximum period of time, after certain events, that legal proceedings based on those events may be initiated. In civil law systems, similar provisions are usually part of the civil code or criminal code and are often known collectively as "periods of prescription" or "prescriptive periods."

A common law legal system might have a statute limiting the time for prosecution of crimes called misdemeanors to two years after the offense occurred. In that statute, if a person is discovered to have committed a misdemeanor three years ago, the time has expired for the prosecution of the misdemeanor.

United States

· History of competition law
· Monopoly

· Coercive monopoly
· Natural monopoly
· Barriers to entry
· Market power
· SSNIP test
· Relevant market
· Merger control

Anti-competitive practices

· Monopolization
· Collusion

· Formation of cartels
· Price fixing
· Bid rigging
· Product bundling and tying
· Refusal to deal

· Group boycott
· Exclusive dealing
· Dividing territories
· Conscious parallelism
· Predatory pricing
· Misuse of patents and copyrights

Laws and doctrines

United States

- Sherman Antitrust Act
- Clayton Antitrust Act
- Robinson-Patman Act
- FTC Act
- Hart-Scott-Rodino Act
- Merger guidelines
- Essential facilities doctrine
- Noerr-Pennington doctrine
- Parker immunity doctrine
- Rule of reason

Europe

- UK competition law
- Irish competition law

Australia

- Trade Practices Act 1974

Enforcement authorities and organizations

Competition law history refers to attempts by governments to regulate competitive markets for goods and services, leading up to the modern competition or antitrust laws around the world today. The earliest records traces back to the efforts of Roman legislators to control price fluctuations and unfair trade practices. Through the Middle Ages in Europe, Kings and Queens repeatedly cracked down on monopolies, including those created through state legislation.

- International Competition Network
- List of competition regulators

Business

There are many ways in which a business may be owned under the legal system of England and Wales. Different types of ownership are suitable for organisations depending on the degree of control the owners wish to have over the business. The choice of ownership methor also relates to the organisations ability to raise funds for the business activities.

Service provider

A service provider is an entity that provides services to other entities. Usually this refers to a business that provides subscription or web service to other businesses or individuals. Examples of these services include Internet access, Mobile phone operator, and web application hosting.

Plea bargain

A plea bargain is an agreement in a criminal case where by the prosecutor offers the defendant the opportunity to plead guilty, usually to a lesser charge or to the original criminal charge with a recommendation of a lighter than the maximum sentence. A plea bargain gives criminal defendants the opportunity to avoid sitting through a trial risking conviction on the original more serious charge. For example, a criminal defendant charged with a felony theft charge, the conviction of which would require imprisonment in state prison, may be offered the opportunity to plead guilty to a misdemeanor theft charge, which may not carry jail time.

Probable cause

The right of the people to be secure in their persons, houses, papers, and effects, against unreasonable searches and seizures, shall not be violated, and no Warrants shall issue, but upon Probable cause, supported by Oath or affirmation, and particularly describing the place to be searched, and the persons or things to be seized.

The most well-known definition of Probable cause is "a reasonable belief that a person has committed a crime". Another common definition is "a reasonable amount of suspicion, supported by circumstances sufficiently strong to justify a prudent and cautious person"s belief that certain facts are probably true".

Guarantee

The act of becoming a surety is also called a Guarantee. Traditionally a Guarantee was distinguished from a surety in that the surety"s liability was joint and primary with the principal, whereas the guaranty"s liability was ancillary and derivative, but many jurisdictions have abolished this distinction

Sarbanes-Oxley Act

The Sarbanes-Oxley Act of 2002 (Pub.L. 107-204, 116 Stat. 745, enacted July 30, 2002), also known as the Public Company Accounting Reform and Investor Protection Act of 2002 and commonly called Sarbanes-Oxley, Sarbox or SOX, is a United States federal law enacted on July 30, 2002, as a reaction to a number of major corporate and accounting scandals including those affecting Enron, Tyco International, Adelphia, Peregrine Systems and WorldCom.

Sentencing guidelines

The Federal Sentencing guidelines are rules that set out a uniform sentencing policy for convicted felons in the United States federal courts system.

The Guidelines are the product of the United States Sentencing Commission and are part of an overall federal sentencing reform package that took effect in the mid-1960s. The implementation of this reform package was the result of bipartisan cooperation, led chiefly by Senator Edward Kennedy, as Chair of the Senate Judiciary Committee, and Attorney General Edwin Meese.

United States Sentencing Commission

The United States Sentencing Commission is an independent agency of the judicial branch of the federal government of the United States. It is responsible for articulating the sentencing guidelines for the United States federal courts. The Commission promulgates the Federal Sentencing Guidelines, which replaced the prior system of indeterminate sentencing that allowed trial judges to give sentences ranging from probation to the maximum statutory punishment for the offense.

Terrorism	Terrorism is a policy or ideology of violence intended to intimidate or cause terror for the purpose of "exerting pressure on decision making by state bodies." The term "terror" is largely used to indicate clandestine, low-intensity violence that targets civilians and generates public fear. Thus "terror" is distinct from asymmetric warfare, and violates the concept of a common law of war in which civilian life is regarded. The term "-ism" is used to indicate an ideology --typically one that claims its attacks are in the domain of a "just war" concept, though most condemn such as crimes against humanity.
Privacy	Privacy is the ability of an individual or group to seclude themselves or information about themselves and thereby reveal themselves selectively. The boundaries and content of what is considered private differ among cultures and individuals, but share basic common themes. Privacy is sometimes related to anonymity, the wish to remain unnoticed or unidentified in the public realm.
USA Patriot Act	The USA Patriot Act, commonly known as the "Patriot Act", is a statute enacted by the United States Government that President George W. Bush signed into law on October 26, 2001. The contrived acronym stands for Uniting and Strengthening America by Providing Appropriate Tools Required to Intercept and Obstruct Terrorism Act of 2001 (Public Law Pub.L. 107-56.)
Freedom of contract	Freedom of contract or contractualism is the freedom of individuals to bargain among themselves the terms of their own contracts, without government interference. Anything more than minimal regulations and taxes may be seen as infringements. It is the underpinning of the theory of laissez-faire economics.
Trademark	A trademark or trade mark is a distinctive sign or indicator used by an individual, business organization and to distinguish its products or services from those of other entities. A trademark is designated by the following symbols: · â„¢ (for an unregistered trademark that is, a mark used to promote or brand goods); · â„ (for an unregistered service mark, that is, a mark used to promote or brand services); and · Â® (for a registered trademark) A trademark is a type of intellectual property, and typically a name, word, phrase, logo, symbol, design, image, or a combination of these elements. There is also a range of non-conventional trademark s comprising marks which do not fall into these standard categories. The owner of a registered trademark may commence legal proceedings for trademark infringement to prevent unauthorized use of that trademark
Trademark Infringement	Trademark infringement is a violation of the exclusive rights attaching to a trademark without the authorization of the trademark owner or any licensees (provided that such authorization was within the scope of the license.) Infringement may occur when one party, the "infringer", uses a trademark which is identical or confusingly similar to a trademark owned by another party, in relation to products or services which are identical or similar to the products or services which the registration covers. An owner of a trademark may commence legal proceedings against a party which infringes its registration.

Duty

Duty (from "due," that which is owing, O. Fr. deu, did, past participle of devoir; Lat. debere, debitum; cf.

Obligation

An obligation is a requirement to take some course of action, whether legal or moral. There are also obligation s in other normative contexts, such as obligation s of etiquette, social obligation s, and possibly in terms of politics, where obligation s are requirements which must be fulfilled. These are generally legal obligation s, which can incur a penalty for unfulfilment, although certain people are obliged to carry out certain actions for other reasons as well, whether as a tradition or for social reasons.

Parol evidence

The Parol evidence rule is the legal application of a rule of substantive law in contract cases that prevents a party to a written contract from contradicting (or sometimes adding to) the terms of the contract by seeking the admission of evidence "extrinsic" (outside) to the contract. For example, Carl agrees in writing to sell Betty a car for $1,000. Betty argues that Carl told her that she would only need to pay Carl $800.

Parol evidence rule

The Parol evidence rule is the legal application of a rule of substantive law in contract cases that prevents a party to a written contract from contradicting (or sometimes adding to) the terms of the contract by seeking the admission of evidence "extrinsic" (outside) to the contract. For example, Carl agrees in writing to sell Betty a car for $1,000. Betty argues that Carl told her that she would only need to pay Carl $800.

Statute

A statute is a formal written enactment of a legislative authority that governs a country, state, city, or county. Typically, statute s command or prohibit something, or declare policy. The word is often used to distinguish law made by legislative bodies from case law and the regulations issued by Government agencies.

Statute of Frauds

The Statute of Frauds refers to the requirement that certain kinds of contracts be made in writing and signed.

Traditionally, the Statute of Frauds requires a writing signed by the defendant in the following circumstances:

· Contracts in consideration of marriage.
· Contracts which cannot be performed within one year.
· Contracts for the transfer of an interest in land.
· Contracts by the executor of a will to pay a debt of the estate with their own money.
· Contracts for the sale of goods above a certain value.
· Contracts in which one party becomes a surety (acts as guarantor) for another party"s debt or other obligation.

This can be remembered by the mnemonic "MY LEGS": Marriage, one year, land, executor, goods, surety.

The term Statute of Frauds comes from an English Act of Parliament passed in 1677 (authored by Sir Leoline Jenkins and passed by the Cavalier Parliament), and more properly called An Act for Prevention of Frauds and Perjuries. Many common law jurisdictions have made similar statutory provisions, while a number of civil law jurisdictions have equivalent legislation incorporated into their civil codes.

Statutory law	Statutory law or statute law is written law (as opposed to oral or customary law) set down by a legislature (as opposed to regulatory law promulgated by the executive branch or common law of the judiciary.) Statutes are enacted in response to a perceived need to clarify the functioning of government, improve civil order, to codify existing law, or for an individual or company to obtain special treatment. Examples of statutory law comprehend traditional civil law and modern civil code systems in contrast to common law.
Uniform Commercial Code	The Uniform Commercial Code is one of a number of uniform acts that have been promulgated in conjunction with efforts to harmonize the law of sales and other commercial transactions in all 50 states within the United States of America. This objective is deemed important because of the prevalence today of commercial transactions that extend beyond one state (for example, where the goods are manufactured in state A, warehoused in state B, sold from state C and delivered in state D.) The Uniform Commercial Code deals primarily with transactions involving personal property (movable property), not real property (immovable property.)
Consideration	Consideration is the legal concept of value in connection with contracts. It is anything of value in the common sense, promised to another when making a contract. It can take the form of money, physical objects, services, promised actions, or even abstinence from a future action.
Contract	Agreement is said to be reached when an offer capable of immediate acceptance is met with a "mirror image" acceptance (ie, an unqualified acceptance). The parties must have the necessary capacity to Contract and the Contract must not be either trifling, indeterminate, impossible or illegal. Contract law is based on the principle expressed in the Latin phrase pacta sunt servanda .
Lease	A Lease is a contract conferring a right on one person to possess property belonging to another person (called a landlord or lessor) to the exclusion of the owner landlord, and all others except with the invitation of the tenant. It is a rental agreement between landlord and tenant. The relationship between the tenant and the landlord is called a tenancy, and the right to possession by the tenant is sometimes called a Leasehold interest.
Reasonable person standard	The reasonable person is a legal fiction of the common law representing an objective standard against which any individual"s conduct can be measured. It is used to determine if a breach of the standard of care has occurred, provided a duty of care can be proven. The Reasonable person standard holds: each person owes a duty to behave as a reasonable person would under the same or similar circumstances.
Chief brand officer	A Chief brand officer is a relatively new executive level position at a corporation, company, organization typically reporting directly to the CEO or board of directors. The Chief brand officer is responsible for a brand"s image, experience, and promise, and propagating it throughout all aspects of the company. The brand officer oversees marketing, advertising, design, public relations and customer service departments.

Offeree

Offer and acceptance analysis is a traditional approach in contract law used to determine whether an agreement exists between two parties. As a contract is an agreement, an offer is an indication by one person (the "offeror") to another (the "Offeree") of the offeror"s willingness to enter into a contract on certain terms without further negotiations. A contract is said to come into existence when acceptance of an offer (agreement to the terms in it) has been communicated to the offeror by the Offeree.

Offeror

Offer and acceptance analysis is a traditional approach in contract law used to determine whether an agreement exists between two parties. As a contract is an agreement, an offer is an indication by one person (the "Offeror") to another (the "offeree") of the Offeror"s willingness to enter into a contract on certain terms without further negotiations. A contract is said to come into existence when acceptance of an offer (agreement to the terms in it) has been communicated to the Offeror by the offeree.

Security interest

A Security interest is a property interest created by agreement or by operation of law over assets to secure the performance of an obligation, usually the payment of a debt. It gives the beneficiary of the Security interest certain preferential rights in the disposition of secured assets. Such rights vary according to the type of Security interest, but in most cases, a holder of the Security interest is entitled to seize, and usually sell, the property to discharge the debt that the Security interest secures.

Employment

Employment is a contract between two parties, one being the employer and the other being the employee. An employee may be defined as: "A person in the service of another under any contract of hire, express or implied, oral or written, where the employer has the power or right to control and direct the employee in the material details of how the work is to be performed." Black"s Law Dictionary page 471 (5th ed. 1979).

Estoppel

Estoppel is a legal doctrine at common law, where a party is barred from claiming or denying an argument on an equitable ground. Estoppel complements the requirement of consideration in contract law. In general, Estoppel protects an aggrieved party, if the counter-party induced an expectation from the aggrieved party, and the aggrieved party reasonably relied on the expectation and would suffer detriment if the expectation is not met.

Bill of lading

A Bill of lading (sometimes referred to as a Bill of lading,or B/L) is a document issued by a carrier to a shipper, acknowledging that specified goods have been received on board as cargo for conveyance to a named place for delivery to the consignee who is usually identified. A through Bill of lading involves the use of at least two different modes of transport from road, rail, air, and sea. The term derives from the noun "bill", a schedule of costs for services supplied or to be supplied, and from the verb "to lade" which means to load a cargo onto a ship or other form of transport.

Letter of credit

A standard, commercial Letter of credit is a document issued mostly by a financial institution, used primarily in trade finance, which usually provides an irrevocable payment undertaking.

The LC can also be the source of payment for a transaction, meaning that redeeming the Letter of credit will pay an exporter. Letters of credit are used primarily in international trade transactions of significant value, for deals between a supplier in one country and a customer in another.

Rescission	In contract law, rescission has been defined as the unmaking of a contract between parties. rescission is the unwinding of a transaction. This is done to bring the parties, as far as possible, back to the position in which they were before they entered into a contract (the "status quo ante".)
Revocation	Revocation is the act of recall or annulment. It is the reversal of an act, the recalling of a grant, or the making void of some deed previously existing. In the law of contracts, revocation is a type of remedy for buyers when the buyer accepts a nonconforming good from the seller.
Ratification	Ratification is the act of approving and paying for supplies or services provided to and accepted by the government as a result of an unauthorized commitment. It gives official sanction or approval to a formal document such as a treaty or constitution. It includes the process of adopting an international treaty by the legislature, a constitution, or another nationally binding document (such as an amendment to a constitution) by the agreement of multiple sub-national entities.
Unconscionability	Unconscionability is a term used in contract law to describe a defense against the enforcement of a contract based on the presence of terms unfair to one party. Typically, such a contract is held to be unenforceable because the consideration offered is lacking or is so obviously inadequate that to enforce the contract would be unfair to the party seeking to escape the contract. In and of itself, inadequate consideration is likely not enough to make a contract unenforceable.
Voidable	In law, a transaction or action which is voidable is valid, but may be annulled by one of the parties to the transaction. voidable is usually used in distinction to void ab initio (or void from the outset) and unenforceable. The act of invalidating the contract by the party exercising its rights to anul the voidable contract is usually referred to either as voiding the contract (in the United States and Canada) or avoiding the contract (in the United Kingdom, Australia and other common law countries.)
Quantum meruit	Quantum meruit is a Latin phrase meaning "as much as he has deserved". This claim is also referred to as "unjust enrichment." In the context of contract law, it means something along the lines of "reasonable value of services". In the United States, the elements of quantum meruit are determined by state common law.
Unjust enrichment	Unjust enrichment is a legal term denoting a particular type of causative event in which one party is unjustly enriched at the expense of another, and an obligation to make restitution arises, regardless of liability for wrongdoing. Liability under the principle of unjust enrichment is wholly independent of liability for wrongdoing. Claims in unjust enrichment do not depend upon proof of any wrong.

Plain meaning rule	The Plain meaning rule is a type of statutory construction, which dictates that statutes are to be interpreted using the ordinary meaning of the language of the statute unless a statute explicitly defines some of its terms otherwise. In other words, the law is to read, word for word and should not divert from its true meaning. It is the mechanism that underlines textualism and, to a certain extent, originalism.

Contract

Agreement is said to be reached when an offer capable of immediate acceptance is met with a "mirror image" acceptance (ie, an unqualified acceptance). The parties must have the necessary capacity to Contract and the Contract must not be either trifling, indeterminate, impossible or illegal. Contract law is based on the principle expressed in the Latin phrase pacta sunt servanda .

Lease

A Lease is a contract conferring a right on one person to possess property belonging to another person (called a landlord or lessor) to the exclusion of the owner landlord, and all others except with the invitation of the tenant. It is a rental agreement between landlord and tenant. The relationship between the tenant and the landlord is called a tenancy, and the right to possession by the tenant is sometimes called a Leasehold interest.

Offeree

Offer and acceptance analysis is a traditional approach in contract law used to determine whether an agreement exists between two parties. As a contract is an agreement, an offer is an indication by one person (the "offeror") to another (the "Offeree") of the offeror"s willingness to enter into a contract on certain terms without further negotiations. A contract is said to come into existence when acceptance of an offer (agreement to the terms in it) has been communicated to the offeror by the Offeree.

Offeror

Offer and acceptance analysis is a traditional approach in contract law used to determine whether an agreement exists between two parties. As a contract is an agreement, an offer is an indication by one person (the "Offeror") to another (the "offeree") of the Offeror"s willingness to enter into a contract on certain terms without further negotiations. A contract is said to come into existence when acceptance of an offer (agreement to the terms in it) has been communicated to the Offeror by the offeree.

Parol evidence

The Parol evidence rule is the legal application of a rule of substantive law in contract cases that prevents a party to a written contract from contradicting (or sometimes adding to) the terms of the contract by seeking the admission of evidence "extrinsic" (outside) to the contract. For example, Carl agrees in writing to sell Betty a car for $1,000. Betty argues that Carl told her that she would only need to pay Carl $800.

Parol evidence rule

The Parol evidence rule is the legal application of a rule of substantive law in contract cases that prevents a party to a written contract from contradicting (or sometimes adding to) the terms of the contract by seeking the admission of evidence "extrinsic" (outside) to the contract. For example, Carl agrees in writing to sell Betty a car for $1,000. Betty argues that Carl told her that she would only need to pay Carl $800.

Statute

A statute is a formal written enactment of a legislative authority that governs a country, state, city, or county. Typically, statute s command or prohibit something, or declare policy. The word is often used to distinguish law made by legislative bodies from case law and the regulations issued by Government agencies.

Statute of Frauds

The Statute of Frauds refers to the requirement that certain kinds of contracts be made in writing and signed.

Traditionally, the Statute of Frauds requires a writing signed by the defendant in the following circumstances:

· Contracts in consideration of marriage.
· Contracts which cannot be performed within one year.
· Contracts for the transfer of an interest in land.
· Contracts by the executor of a will to pay a debt of the estate with their own money.
· Contracts for the sale of goods above a certain value.
· Contracts in which one party becomes a surety (acts as guarantor) for another party"s debt or other obligation.

This can be remembered by the mnemonic "MY LEGS": Marriage, one year, land, executor, goods, surety.

The term Statute of Frauds comes from an English Act of Parliament passed in 1677 (authored by Sir Leoline Jenkins and passed by the Cavalier Parliament), and more properly called An Act for Prevention of Frauds and Perjuries. Many common law jurisdictions have made similar statutory provisions, while a number of civil law jurisdictions have equivalent legislation incorporated into their civil codes.

Chief brand officer

A Chief brand officer is a relatively new executive level position at a corporation, company, organization typically reporting directly to the CEO or board of directors. The Chief brand officer is responsible for a brand"s image, experience, and promise, and propagating it throughout all aspects of the company. The brand officer oversees marketing, advertising, design, public relations and customer service departments.

Consideration

Consideration is the legal concept of value in connection with contracts. It is anything of value in the common sense, promised to another when making a contract. It can take the form of money, physical objects, services, promised actions, or even abstinence from a future action.

Revocation

Revocation is the act of recall or annulment. It is the reversal of an act, the recalling of a grant, or the making void of some deed previously existing.

In the law of contracts, revocation is a type of remedy for buyers when the buyer accepts a nonconforming good from the seller.

Estoppel

Estoppel is a legal doctrine at common law, where a party is barred from claiming or denying an argument on an equitable ground. Estoppel complements the requirement of consideration in contract law. In general, Estoppel protects an aggrieved party, if the counter-party induced an expectation from the aggrieved party, and the aggrieved party reasonably relied on the expectation and would suffer detriment if the expectation is not met.

Option

In finance, an option is a contract between a buyer and a seller that gives the buyer the right--but not the obligation--to buy or to sell a particular asset (the underlying asset) at a later day at an agreed price. In return for granting the option, the seller collects a payment (the premium) from the buyer. A call option gives the buyer the right to buy the underlying asset; a put option gives the buyer of the option the right to sell the underlying asset.

Subscription business model	The subscription business model is a business model where a customer must pay a subscription price to have access to the product/service. The model was pioneered by magazines and newspapers, but is now used by many businesses and websites. Rather than selling products individually, a subscription sells periodic (monthly or yearly or seasonal) use or access to a product or service, or, in the case of such non-profit organizations as opera companies or symphony orchestras, it sells tickets to the entire run of five to fifteen scheduled performances for an entire season.
Mirror image rule	In the law of contracts, the Mirror image rule, also referred to as an unequivocal and absolute acceptance requirement states that an offer must be accepted exactly without modifications. The offeror is the master of his own offer. An attempt to accept the offer on different terms instead creates a counter-offer, and this constitutes a rejection of the original offer.
Operation of law	The phrase "by Operation of law" is a legal term that indicates that a right or liability has been created for a party, irrespective of the intent of that party, because it is dictated by existing legal principles. For example, if a person dies without a will, his heirs are determined by Operation of law. Similarly, if a person marries or has a child after his or her will has been executed, the law writes this pretermitted spouse or pretermitted heir into the will if no provision for this situation was specifically included.
Impossibility	In contract law, Impossibility is an excuse for the nonperformance of duties under a contract, based on a change in circumstances (or the discovery of preexisting circumstances), the nonoccurrence of which was an underlying assumption of the contract, that makes performance of the contract literally impossible. For such a defense to be raised, performance must not merely be difficult or unexpectedly costly for one party; there must be no way for it to actually be accomplished. For example, if Rachel contracts to pay Joey $1000 to paint her house on October 1, but the house burns to the ground before the end of September, Rachel is excused from her duty to pay Joey the $1000, and he is excused from his duty to paint her house; however, Joey may still be able to sue for the unjust enrichment of any benefit conferred on Rachel before her house burned down.
Negotiable instrument	A Negotiable instrument is a specialized type of "contract" for the payment of money that is unconditional and capable of transfer by negotiation. Common examples include cheques, banknotes (paper money), and commercial paper. A Negotiable instrument is not a contract, as contract formation requires an offer, acceptance, and consideration, none of which is an element of a Negotiable instrument.
Mailbox rule	In common law contracts, the Mailbox rule (called the postal rule or postal acceptance rule in the UK, Australia and New Zealand, or deposited acceptance rule) determines the timing of acceptance of an offer when mail is contemplated as the medium of acceptance. The general principle is that a contract is formed when acceptance is actually communicated to the offeror. The Mailbox rule is an exception to the general principle.

Uniform Electronic Transactions Act

The Uniform Electronic Transactions Act is one of the several United States Uniform Acts proposed by the National Conference of Commissioners on Uniform State Laws (NCCUSL.) Since then 46 States, the District of Columbia, Puerto Rico, and the U.S. Virgin Islands have adopted it into their own laws. Its overarching purpose is to bring into line the differing State laws over such areas as retention of paper records (checks in particular), and the validity of electronic signatures, thereby supporting the validity of electronic contracts as a viable medium of agreement.

United States

· History of competition law
· Monopoly

· Coercive monopoly
· Natural monopoly
· Barriers to entry
· Market power
· SSNIP test
· Relevant market
· Merger control

Anti-competitive practices

· Monopolization
· Collusion

· Formation of cartels
· Price fixing
· Bid rigging
· Product bundling and tying
· Refusal to deal

· Group boycott
· Exclusive dealing
· Dividing territories
· Conscious parallelism
· Predatory pricing
· Misuse of patents and copyrights

Laws and doctrines

United States

- Sherman Antitrust Act
- Clayton Antitrust Act
- Robinson-Patman Act
- FTC Act
- Hart-Scott-Rodino Act
- Merger guidelines
- Essential facilities doctrine
- Noerr-Pennington doctrine
- Parker immunity doctrine
- Rule of reason

Europe

- UK competition law
- Irish competition law

Australia

- Trade Practices Act 1974

Enforcement authorities and organizations

Competition law history refers to attempts by governments to regulate competitive markets for goods and services, leading up to the modern competition or antitrust laws around the world today. The earliest records traces back to the efforts of Roman legislators to control price fluctuations and unfair trade practices. Through the Middle Ages in Europe, Kings and Queens repeatedly cracked down on monopolies, including those created through state legislation.

- International Competition Network
- List of competition regulators

Forbearance

In the context of a mortgage process, Forbearance is a special agreement between the lender and the borrower to delay a foreclosure.

Loan borrowers sometimes have problems making payments. This may cause the lender to start the foreclosure process.

Lease

A Lease is a contract conferring a right on one person to possess property belonging to another person (called a landlord or lessor) to the exclusion of the owner landlord, and all others except with the invitation of the tenant. It is a rental agreement between landlord and tenant. The relationship between the tenant and the landlord is called a tenancy, and the right to possession by the tenant is sometimes called a Leasehold interest.

Cash

Two primary accounting methods, cash and accrual basis, are used to calculate taxable income for U.S. federal income taxes. According to the Internal Revenue Code, a taxpayer may compute taxable income by:

· the cash receipts and disbursements method;
· an accrual method;
· any other method permitted by the chapter; or
· any combination of the foregoing methods permitted under regulations prescribed by the Secretary.

As a general rule, a taxpayer must compute taxable income using the same accounting method he uses to compute income in keeping his books.

Consideration

Consideration is the legal concept of value in connection with contracts. It is anything of value in the common sense, promised to another when making a contract. It can take the form of money, physical objects, services, promised actions, or even abstinence from a future action.

Contract

Agreement is said to be reached when an offer capable of immediate acceptance is met with a "mirror image" acceptance (ie, an unqualified acceptance). The parties must have the necessary capacity to Contract and the Contract must not be either trifling, indeterminate, impossible or illegal. Contract law is based on the principle expressed in the Latin phrase pacta sunt servanda .

Duty

Duty (from "due," that which is owing, O. Fr. deu, did, past participle of devoir; Lat. debere, debitum; cf.

Obligation

An obligation is a requirement to take some course of action, whether legal or moral. There are also obligation s in other normative contexts, such as obligation s of etiquette, social obligation s, and possibly in terms of politics, where obligation s are requirements which must be fulfilled. These are generally legal obligation s, which can incur a penalty for unfulfilment, although certain people are obliged to carry out certain actions for other reasons as well, whether as a tradition or for social reasons.

Rescission

In contract law, rescission has been defined as the unmaking of a contract between parties. rescission is the unwinding of a transaction. This is done to bring the parties, as far as possible, back to the position in which they were before they entered into a contract (the "status quo ante".)

Unconscionability	Unconscionability is a term used in contract law to describe a defense against the enforcement of a contract based on the presence of terms unfair to one party. Typically, such a contract is held to be unenforceable because the consideration offered is lacking or is so obviously inadequate that to enforce the contract would be unfair to the party seeking to escape the contract. In and of itself, inadequate consideration is likely not enough to make a contract unenforceable.
Chief brand officer	A Chief brand officer is a relatively new executive level position at a corporation, company, organization typically reporting directly to the CEO or board of directors. The Chief brand officer is responsible for a brand"s image, experience, and promise, and propagating it throughout all aspects of the company. The brand officer oversees marketing, advertising, design, public relations and customer service departments.
Security interest	A Security interest is a property interest created by agreement or by operation of law over assets to secure the performance of an obligation, usually the payment of a debt. It gives the beneficiary of the Security interest certain preferential rights in the disposition of secured assets. Such rights vary according to the type of Security interest, but in most cases, a holder of the Security interest is entitled to seize, and usually sell, the property to discharge the debt that the Security interest secures.
Illusory Promise	In contract law, an Illusory promise is one that courts will not enforce. This is in contrast with a contract, which is a promise that courts will enforce. A promise may be illusory for a number of reasons.
Statute	A statute is a formal written enactment of a legislative authority that governs a country, state, city, or county. Typically, statute s command or prohibit something, or declare policy. The word is often used to distinguish law made by legislative bodies from case law and the regulations issued by Government agencies.
Statute of Frauds	The Statute of Frauds refers to the requirement that certain kinds of contracts be made in writing and signed. Traditionally, the Statute of Frauds requires a writing signed by the defendant in the following circumstances: · Contracts in consideration of marriage. · Contracts which cannot be performed within one year. · Contracts for the transfer of an interest in land. · Contracts by the executor of a will to pay a debt of the estate with their own money. · Contracts for the sale of goods above a certain value. · Contracts in which one party becomes a surety (acts as guarantor) for another party"s debt or other obligation. This can be remembered by the mnemonic "MY LEGS": Marriage, one year, land, executor, goods, surety.

The term Statute of Frauds comes from an English Act of Parliament passed in 1677 (authored by Sir Leoline Jenkins and passed by the Cavalier Parliament), and more properly called An Act for Prevention of Frauds and Perjuries. Many common law jurisdictions have made similar statutory provisions, while a number of civil law jurisdictions have equivalent legislation incorporated into their civil codes.

Estoppel

Estoppel is a legal doctrine at common law, where a party is barred from claiming or denying an argument on an equitable ground. Estoppel complements the requirement of consideration in contract law. In general, Estoppel protects an aggrieved party, if the counter-party induced an expectation from the aggrieved party, and the aggrieved party reasonably relied on the expectation and would suffer detriment if the expectation is not met.

Statute of limitations

A statute of limitations is a statute in a common law legal system that sets forth the maximum period of time, after certain events, that legal proceedings based on those events may be initiated. In civil law systems, similar provisions are usually part of the civil code or criminal code and are often known collectively as "periods of prescription" or "prescriptive periods."

A common law legal system might have a statute limiting the time for prosecution of crimes called misdemeanors to two years after the offense occurred. In that statute, if a person is discovered to have committed a misdemeanor three years ago, the time has expired for the prosecution of the misdemeanor.

Parol evidence

The Parol evidence rule is the legal application of a rule of substantive law in contract cases that prevents a party to a written contract from contradicting (or sometimes adding to) the terms of the contract by seeking the admission of evidence "extrinsic" (outside) to the contract. For example, Carl agrees in writing to sell Betty a car for $1,000. Betty argues that Carl told her that she would only need to pay Carl $800.

Parol evidence rule

The Parol evidence rule is the legal application of a rule of substantive law in contract cases that prevents a party to a written contract from contradicting (or sometimes adding to) the terms of the contract by seeking the admission of evidence "extrinsic" (outside) to the contract. For example, Carl agrees in writing to sell Betty a car for $1,000. Betty argues that Carl told her that she would only need to pay Carl $800.

Employment

Employment is a contract between two parties, one being the employer and the other being the employee. An employee may be defined as: "A person in the service of another under any contract of hire, express or implied, oral or written, where the employer has the power or right to control and direct the employee in the material details of how the work is to be performed." Black"s Law Dictionary page 471 (5th ed. 1979).

Employment discrimination

Employment discrimination (or workplace discrimination) is discrimination in hiring, promotion, job assignment, termination, and compensation. It includes various types of harassment.

Many jurisdictions prohibit some types of Employment discrimination, often by forbidding discrimination based on certain traits ("protected categories").

Public policy	Public policy can be generally defined as the course of action or inaction taken by governmental entities with regard to a particular issue or set of issues. Other scholars define it as a system of "courses of action, regulatory measures, laws, and funding priorities concerning a given topic promulgated by a governmental entity or its representatives." public policy is commonly embodied "in constitutions, legislative acts, and judicial decisions." In the United States, this concept refers not only to the end result of policies, but more broadly to the decision-making and analysis of governmental decisions. public policy is also considered an academic discipline, as it is studied by professors and students at public policy schools of major universities throughout the country.
Subscription business model	The subscription business model is a business model where a customer must pay a subscription price to have access to the product/service. The model was pioneered by magazines and newspapers, but is now used by many businesses and websites. Rather than selling products individually, a subscription sells periodic (monthly or yearly or seasonal) use or access to a product or service, or, in the case of such non-profit organizations as opera companies or symphony orchestras, it sells tickets to the entire run of five to fifteen scheduled performances for an entire season.
Tort	Tort law is a body of law that addresses, and provides remedies for, civil wrongs not arising out of contractual obligations. A person who suffers legal damages may be able to use Tort law to receive compensation from someone who is legally responsible, or "liable," for those injuries. Generally speaking, Tort law defines what constitutes a legal injury and establishes the circumstances under which one person may be held liable for another"s injury.

Lease

A Lease is a contract conferring a right on one person to possess property belonging to another person (called a landlord or lessor) to the exclusion of the owner landlord, and all others except with the invitation of the tenant. It is a rental agreement between landlord and tenant. The relationship between the tenant and the landlord is called a tenancy, and the right to possession by the tenant is sometimes called a Leasehold interest.

Statute

A statute is a formal written enactment of a legislative authority that governs a country, state, city, or county. Typically, statute s command or prohibit something, or declare policy. The word is often used to distinguish law made by legislative bodies from case law and the regulations issued by Government agencies.

Statute of Frauds

The Statute of Frauds refers to the requirement that certain kinds of contracts be made in writing and signed.

Traditionally, the Statute of Frauds requires a writing signed by the defendant in the following circumstances:

· Contracts in consideration of marriage.
· Contracts which cannot be performed within one year.
· Contracts for the transfer of an interest in land.
· Contracts by the executor of a will to pay a debt of the estate with their own money.
· Contracts for the sale of goods above a certain value.
· Contracts in which one party becomes a surety (acts as guarantor) for another party"s debt or other obligation.

This can be remembered by the mnemonic "MY LEGS": Marriage, one year, land, executor, goods, surety.

The term Statute of Frauds comes from an English Act of Parliament passed in 1677 (authored by Sir Leoline Jenkins and passed by the Cavalier Parliament), and more properly called An Act for Prevention of Frauds and Perjuries. Many common law jurisdictions have made similar statutory provisions, while a number of civil law jurisdictions have equivalent legislation incorporated into their civil codes.

Consideration

Consideration is the legal concept of value in connection with contracts. It is anything of value in the common sense, promised to another when making a contract. It can take the form of money, physical objects, services, promised actions, or even abstinence from a future action.

Contract

Agreement is said to be reached when an offer capable of immediate acceptance is met with a "mirror image" acceptance (ie, an unqualified acceptance). The parties must have the necessary capacity to Contract and the Contract must not be either trifling, indeterminate, impossible or illegal. Contract law is based on the principle expressed in the Latin phrase pacta sunt servanda .

Voidable

In law, a transaction or action which is voidable is valid, but may be annulled by one of the parties to the transaction. voidable is usually used in distinction to void ab initio (or void from the outset) and unenforceable.

The act of invalidating the contract by the party exercising its rights to anul the voidable contract is usually referred to either as voiding the contract (in the United States and Canada) or avoiding the contract (in the United Kingdom, Australia and other common law countries.)

Estoppel — Estoppel is a legal doctrine at common law, where a party is barred from claiming or denying an argument on an equitable ground. Estoppel complements the requirement of consideration in contract law. In general, Estoppel protects an aggrieved party, if the counter-party induced an expectation from the aggrieved party, and the aggrieved party reasonably relied on the expectation and would suffer detriment if the expectation is not met.

Misrepresentation — Misrepresentation is a contract law concept. It means a false statement of fact made by one party to another party, which has the effect of inducing that party into the contract. For example, under certain circumstances, false statements or promises made by a seller of goods regarding the quality or nature of the product that the seller has may constitute Misrepresentation.

Ratification — Ratification is the act of approving and paying for supplies or services provided to and accepted by the government as a result of an unauthorized commitment. It gives official sanction or approval to a formal document such as a treaty or constitution. It includes the process of adopting an international treaty by the legislature, a constitution, or another nationally binding document (such as an amendment to a constitution) by the agreement of multiple sub-national entities.

Chief brand officer — A Chief brand officer is a relatively new executive level position at a corporation, company, organization typically reporting directly to the CEO or board of directors. The Chief brand officer is responsible for a brand"s image, experience, and promise, and propagating it throughout all aspects of the company. The brand officer oversees marketing, advertising, design, public relations and customer service departments.

Negotiable instrument — A Negotiable instrument is a specialized type of "contract" for the payment of money that is unconditional and capable of transfer by negotiation. Common examples include cheques, banknotes (paper money), and commercial paper.

A Negotiable instrument is not a contract, as contract formation requires an offer, acceptance, and consideration, none of which is an element of a Negotiable instrument.

Parol evidence — The Parol evidence rule is the legal application of a rule of substantive law in contract cases that prevents a party to a written contract from contradicting (or sometimes adding to) the terms of the contract by seeking the admission of evidence "extrinsic" (outside) to the contract. For example, Carl agrees in writing to sell Betty a car for $1,000. Betty argues that Carl told her that she would only need to pay Carl $800.

Parol evidence rule — The Parol evidence rule is the legal application of a rule of substantive law in contract cases that prevents a party to a written contract from contradicting (or sometimes adding to) the terms of the contract by seeking the admission of evidence "extrinsic" (outside) to the contract. For example, Carl agrees in writing to sell Betty a car for $1,000. Betty argues that Carl told her that she would only need to pay Carl $800.

Valid

The term valid ity in logic applies to arguments or statements.

An argument is valid if and only if the truth of its premises entails the truth of its conclusion, it would be self-contradictory to affirm the premises and deny the conclusion. The corresponding conditional of a valid argument is a logical truth and the negation of its corresponding conditional is a contradiction.

Arbitration

Arbitration, a form of alternative dispute resolution (ADR), is a legal technique for the resolution of disputes outside the courts, wherein the parties to a dispute refer it to one or more persons (the "arbitrators", "arbiters" or "arbitral tribunal"), by whose decision (the "award") they agree to be bound. It is a settlement technique in which a third party reviews the case and imposes a decision that is legally binding for both sides. Other forms of ADR include mediation (a form of settlement negotiation facilitated by a neutral third party) and non-binding resolution by experts.

Usury

Usury originally meant the charging of interest on loans. This would have included charging a fee for the use of money, such as at a bureau de change. After countries legislated to limit the rate of interest on loans, Usury came to mean the interest above the lawful rate.

Employment

Employment is a contract between two parties, one being the employer and the other being the employee. An employee may be defined as: "A person in the service of another under any contract of hire, express or implied, oral or written, where the employer has the power or right to control and direct the employee in the material details of how the work is to be performed." Black"s Law Dictionary page 471 (5th ed. 1979).

Public policy

Public policy can be generally defined as the course of action or inaction taken by governmental entities with regard to a particular issue or set of issues. Other scholars define it as a system of "courses of action, regulatory measures, laws, and funding priorities concerning a given topic promulgated by a governmental entity or its representatives." public policy is commonly embodied "in constitutions, legislative acts, and judicial decisions."

In the United States, this concept refers not only to the end result of policies, but more broadly to the decision-making and analysis of governmental decisions. public policy is also considered an academic discipline, as it is studied by professors and students at public policy schools of major universities throughout the country.

Business

There are many ways in which a business may be owned under the legal system of England and Wales. Different types of ownership are suitable for organisations depending on the degree of control the owners wish to have over the business. The choice of ownership methor also relates to the organisations ability to raise funds for the business activities.

Consumer protection

Consumer protection laws are designed to ensure fair competition and the free flow of truthful information in the marketplace. The laws are designed to prevent businesses that engage in fraud or specified unfair practices from gaining an advantage over competitors and may provide additional protection for the weak and those unable to take care of themselves. Consumer protection laws are a form of government regulation which protects the interests of consumers.

Unconscionability	Unconscionability is a term used in contract law to describe a defense against the enforcement of a contract based on the presence of terms unfair to one party. Typically, such a contract is held to be unenforceable because the consideration offered is lacking or is so obviously inadequate that to enforce the contract would be unfair to the party seeking to escape the contract. In and of itself, inadequate consideration is likely not enough to make a contract unenforceable.
Arbitration clause	An Arbitration clause is a commonly used clause in a contract that requires the parties to resolve their disputes through an arbitration process. Although such a clause may or may not specify that arbitration occur within a specific jurisdiction, it always binds the parties to a type of resolution outside of the courts, and is therefore considered a kind of forum selection clause. In the United States, the federal government has expressed a policy of support of Arbitration clauses, because they reduce the burden on court systems to resolve disputes.
Pari delicto	In pari delicto, Latin for "in equal fault " is a legal term used to indicate that two persons or entities are equally at fault, whether the malfeasance in question is a crime or tort. The phrase is most commonly used by courts when relief is being denied to both parties in a civil action because of wrongdoing by both parties. The phrase means, in essence, that since both parties are equally at fault, the court will not involve itself in resolving one side"s claim over the other, and whoever possesses whatever is in dispute may continue to do so in the absence of a superior claim.
Duress	Duress or coercion (as a term of jurisprudence) is a possible legal defense, one of four of the most important justification defenses, by which defendants argue that they should not be held liable because the actions that broke the law were only performed out of an immediate fear of injury. Black"s Law Dictionary (6th ed). defines Duress as "any unlawful threat or coercion used...
Employment discrimination	Employment discrimination (or workplace discrimination) is discrimination in hiring, promotion, job assignment, termination, and compensation. It includes various types of harassment. Many jurisdictions prohibit some types of Employment discrimination, often by forbidding discrimination based on certain traits ("protected categories").
Protected class	Protected class is a term used in United States anti-discrimination law. The term describes groups of people who are protected from discrimination and harassment. The following characteristics are considered " Protected class es" and persons cannot be discriminated against based on these characteristics:

· Race - Federal: Civil Rights Act of 1964 and The Civil Rights Act of 1866
· Ethnicity
· Religion or sect - Federal: Civil Rights Act of 1964
· Color - Federal: Civil Rights Act of 1964
· National origin - Federal: Civil Rights Act of 1964
· Age (40 and over) - Federal: Age Discrimination in Employment Act of 1967
· Sex - Federal: Equal Pay Act of 1963 ' Civil Rights Act of 1964
· Familial status (Housing, cannot discriminate for having children, exception for senior housing)
· Sexual orientation (in some jurisdictions and not in others)
· Disability status - Federal: Vocational Rehabilitation and Other Rehabilitation Services of 1973 ' Americans with Disabilities Act of 1990
· Veteran status - Federal Vietnam Era Veterans Readjustment Assistance Act of 1974
· Genetic Information - Federal: Genetic Information Nondiscrimination Act .

Undue influence

Undue influence is an equitable doctrine that involves one person taking advantage of a position of power over another person. It is where free will to bargain is not possible.

If undue influence is proved in a contract, in USA law, the contract is voidable by the innocent party, and the remedy is rescission.

Numerary

Numerary is a civil designation for persons who are incorporated in a fixed or permanent way to a society or group: regular member of the working staff, permanent staff distinguished from a super Numerary .

The term Numerary and its counterpart, "super Numerary ," originated in Spanish and Latin American academy and government; it is now also used in countries all over the world, such as France, the U.S., England, Italy, etc.

There are Numerary members of surgical organizations, of universities, of gastronomical associations, etc.

Rescission	In contract law, rescission has been defined as the unmaking of a contract between parties. rescission is the unwinding of a transaction. This is done to bring the parties, as far as possible, back to the position in which they were before they entered into a contract (the "status quo ante".)
Cash	Two primary accounting methods, cash and accrual basis, are used to calculate taxable income for U.S. federal income taxes. According to the Internal Revenue Code, a taxpayer may compute taxable income by: · the cash receipts and disbursements method; · an accrual method; · any other method permitted by the chapter; or · any combination of the foregoing methods permitted under regulations prescribed by the Secretary. As a general rule, a taxpayer must compute taxable income using the same accounting method he uses to compute income in keeping his books.
Contract	Agreement is said to be reached when an offer capable of immediate acceptance is met with a "mirror image" acceptance (ie, an unqualified acceptance). The parties must have the necessary capacity to Contract and the Contract must not be either trifling, indeterminate, impossible or illegal. Contract law is based on the principle expressed in the Latin phrase pacta sunt servanda .
Unilateralism	Unilateralism is any doctrine or agenda that supports one-sided action. Such action may be in disregard for other parties, or as an expression of a commitment toward a direction which other parties may find agreeable. Unilateralism is a neologism, (used in all countries) coined to be an antonym for multilateralism --the doctrine which asserts the benefits of participation from as many parties as possible.
Unilateral Mistake	In contract law a mistake is an erroneous belief, at contracting, that certain facts are true. It may be used as grounds to invalidate the agreement. Common law has identified two different types of mistake in contract: "Unilateral mistake" and "mutual mistake," sometimes called "common mistake." A Unilateral mistake is where only one party to a contract is mistaken as to the terms or subject-matter contained in a contract.
Misrepresentation	Misrepresentation is a contract law concept. It means a false statement of fact made by one party to another party, which has the effect of inducing that party into the contract. For example, under certain circumstances, false statements or promises made by a seller of goods regarding the quality or nature of the product that the seller has may constitute Misrepresentation.
Puffery	Puffery as a legal term refers to promotional statements and claims that express subjective rather than objective views, such that no reasonable person would take literally. Puffery is especially featured in testimonials. In a legal context, the term originated in the English Court of Appeal case Carlill v Carbolic Smoke Ball Company, which centred on whether a monetary reimbursement should be paid when an influenza preventative device failed to work.

Estoppel	Estoppel is a legal doctrine at common law, where a party is barred from claiming or denying an argument on an equitable ground. Estoppel complements the requirement of consideration in contract law. In general, Estoppel protects an aggrieved party, if the counter-party induced an expectation from the aggrieved party, and the aggrieved party reasonably relied on the expectation and would suffer detriment if the expectation is not met.
Service provider	A service provider is an entity that provides services to other entities. Usually this refers to a business that provides subscription or web service to other businesses or individuals. Examples of these services include Internet access, Mobile phone operator, and web application hosting.
Arbitration	Arbitration, a form of alternative dispute resolution (ADR), is a legal technique for the resolution of disputes outside the courts, wherein the parties to a dispute refer it to one or more persons (the "arbitrators", "arbiters" or "arbitral tribunal"), by whose decision (the "award") they agree to be bound. It is a settlement technique in which a third party reviews the case and imposes a decision that is legally binding for both sides. Other forms of ADR include mediation (a form of settlement negotiation facilitated by a neutral third party) and non-binding resolution by experts.
Unjust enrichment	Unjust enrichment is a legal term denoting a particular type of causative event in which one party is unjustly enriched at the expense of another, and an obligation to make restitution arises, regardless of liability for wrongdoing. Liability under the principle of unjust enrichment is wholly independent of liability for wrongdoing. Claims in unjust enrichment do not depend upon proof of any wrong.
Chief brand officer	A Chief brand officer is a relatively new executive level position at a corporation, company, organization typically reporting directly to the CEO or board of directors. The Chief brand officer is responsible for a brand''s image, experience, and promise, and propagating it throughout all aspects of the company. The brand officer oversees marketing, advertising, design, public relations and customer service departments.
Employment	Employment is a contract between two parties, one being the employer and the other being the employee. An employee may be defined as: "A person in the service of another under any contract of hire, express or implied, oral or written, where the employer has the power or right to control and direct the employee in the material details of how the work is to be performed." Black''s Law Dictionary page 471 (5th ed. 1979).
Damages	Damages for breach of contract is a common law remedy, available as of right. It is designed to compensate the victim for their actual loss as a result of the wrongdoer''s breach rather than to punish the wrongdoer. If no loss has been occasioned by the plaintiff, only nominal Damages will be awarded.
Undue influence	Undue influence is an equitable doctrine that involves one person taking advantage of a position of power over another person. It is where free will to bargain is not possible.

If undue influence is proved in a contract, in USA law, the contract is voidable by the innocent party, and the remedy is rescission.

Punitive Damages

Punitive Damages are damages not awarded in order to compensate the plaintiff, but in order to reform or deter the defendant and similar persons from pursuing a course of action such as that which damaged the plaintiff.
punitive Damages are often awarded where compensatory damages are deemed an inadequate remedy. The court may impose them to prevent under-compensation of plaintiffs, to allow redress for undetectable torts and taking some strain away from the criminal justice system.

Duress

Duress or coercion (as a term of jurisprudence) is a possible legal defense, one of four of the most important justification defenses, by which defendants argue that they should not be held liable because the actions that broke the law were only performed out of an immediate fear of injury. Black"s Law Dictionary (6th ed). defines Duress as "any unlawful threat or coercion used...

Lease

A Lease is a contract conferring a right on one person to possess property belonging to another person (called a landlord or lessor) to the exclusion of the owner landlord, and all others except with the invitation of the tenant. It is a rental agreement between landlord and tenant. The relationship between the tenant and the landlord is called a tenancy, and the right to possession by the tenant is sometimes called a Leasehold interest.

Rebuttable presumption

Both in common law and in civil law, a rebuttable presumption is an assumption made by a court, one that is taken to be true unless someone comes forward to contest it and prove otherwise. A rebuttable presumption is often associated with prima facie evidence.
rebuttable presumption s in criminal law are somewhat controversial in that they do effectively reverse the presumption of innocence in some cases.

Statute

A statute is a formal written enactment of a legislative authority that governs a country, state, city, or county. Typically, statute s command or prohibit something, or declare policy. The word is often used to distinguish law made by legislative bodies from case law and the regulations issued by Government agencies.

Statute of Frauds

The Statute of Frauds refers to the requirement that certain kinds of contracts be made in writing and signed.
Traditionally, the Statute of Frauds requires a writing signed by the defendant in the following circumstances:

· Contracts in consideration of marriage.
· Contracts which cannot be performed within one year.
· Contracts for the transfer of an interest in land.
· Contracts by the executor of a will to pay a debt of the estate with their own money.
· Contracts for the sale of goods above a certain value.
· Contracts in which one party becomes a surety (acts as guarantor) for another party"s debt or other obligation.

This can be remembered by the mnemonic "MY LEGS": Marriage, one year, land, executor, goods, surety.

The term Statute of Frauds comes from an English Act of Parliament passed in 1677 (authored by Sir Leoline Jenkins and passed by the Cavalier Parliament), and more properly called An Act for Prevention of Frauds and Perjuries. Many common law jurisdictions have made similar statutory provisions, while a number of civil law jurisdictions have equivalent legislation incorporated into their civil codes.

Unconscionability

Unconscionability is a term used in contract law to describe a defense against the enforcement of a contract based on the presence of terms unfair to one party. Typically, such a contract is held to be unenforceable because the consideration offered is lacking or is so obviously inadequate that to enforce the contract would be unfair to the party seeking to escape the contract.

In and of itself, inadequate consideration is likely not enough to make a contract unenforceable.

Uniform Commercial Code

The Uniform Commercial Code is one of a number of uniform acts that have been promulgated in conjunction with efforts to harmonize the law of sales and other commercial transactions in all 50 states within the United States of America. This objective is deemed important because of the prevalence today of commercial transactions that extend beyond one state (for example, where the goods are manufactured in state A, warehoused in state B, sold from state C and delivered in state D.) The Uniform Commercial Code deals primarily with transactions involving personal property (movable property), not real property (immovable property.)

State Court

In the United States, a state court has jurisdiction over disputes with some connection to a U.S. state. Cases are heard before and evidence is presented in a trial court, which is usually located in a courthouse in the county seat. Territory outside of any state in the United States, such as the District of Columbia or American Samoa, often have courts established under federal or territorial law which substitute for a state court system, distinct from the ordinary federal court system.

United Nations Convention on Contracts for the International Sale of Goods

The United Nations Convention on Contracts for the International Sale of Goods is a treaty offering a uniform international sales law that, as of July 2008, had been ratified by 71 countries that account for a significant proportion of world trade, making it one of the most successful international uniform laws. Japan is the most recent State to have ratified the Convention.

It allows exporters to avoid choice of law issues as it offers "accepted substantive rules on which contracting parties, courts, and arbitrators may rely".

Parol evidence

The Parol evidence rule is the legal application of a rule of substantive law in contract cases that prevents a party to a written contract from contradicting (or sometimes adding to) the terms of the contract by seeking the admission of evidence "extrinsic" (outside) to the contract. For example, Carl agrees in writing to sell Betty a car for $1,000. Betty argues that Carl told her that she would only need to pay Carl $800.

Parol evidence rule

The Parol evidence rule is the legal application of a rule of substantive law in contract cases that prevents a party to a written contract from contradicting (or sometimes adding to) the terms of the contract by seeking the admission of evidence "extrinsic" (outside) to the contract. For example, Carl agrees in writing to sell Betty a car for $1,000. Betty argues that Carl told her that she would only need to pay Carl $800.

Statute

A statute is a formal written enactment of a legislative authority that governs a country, state, city, or county. Typically, statute s command or prohibit something, or declare policy. The word is often used to distinguish law made by legislative bodies from case law and the regulations issued by Government agencies.

Statute of Frauds

The Statute of Frauds refers to the requirement that certain kinds of contracts be made in writing and signed.

Traditionally, the Statute of Frauds requires a writing signed by the defendant in the following circumstances:

· Contracts in consideration of marriage.
· Contracts which cannot be performed within one year.
· Contracts for the transfer of an interest in land.
· Contracts by the executor of a will to pay a debt of the estate with their own money.
· Contracts for the sale of goods above a certain value.
· Contracts in which one party becomes a surety (acts as guarantor) for another party"s debt or other obligation.

This can be remembered by the mnemonic "MY LEGS": Marriage, one year, land, executor, goods, surety.

The term Statute of Frauds comes from an English Act of Parliament passed in 1677 (authored by Sir Leoline Jenkins and passed by the Cavalier Parliament), and more properly called An Act for Prevention of Frauds and Perjuries. Many common law jurisdictions have made similar statutory provisions, while a number of civil law jurisdictions have equivalent legislation incorporated into their civil codes.

Uniform Commercial Code	The Uniform Commercial Code is one of a number of uniform acts that have been promulgated in conjunction with efforts to harmonize the law of sales and other commercial transactions in all 50 states within the United States of America. This objective is deemed important because of the prevalence today of commercial transactions that extend beyond one state (for example, where the goods are manufactured in state A, warehoused in state B, sold from state C and delivered in state D.) The Uniform Commercial Code deals primarily with transactions involving personal property (movable property), not real property (immovable property.)
Contract	Agreement is said to be reached when an offer capable of immediate acceptance is met with a "mirror image" acceptance (ie, an unqualified acceptance). The parties must have the necessary capacity to Contract and the Contract must not be either trifling, indeterminate, impossible or illegal. Contract law is based on the principle expressed in the Latin phrase pacta sunt servanda .
Estoppel	Estoppel is a legal doctrine at common law, where a party is barred from claiming or denying an argument on an equitable ground. Estoppel complements the requirement of consideration in contract law. In general, Estoppel protects an aggrieved party, if the counter-party induced an expectation from the aggrieved party, and the aggrieved party reasonably relied on the expectation and would suffer detriment if the expectation is not met.
Lease	A Lease is a contract conferring a right on one person to possess property belonging to another person (called a landlord or lessor) to the exclusion of the owner landlord, and all others except with the invitation of the tenant. It is a rental agreement between landlord and tenant. The relationship between the tenant and the landlord is called a tenancy, and the right to possession by the tenant is sometimes called a Leasehold interest.
Real property	In the common law, real property refers to one of the three main classes of property, the other two classes being personal property and intellectual property. real property generally encompasses land, land improvements resulting from human effort including buildings and machinery sited on land, and various property rights over the preceding. The concept is variously named and defined in other jurisdictions: heritable property in Scotland, immobilier in France, and immovable property in Canada, United States, India, Pakistan, Bangladesh, Malta, Cyprus, and in countries where civil law systems prevail, including most of Europe, Russia, and South America.
Collateral Contract	A Collateral contract is a contract where the consideration is the entry into another contract, and co-exists side by side with the main contract. For example, a Collateral contract is formed when one party pays the other party a certain sum for entry into another contract. A Collateral contract may be between one of the parties and a third party.
Consideration	Consideration is the legal concept of value in connection with contracts. It is anything of value in the common sense, promised to another when making a contract. It can take the form of money, physical objects, services, promised actions, or even abstinence from a future action.
Duty	Duty (from "due," that which is owing, O. Fr. deu, did, past participle of devoir; Lat. debere, debitum; cf.

Obligation	An obligation is a requirement to take some course of action, whether legal or moral. There are also obligation s in other normative contexts, such as obligation s of etiquette, social obligation s, and possibly in terms of politics, where obligation s are requirements which must be fulfilled. These are generally legal obligation s, which can incur a penalty for unfulfilment, although certain people are obliged to carry out certain actions for other reasons as well, whether as a tradition or for social reasons.
Specific performance	In the law of Remedy, an order of specific performance is an order of the court which requires a party to perform a specific act, usually what is stated in a contract. While specific performance can be in the form of any type of forced action, it is usually used to complete a previously established transaction, thus being the most effective remedy in protecting the expectation interest of the innocent party to a contract. It is usually the opposite of a prohibitory injunction but there are mandatory injunctions which have a similar effect to specific performance.
Chief brand officer	A Chief brand officer is a relatively new executive level position at a corporation, company, organization typically reporting directly to the CEO or board of directors. The Chief brand officer is responsible for a brand''s image, experience, and promise, and propagating it throughout all aspects of the company. The brand officer oversees marketing, advertising, design, public relations and customer service departments.
Postnuptial Agreement	A Postnuptial agreement is a written contract executed after a couple gets married to settle the couple''s affairs and assets in the event of a separation or divorce. It is normally "notarized" or acknowledged, and is usually the subject of statute of frauds. Like the contents of a prenuptial agreement, it can vary widely, but commonly includes provisions for division of property and spousal support in the event of divorce, death of one of the spouses, or breakup of marriage.
Prenuptial	A prenuptial agreement, antenuptial agreement commonly abbreviated to prenup or prenupt, is a contract entered into prior to marriage or civil union by the people intending to marry. The content of a prenuptial agreement can vary widely, but commonly includes provisions for division of property and spousal support in the event of divorce or breakup of marriage. Many countries, including Canada, France, Italy, and Germany, have matrimonial regimes, in addition to in lieu of prenuptial agreements.
Subscription business model	The subscription business model is a business model where a customer must pay a subscription price to have access to the product/service. The model was pioneered by magazines and newspapers, but is now used by many businesses and websites. Rather than selling products individually, a subscription sells periodic (monthly or yearly or seasonal) use or access to a product or service, or, in the case of such non-profit organizations as opera companies or symphony orchestras, it sells tickets to the entire run of five to fifteen scheduled performances for an entire season.

Security interest	A Security interest is a property interest created by agreement or by operation of law over assets to secure the performance of an obligation, usually the payment of a debt. It gives the beneficiary of the Security interest certain preferential rights in the disposition of secured assets. Such rights vary according to the type of Security interest, but in most cases, a holder of the Security interest is entitled to seize, and usually sell, the property to discharge the debt that the Security interest secures.
Voidable	In law, a transaction or action which is voidable is valid, but may be annulled by one of the parties to the transaction. voidable is usually used in distinction to void ab initio (or void from the outset) and unenforceable. The act of invalidating the contract by the party exercising its rights to anul the voidable contract is usually referred to either as voiding the contract (in the United States and Canada) or avoiding the contract (in the United Kingdom, Australia and other common law countries.)

Delegation	Delegation is the assignment of authority and responsibility to another person to carry out specific activities. However the person who delegated the work remains accountable for the outcome of the delegated work. Delegation empowers a subordinate to make decisions, i.e. it is a shift of decision-making authority from one organizational level to a lower one.
Duty	Duty (from "due," that which is owing, O. Fr. deu, did, past participle of devoir; Lat. debere, debitum; cf.
Mortgage loan	A Mortgage loan is a loan secured by real property through the use of a document which evidences the existence of the loan and the encumbrance of that realty through the granting of a mortgage which secures the loan. However, the word mortgage alone, in everyday usage, is most often used to mean Mortgage loan. A home buyer or builder can obtain financing (a loan) either to purchase or secure against the property from a financial institution, such as a bank, either directly or indirectly through intermediaries.
Obligation	An obligation is a requirement to take some course of action, whether legal or moral. There are also obligation s in other normative contexts, such as obligation s of etiquette, social obligation s, and possibly in terms of politics, where obligation s are requirements which must be fulfilled. These are generally legal obligation s, which can incur a penalty for unfulfilment, although certain people are obliged to carry out certain actions for other reasons as well, whether as a tradition or for social reasons.
Obligee	Delegation is a term used in the law of contracts to describe the act of giving another person the responsibility of carrying out the performance agreed to in a contract. Three parties are concerned with this act - the party who had incurred the obligation to perform under the contract is called the delegator; the party who assumes the responsibility of performing this duty is called the delegatee; and the party to whom this performance is owed is called the Obligee. The term is also a concept of Administrative Law.
Obligor	Assignment of rights under a contract is the complete transfer of the rights to receive the benefits accruing to one of the parties to that contract. For example, if party A contracts with Party B to sell his car to him for $10, party A can later assign the benefits of the contract - the right to be paid $10 - to party C. In this scenario, party A is the obligee/assignor, party B is an Obligor, and party C is the assignee. Such an assignment may be donative (essentially given as a gift), or it may be contractually exchanged for consideration.
Privity	The doctrine of privity in contract law provides that a contract cannot confer rights or impose obligations arising under it on any person or agent except the parties to it. The premise is that only parties to contracts should be able to sue to enforce their rights or claim damages as such. However, the doctrine has proven problematic due to its implications upon contracts made for the benefit of third parties who are unable to enforce the obligations of the contracting parties.

Statute	A statute is a formal written enactment of a legislative authority that governs a country, state, city, or county. Typically, statute s command or prohibit something, or declare policy. The word is often used to distinguish law made by legislative bodies from case law and the regulations issued by Government agencies.
Statute of Frauds	The Statute of Frauds refers to the requirement that certain kinds of contracts be made in writing and signed. Traditionally, the Statute of Frauds requires a writing signed by the defendant in the following circumstances: · Contracts in consideration of marriage. · Contracts which cannot be performed within one year. · Contracts for the transfer of an interest in land. · Contracts by the executor of a will to pay a debt of the estate with their own money. · Contracts for the sale of goods above a certain value. · Contracts in which one party becomes a surety (acts as guarantor) for another party"s debt or other obligation. This can be remembered by the mnemonic "MY LEGS": Marriage, one year, land, executor, goods, surety. The term Statute of Frauds comes from an English Act of Parliament passed in 1677 (authored by Sir Leoline Jenkins and passed by the Cavalier Parliament), and more properly called An Act for Prevention of Frauds and Perjuries. Many common law jurisdictions have made similar statutory provisions, while a number of civil law jurisdictions have equivalent legislation incorporated into their civil codes.
Third party beneficiary	A third party beneficiary, in the law of contracts, is a person who may have the right to sue on a contract, despite not having originally been a party to the contract. This right arises where the third party is the intended beneficiary of the contract, as opposed to an incidental beneficiary. It vests when the third party relies on or assents to the relationship, and gives the third party the right to sue either the promisor or the promisee of the contract, depending on the circumstances under which the relationship was created.
Contract	Agreement is said to be reached when an offer capable of immediate acceptance is met with a "mirror image" acceptance (ie, an unqualified acceptance). The parties must have the necessary capacity to Contract and the Contract must not be either trifling, indeterminate, impossible or illegal. Contract law is based on the principle expressed in the Latin phrase pacta sunt servanda .
Estoppel	Estoppel is a legal doctrine at common law, where a party is barred from claiming or denying an argument on an equitable ground. Estoppel complements the requirement of consideration in contract law. In general, Estoppel protects an aggrieved party, if the counter-party induced an expectation from the aggrieved party, and the aggrieved party reasonably relied on the expectation and would suffer detriment if the expectation is not met.

Arbitration	Arbitration, a form of alternative dispute resolution (ADR), is a legal technique for the resolution of disputes outside the courts, wherein the parties to a dispute refer it to one or more persons (the "arbitrators", "arbiters" or "arbitral tribunal"), by whose decision (the "award") they agree to be bound. It is a settlement technique in which a third party reviews the case and imposes a decision that is legally binding for both sides. Other forms of ADR include mediation (a form of settlement negotiation facilitated by a neutral third party) and non-binding resolution by experts.
Lease	A Lease is a contract conferring a right on one person to possess property belonging to another person (called a landlord or lessor) to the exclusion of the owner landlord, and all others except with the invitation of the tenant. It is a rental agreement between landlord and tenant. The relationship between the tenant and the landlord is called a tenancy, and the right to possession by the tenant is sometimes called a Leasehold interest.
Uniform Commercial Code	The Uniform Commercial Code is one of a number of uniform acts that have been promulgated in conjunction with efforts to harmonize the law of sales and other commercial transactions in all 50 states within the United States of America. This objective is deemed important because of the prevalence today of commercial transactions that extend beyond one state (for example, where the goods are manufactured in state A, warehoused in state B, sold from state C and delivered in state D.) The Uniform Commercial Code deals primarily with transactions involving personal property (movable property), not real property (immovable property.)
Damages	Damages for breach of contract is a common law remedy, available as of right. It is designed to compensate the victim for their actual loss as a result of the wrongdoer"s breach rather than to punish the wrongdoer. If no loss has been occasioned by the plaintiff, only nominal Damages will be awarded.
Vesting	In law, Vesting is to give an immediately secured right of present or future enjoyment. One has a vested right to an asset that cannot be taken away by any third party, even though one may not yet possess the asset. When the right, interest or title to the present or future possession of a legal estate can be transferred to any other party, it is termed a vested interest.

Condition precedent	Condition precedent refers to an event or state of affairs that is required before something else will occur. In contract law a Condition precedent is an event which must occur, unless its non-occurrence is excused, before performance under a contract becomes due, i.e., before any contractual duty arises. For instance, in the sentence "I will only go to heaven after I have died" my death is a Condition precedent to my going to heaven (although it is also possible in this example for the occurrence of other conditions precedent to be needed before I go to heaven: it is not stated that I will necessarily go to heaven if I die).
Duty	Duty (from "due," that which is owing, O. Fr. deu, did, past participle of devoir; Lat. debere, debitum; cf.
Lease	A Lease is a contract conferring a right on one person to possess property belonging to another person (called a landlord or lessor) to the exclusion of the owner landlord, and all others except with the invitation of the tenant. It is a rental agreement between landlord and tenant. The relationship between the tenant and the landlord is called a tenancy, and the right to possession by the tenant is sometimes called a Leasehold interest.
Obligation	An obligation is a requirement to take some course of action, whether legal or moral. There are also obligation s in other normative contexts, such as obligation s of etiquette, social obligation s, and possibly in terms of politics, where obligation s are requirements which must be fulfilled. These are generally legal obligation s, which can incur a penalty for unfulfilment, although certain people are obliged to carry out certain actions for other reasons as well, whether as a tradition or for social reasons.
Security interest	A Security interest is a property interest created by agreement or by operation of law over assets to secure the performance of an obligation, usually the payment of a debt. It gives the beneficiary of the Security interest certain preferential rights in the disposition of secured assets. Such rights vary according to the type of Security interest, but in most cases, a holder of the Security interest is entitled to seize, and usually sell, the property to discharge the debt that the Security interest secures.
Contract	Agreement is said to be reached when an offer capable of immediate acceptance is met with a "mirror image" acceptance (ie, an unqualified acceptance). The parties must have the necessary capacity to Contract and the Contract must not be either trifling, indeterminate, impossible or illegal. Contract law is based on the principle expressed in the Latin phrase pacta sunt servanda .
Condition subsequent	Condition subsequent refers to an event or state of affairs, such that its occurrence will bring an end to something else. Alternatively, an event or state of affairs that must continue to exist for something else to continue "When I run out of fuel, the fire will die down" or "so long as I have fuel, the fire will continue." In both cases, running out of fuel is a Condition subsequent to the continuance of the fire. In contract law, a contract may be frustrated on the occurrence of a Condition subsequent: in a contract to provide a music hall for a musical performance, the burning down of the music hall may frustrate the contract and automatically bring it to an end.

Partnership

A Partnership is a type of business entity in which partners (owners) share with each other the profits or losses of the business. Partnership s are often favored over corporations for taxation purposes, as the Partnership structure does not generally incur a tax on profits before it is distributed to the partners (i.e. there is no dividend tax levied.) However, depending on the Partnership structure and the jurisdiction in which it operates, owners of a Partnership may be exposed to greater personal liability than they would as shareholders of a corporation.

Reasonable person standard

The reasonable person is a legal fiction of the common law representing an objective standard against which any individual"s conduct can be measured. It is used to determine if a breach of the standard of care has occurred, provided a duty of care can be proven.

The Reasonable person standard holds: each person owes a duty to behave as a reasonable person would under the same or similar circumstances.

Impossibility

In contract law, Impossibility is an excuse for the nonperformance of duties under a contract, based on a change in circumstances (or the discovery of preexisting circumstances), the nonoccurrence of which was an underlying assumption of the contract, that makes performance of the contract literally impossible. For such a defense to be raised, performance must not merely be difficult or unexpectedly costly for one party; there must be no way for it to actually be accomplished.

For example, if Rachel contracts to pay Joey $1000 to paint her house on October 1, but the house burns to the ground before the end of September, Rachel is excused from her duty to pay Joey the $1000, and he is excused from his duty to paint her house; however, Joey may still be able to sue for the unjust enrichment of any benefit conferred on Rachel before her house burned down.

Statute

A statute is a formal written enactment of a legislative authority that governs a country, state, city, or county. Typically, statute s command or prohibit something, or declare policy. The word is often used to distinguish law made by legislative bodies from case law and the regulations issued by Government agencies.

Statute of Frauds

The Statute of Frauds refers to the requirement that certain kinds of contracts be made in writing and signed.

Traditionally, the Statute of Frauds requires a writing signed by the defendant in the following circumstances:

· Contracts in consideration of marriage.
· Contracts which cannot be performed within one year.
· Contracts for the transfer of an interest in land.
· Contracts by the executor of a will to pay a debt of the estate with their own money.
· Contracts for the sale of goods above a certain value.
· Contracts in which one party becomes a surety (acts as guarantor) for another party"s debt or other obligation.

This can be remembered by the mnemonic "MY LEGS": Marriage, one year, land, executor, goods, surety.

The term Statute of Frauds comes from an English Act of Parliament passed in 1677 (authored by Sir Leoline Jenkins and passed by the Cavalier Parliament), and more properly called An Act for Prevention of Frauds and Perjuries. Many common law jurisdictions have made similar statutory provisions, while a number of civil law jurisdictions have equivalent legislation incorporated into their civil codes.

Estoppel

Estoppel is a legal doctrine at common law, where a party is barred from claiming or denying an argument on an equitable ground. Estoppel complements the requirement of consideration in contract law. In general, Estoppel protects an aggrieved party, if the counter-party induced an expectation from the aggrieved party, and the aggrieved party reasonably relied on the expectation and would suffer detriment if the expectation is not met.

United Nations Convention on Contracts for the International Sale of Goods

The United Nations Convention on Contracts for the International Sale of Goods is a treaty offering a uniform international sales law that, as of July 2008, had been ratified by 71 countries that account for a significant proportion of world trade, making it one of the most successful international uniform laws. Japan is the most recent State to have ratified the Convention.

It allows exporters to avoid choice of law issues as it offers "accepted substantive rules on which contracting parties, courts, and arbitrators may rely".

Novation

Novation is a term used in contract law and business law to describe the act of either replacing an obligation to perform with a new obligation, or replacing a party to an agreement with a new party. In contrast to an assignment, which is valid so long as the obligee (person receiving the benefit of the bargain) is given notice, a Novation is valid only with the consent of all parties to the original agreement: the obligee must consent to the replacement of the original obligor with the new obligor. A contract transferred by the Novation process transfers all duties and obligations from the original obligor to the new obligor.

Parol evidence

The Parol evidence rule is the legal application of a rule of substantive law in contract cases that prevents a party to a written contract from contradicting (or sometimes adding to) the terms of the contract by seeking the admission of evidence "extrinsic" (outside) to the contract. For example, Carl agrees in writing to sell Betty a car for $1,000. Betty argues that Carl told her that she would only need to pay Carl $800.

Parol evidence rule

The Parol evidence rule is the legal application of a rule of substantive law in contract cases that prevents a party to a written contract from contradicting (or sometimes adding to) the terms of the contract by seeking the admission of evidence "extrinsic" (outside) to the contract. For example, Carl agrees in writing to sell Betty a car for $1,000. Betty argues that Carl told her that she would only need to pay Carl $800.

Rescission

In contract law, rescission has been defined as the unmaking of a contract between parties. rescission is the unwinding of a transaction. This is done to bring the parties, as far as possible, back to the position in which they were before they entered into a contract (the "status quo ante".)

Writ

In law, a writ is a formal writ ten order issued by a body with administrative or judicial jurisdiction; in modern usage, this public body is generally a court. Warrants, prerogative writ s and subpoenas are types of writ s; there are many others.

Originally, a writ was a letter or command from the Sovereign, or from some person with appropriate jurisdiction.

Writ of attachment

A Writ of attachment is a court order to "attach" or seize an asset. It is issued by a court to a law enforcement officer or sheriff. The Writ of attachment is issued in order to satisfy a judgment issued by the court.

Chief brand officer

A Chief brand officer is a relatively new executive level position at a corporation, company, organization typically reporting directly to the CEO or board of directors. The Chief brand officer is responsible for a brand''s image, experience, and promise, and propagating it throughout all aspects of the company. The brand officer oversees marketing, advertising, design, public relations and customer service departments.

Consideration

Consideration is the legal concept of value in connection with contracts. It is anything of value in the common sense, promised to another when making a contract. It can take the form of money, physical objects, services, promised actions, or even abstinence from a future action.

Personal property

Personal property is a type of property. In the common law systems Personal property may also be called chattels or personalty. It is distinguished from real property, or real estate.

Personal property may be classified in a variety of ways. Tangible Personal property refers to any type of property that can generally be moved (i.e., it is not attached to real property or land), touched or felt. These generally include items such as furniture, clothing, jewelry, art, writings, or household goods. In some cases, there can be formal title documents that show the ownership and transfer rights of that property after a person''s death (for example, motor vehicles, boats, etc.) In many cases, however, tangible Personal property will not be "titled" in an owner''s name and is presumed to be whatever property he or she was in possession of at the time of his or her death.

Intangible Personal property or "intangibles" refers to Personal property that cannot actually be moved, touched or felt, but instead represents something of value such as negotiable instruments, securities, goods, and intangible assets including chose in action.

Real property

In the common law, real property refers to one of the three main classes of property, the other two classes being personal property and intellectual property. real property generally encompasses land, land improvements resulting from human effort including buildings and machinery sited on land, and various property rights over the preceding.

The concept is variously named and defined in other jurisdictions: heritable property in Scotland, immobilier in France, and immovable property in Canada, United States, India, Pakistan, Bangladesh, Malta, Cyprus, and in countries where civil law systems prevail, including most of Europe, Russia, and South America.

Bank Secrecy Act

The Bank Secrecy Act of 1970 (or Bank Secrecy Act, or otherwise known as the Currency and Foreign Transactions Reporting Act) requires financial institutions in the United States to assist U.S. government agencies to detect and prevent money laundering. Specifically, the act requires financial institutions to keep records of [cash purchases of negotiable instruments, and file reports of cash purchases of these negotiable instruments of $3,000 or more (daily aggregate amount), and to report suspicious activity that might signify money laundering, tax evasion, or other criminal activities. Many banks will no longer sell negotiable instruments when purchased with cash, requiring the purchase to be withdrawn from an account at that institution.

Bankruptcy

Bankruptcy is a legally declared inability or impairment of ability of an individual or organization to pay its creditors. Creditors may file a Bankruptcy petition against a debtor ("involuntary Bankruptcy") in an effort to recoup a portion of what they are owed or initiate a restructuring. In the majority of cases, however, Bankruptcy is initiated by the debtor (a "voluntary Bankruptcy" that is filed by the insolvent individual or organization).

Operation of law

The phrase "by Operation of law" is a legal term that indicates that a right or liability has been created for a party, irrespective of the intent of that party, because it is dictated by existing legal principles. For example, if a person dies without a will, his heirs are determined by Operation of law. Similarly, if a person marries or has a child after his or her will has been executed, the law writes this pretermitted spouse or pretermitted heir into the will if no provision for this situation was specifically included.

Statute of limitations

A statute of limitations is a statute in a common law legal system that sets forth the maximum period of time, after certain events, that legal proceedings based on those events may be initiated. In civil law systems, similar provisions are usually part of the civil code or criminal code and are often known collectively as "periods of prescription" or "prescriptive periods."

A common law legal system might have a statute limiting the time for prosecution of crimes called misdemeanors to two years after the offense occurred. In that statute, if a person is discovered to have committed a misdemeanor three years ago, the time has expired for the prosecution of the misdemeanor.

Impracticability

The doctrine of Impracticability in the common law of contracts excuses performance of a duty, where that duty has become unfeasibly difficult or expensive for the party who was to perform. It is similar in some respects to the doctrine of impossibility because it is triggered by the occurrence of a condition, the nonoccurrence of which was a basic assumption of the contract. The major difference between impossibility and Impracticability, however, is that while impossibility excuses performance where the contractual duty cannot physically be performed, the doctrine of Impracticability comes into play where performance is still physically possible, but would be very burdensome for the party whose performance is due.

Negotiable instrument

A Negotiable instrument is a specialized type of "contract" for the payment of money that is unconditional and capable of transfer by negotiation. Common examples include cheques, banknotes (paper money), and commercial paper.

A Negotiable instrument is not a contract, as contract formation requires an offer, acceptance, and consideration, none of which is an element of a Negotiable instrument.

Frustration of Purpose	In the law of contracts, Frustration of purpose is a defense to enforcement of the contract. Frustration of purpose occurs when an unforeseen event undermines a party"s principal purpose for entering into a contract, and both parties knew of this principal purpose at the time the contract was made. Despite frequently arising as a result of government action, any third party (or even nature) can frustrate a contracting party"s primary purpose for entering into the contract.

Damages

Damages for breach of contract is a common law remedy, available as of right. It is designed to compensate the victim for their actual loss as a result of the wrongdoer"s breach rather than to punish the wrongdoer. If no loss has been occasioned by the plaintiff, only nominal Damages will be awarded.

Lease

A Lease is a contract conferring a right on one person to possess property belonging to another person (called a landlord or lessor) to the exclusion of the owner landlord, and all others except with the invitation of the tenant. It is a rental agreement between landlord and tenant. The relationship between the tenant and the landlord is called a tenancy, and the right to possession by the tenant is sometimes called a Leasehold interest.

Business

There are many ways in which a business may be owned under the legal system of England and Wales. Different types of ownership are suitable for organisations depending on the degree of control the owners wish to have over the business. The choice of ownership methor also relates to the organisations ability to raise funds for the business activities.

Contract

Agreement is said to be reached when an offer capable of immediate acceptance is met with a "mirror image" acceptance (ie, an unqualified acceptance). The parties must have the necessary capacity to Contract and the Contract must not be either trifling, indeterminate, impossible or illegal. Contract law is based on the principle expressed in the Latin phrase pacta sunt servanda .

Punitive Damages

Punitive Damages are damages not awarded in order to compensate the plaintiff, but in order to reform or deter the defendant and similar persons from pursuing a course of action such as that which damaged the plaintiff.

punitive Damages are often awarded where compensatory damages are deemed an inadequate remedy. The court may impose them to prevent under-compensation of plaintiffs, to allow redress for undetectable torts and taking some strain away from the criminal justice system.

Real property

In the common law, real property refers to one of the three main classes of property, the other two classes being personal property and intellectual property. real property generally encompasses land, land improvements resulting from human effort including buildings and machinery sited on land, and various property rights over the preceding.

The concept is variously named and defined in other jurisdictions: heritable property in Scotland, immobilier in France, and immovable property in Canada, United States, India, Pakistan, Bangladesh, Malta, Cyprus, and in countries where civil law systems prevail, including most of Europe, Russia, and South America.

Specific performance

In the law of Remedy, an order of specific performance is an order of the court which requires a party to perform a specific act, usually what is stated in a contract. While specific performance can be in the form of any type of forced action, it is usually used to complete a previously established transaction, thus being the most effective remedy in protecting the expectation interest of the innocent party to a contract. It is usually the opposite of a prohibitory injunction but there are mandatory injunctions which have a similar effect to specific performance.

Uniform Commercial Code	The Uniform Commercial Code is one of a number of uniform acts that have been promulgated in conjunction with efforts to harmonize the law of sales and other commercial transactions in all 50 states within the United States of America. This objective is deemed important because of the prevalence today of commercial transactions that extend beyond one state (for example, where the goods are manufactured in state A, warehoused in state B, sold from state C and delivered in state D.) The Uniform Commercial Code deals primarily with transactions involving personal property (movable property), not real property (immovable property.)
Restitution	The law of restitution is the law of gains-based recovery. It is to be contrasted with the law of compensation, which is the law of loss-based recovery. Obligations to make restitution and obligations to pay compensation are each a type of legal response to events in the real world.
Liquidated Damages	Liquidated damages (also referred to as liquidated and ascertained damages) are damages whose amount the parties designate during the formation of a contract for the injured party to collect as compensation upon a specific breach (e.g., late performance). When damages are not predetermined/assessed in advance, then the amount recoverable is said to be "at large" (to be agreed or determined by a court or tribunal in the event of breach). At common law, a Liquidated damages clause will not be enforced if its purpose is to punish the wrongdoer/party in breach rather than to compensate the injured party (in which case it is referred to as a penal or penalty clause).
Security interest	A Security interest is a property interest created by agreement or by operation of law over assets to secure the performance of an obligation, usually the payment of a debt. It gives the beneficiary of the Security interest certain preferential rights in the disposition of secured assets. Such rights vary according to the type of Security interest, but in most cases, a holder of the Security interest is entitled to seize, and usually sell, the property to discharge the debt that the Security interest secures.
Duty	Duty (from "due," that which is owing, O. Fr. deu, did, past participle of devoir; Lat. debere, debitum; cf.
Misrepresentation	Misrepresentation is a contract law concept. It means a false statement of fact made by one party to another party, which has the effect of inducing that party into the contract. For example, under certain circumstances, false statements or promises made by a seller of goods regarding the quality or nature of the product that the seller has may constitute Misrepresentation.
Parol evidence	The Parol evidence rule is the legal application of a rule of substantive law in contract cases that prevents a party to a written contract from contradicting (or sometimes adding to) the terms of the contract by seeking the admission of evidence "extrinsic" (outside) to the contract. For example, Carl agrees in writing to sell Betty a car for $1,000. Betty argues that Carl told her that she would only need to pay Carl $800.

Parol evidence rule	The Parol evidence rule is the legal application of a rule of substantive law in contract cases that prevents a party to a written contract from contradicting (or sometimes adding to) the terms of the contract by seeking the admission of evidence "extrinsic" (outside) to the contract. For example, Carl agrees in writing to sell Betty a car for $1,000. Betty argues that Carl told her that she would only need to pay Carl $800.
Quantum meruit	Quantum meruit is a Latin phrase meaning "as much as he has deserved". This claim is also referred to as "unjust enrichment." In the context of contract law, it means something along the lines of "reasonable value of services". In the United States, the elements of quantum meruit are determined by state common law.
Statute	A statute is a formal written enactment of a legislative authority that governs a country, state, city, or county. Typically, statute s command or prohibit something, or declare policy. The word is often used to distinguish law made by legislative bodies from case law and the regulations issued by Government agencies.
Statute of Frauds	The Statute of Frauds refers to the requirement that certain kinds of contracts be made in writing and signed. Traditionally, the Statute of Frauds requires a writing signed by the defendant in the following circumstances: · Contracts in consideration of marriage. · Contracts which cannot be performed within one year. · Contracts for the transfer of an interest in land. · Contracts by the executor of a will to pay a debt of the estate with their own money. · Contracts for the sale of goods above a certain value. · Contracts in which one party becomes a surety (acts as guarantor) for another party"s debt or other obligation. This can be remembered by the mnemonic "MY LEGS": Marriage, one year, land, executor, goods, surety. The term Statute of Frauds comes from an English Act of Parliament passed in 1677 (authored by Sir Leoline Jenkins and passed by the Cavalier Parliament), and more properly called An Act for Prevention of Frauds and Perjuries. Many common law jurisdictions have made similar statutory provisions, while a number of civil law jurisdictions have equivalent legislation incorporated into their civil codes.
Unjust enrichment	Unjust enrichment is a legal term denoting a particular type of causative event in which one party is unjustly enriched at the expense of another, and an obligation to make restitution arises, regardless of liability for wrongdoing. Liability under the principle of unjust enrichment is wholly independent of liability for wrongdoing. Claims in unjust enrichment do not depend upon proof of any wrong.

Consideration	Consideration is the legal concept of value in connection with contracts. It is anything of value in the common sense, promised to another when making a contract. It can take the form of money, physical objects, services, promised actions, or even abstinence from a future action.
Estoppel	Estoppel is a legal doctrine at common law, where a party is barred from claiming or denying an argument on an equitable ground. Estoppel complements the requirement of consideration in contract law. In general, Estoppel protects an aggrieved party, if the counter-party induced an expectation from the aggrieved party, and the aggrieved party reasonably relied on the expectation and would suffer detriment if the expectation is not met.
United Nations Convention on Contracts for the International Sale of Goods	The United Nations Convention on Contracts for the International Sale of Goods is a treaty offering a uniform international sales law that, as of July 2008, had been ratified by 71 countries that account for a significant proportion of world trade, making it one of the most successful international uniform laws. Japan is the most recent State to have ratified the Convention. It allows exporters to avoid choice of law issues as it offers "accepted substantive rules on which contracting parties, courts, and arbitrators may rely".
Waiver	A waiver is the voluntary relinquishment or surrender of some known right or privilege. While a waiver is often in writing, sometimes a person''s actions can act as a waiver. An example of a written waiver is a disclaimer, which becomes a waiver when accepted.

License	The verb License or grant License means to give permission. The noun License refers to that permission as well as to the document memorializing that permission. License may be granted by a party to another party as an element of an agreement between those parties.
Offeree	Offer and acceptance analysis is a traditional approach in contract law used to determine whether an agreement exists between two parties. As a contract is an agreement, an offer is an indication by one person (the "offeror") to another (the "Offeree") of the offeror"s willingness to enter into a contract on certain terms without further negotiations. A contract is said to come into existence when acceptance of an offer (agreement to the terms in it) has been communicated to the offeror by the Offeree.
Offeror	Offer and acceptance analysis is a traditional approach in contract law used to determine whether an agreement exists between two parties. As a contract is an agreement, an offer is an indication by one person (the "Offeror") to another (the "offeree") of the Offeror"s willingness to enter into a contract on certain terms without further negotiations. A contract is said to come into existence when acceptance of an offer (agreement to the terms in it) has been communicated to the Offeror by the offeree.
Software License	A software license is a legal instrument governing the usage or redistribution of copyright protected software. All software not in the Public domain is copyright protected. A typical software license grants an end-user permission to use one or more copies of software in ways where such a use would otherwise constitute infringement of the software publisher"s exclusive rights under copyright law.
Contract	Agreement is said to be reached when an offer capable of immediate acceptance is met with a "mirror image" acceptance (ie, an unqualified acceptance). The parties must have the necessary capacity to Contract and the Contract must not be either trifling, indeterminate, impossible or illegal. Contract law is based on the principle expressed in the Latin phrase pacta sunt servanda .
Lease	A Lease is a contract conferring a right on one person to possess property belonging to another person (called a landlord or lessor) to the exclusion of the owner landlord, and all others except with the invitation of the tenant. It is a rental agreement between landlord and tenant. The relationship between the tenant and the landlord is called a tenancy, and the right to possession by the tenant is sometimes called a Leasehold interest.
Parol evidence	The Parol evidence rule is the legal application of a rule of substantive law in contract cases that prevents a party to a written contract from contradicting (or sometimes adding to) the terms of the contract by seeking the admission of evidence "extrinsic" (outside) to the contract. For example, Carl agrees in writing to sell Betty a car for $1,000. Betty argues that Carl told her that she would only need to pay Carl $800.
Parol evidence rule	The Parol evidence rule is the legal application of a rule of substantive law in contract cases that prevents a party to a written contract from contradicting (or sometimes adding to) the terms of the contract by seeking the admission of evidence "extrinsic" (outside) to the contract. For example, Carl agrees in writing to sell Betty a car for $1,000. Betty argues that Carl told her that she would only need to pay Carl $800.

Statute

A statute is a formal written enactment of a legislative authority that governs a country, state, city, or county. Typically, statute s command or prohibit something, or declare policy. The word is often used to distinguish law made by legislative bodies from case law and the regulations issued by Government agencies.

Statute of Frauds

The Statute of Frauds refers to the requirement that certain kinds of contracts be made in writing and signed.

Traditionally, the Statute of Frauds requires a writing signed by the defendant in the following circumstances:

· Contracts in consideration of marriage.
· Contracts which cannot be performed within one year.
· Contracts for the transfer of an interest in land.
· Contracts by the executor of a will to pay a debt of the estate with their own money.
· Contracts for the sale of goods above a certain value.
· Contracts in which one party becomes a surety (acts as guarantor) for another party"s debt or other obligation.

This can be remembered by the mnemonic "MY LEGS": Marriage, one year, land, executor, goods, surety.

The term Statute of Frauds comes from an English Act of Parliament passed in 1677 (authored by Sir Leoline Jenkins and passed by the Cavalier Parliament), and more properly called An Act for Prevention of Frauds and Perjuries. Many common law jurisdictions have made similar statutory provisions, while a number of civil law jurisdictions have equivalent legislation incorporated into their civil codes.

Chief brand officer

A Chief brand officer is a relatively new executive level position at a corporation, company, organization typically reporting directly to the CEO or board of directors. The Chief brand officer is responsible for a brand"s image, experience, and promise, and propagating it throughout all aspects of the company. The brand officer oversees marketing, advertising, design, public relations and customer service departments.

Arbitration

Arbitration, a form of alternative dispute resolution (ADR), is a legal technique for the resolution of disputes outside the courts, wherein the parties to a dispute refer it to one or more persons (the "arbitrators", "arbiters" or "arbitral tribunal"), by whose decision (the "award") they agree to be bound. It is a settlement technique in which a third party reviews the case and imposes a decision that is legally binding for both sides. Other forms of ADR include mediation (a form of settlement negotiation facilitated by a neutral third party) and non-binding resolution by experts.

Arbitration clause

An Arbitration clause is a commonly used clause in a contract that requires the parties to resolve their disputes through an arbitration process. Although such a clause may or may not specify that arbitration occur within a specific jurisdiction, it always binds the parties to a type of resolution outside of the courts, and is therefore considered a kind of forum selection clause.

In the United States, the federal government has expressed a policy of support of Arbitration clauses, because they reduce the burden on court systems to resolve disputes.

Consideration	Consideration is the legal concept of value in connection with contracts. It is anything of value in the common sense, promised to another when making a contract. It can take the form of money, physical objects, services, promised actions, or even abstinence from a future action.
Uniform Electronic Transactions Act	The Uniform Electronic Transactions Act is one of the several United States Uniform Acts proposed by the National Conference of Commissioners on Uniform State Laws (NCCUSL.) Since then 46 States, the District of Columbia, Puerto Rico, and the U.S. Virgin Islands have adopted it into their own laws. Its overarching purpose is to bring into line the differing State laws over such areas as retention of paper records (checks in particular), and the validity of electronic signatures, thereby supporting the validity of electronic contracts as a viable medium of agreement.
Sale of Goods	The sale of goods Act 1979 (c.54) is an Act of the Parliament of the United Kingdom which regulates contracts in which goods are sold and bought. The Act consolidates the sale of goods Act 1893 and subsequent legislation, which in turn consolidated the previous common law. The sale of goods Act performs several functions.
Freedom of contract	Freedom of contract or contractualism is the freedom of individuals to bargain among themselves the terms of their own contracts, without government interference. Anything more than minimal regulations and taxes may be seen as infringements. It is the underpinning of the theory of laissez-faire economics.
Impossibility	In contract law, Impossibility is an excuse for the nonperformance of duties under a contract, based on a change in circumstances (or the discovery of preexisting circumstances), the nonoccurrence of which was an underlying assumption of the contract, that makes performance of the contract literally impossible. For such a defense to be raised, performance must not merely be difficult or unexpectedly costly for one party; there must be no way for it to actually be accomplished. For example, if Rachel contracts to pay Joey $1000 to paint her house on October 1, but the house burns to the ground before the end of September, Rachel is excused from her duty to pay Joey the $1000, and he is excused from his duty to paint her house; however, Joey may still be able to sue for the unjust enrichment of any benefit conferred on Rachel before her house burned down.
Misrepresentation	Misrepresentation is a contract law concept. It means a false statement of fact made by one party to another party, which has the effect of inducing that party into the contract. For example, under certain circumstances, false statements or promises made by a seller of goods regarding the quality or nature of the product that the seller has may constitute Misrepresentation.
Unconscionability	Unconscionability is a term used in contract law to describe a defense against the enforcement of a contract based on the presence of terms unfair to one party. Typically, such a contract is held to be unenforceable because the consideration offered is lacking or is so obviously inadequate that to enforce the contract would be unfair to the party seeking to escape the contract. In and of itself, inadequate consideration is likely not enough to make a contract unenforceable.

Employment	Employment is a contract between two parties, one being the employer and the other being the employee. An employee may be defined as: "A person in the service of another under any contract of hire, express or implied, oral or written, where the employer has the power or right to control and direct the employee in the material details of how the work is to be performed." Black"s Law Dictionary page 471 (5th ed. 1979).
Trade secret	A trade secret is a formula, practice, process, design, instrument, pattern by which a business can obtain an economic advantage over competitors or customers. In some jurisdictions, such secrets are referred to as "confidential information" or "classified information". The precise language by which a trade secret is defined varies by jurisdiction (as do the particular types of information that are subject to trade secret protection.)
Uniform Commercial Code	The Uniform Commercial Code is one of a number of uniform acts that have been promulgated in conjunction with efforts to harmonize the law of sales and other commercial transactions in all 50 states within the United States of America. This objective is deemed important because of the prevalence today of commercial transactions that extend beyond one state (for example, where the goods are manufactured in state A, warehoused in state B, sold from state C and delivered in state D.) The Uniform Commercial Code deals primarily with transactions involving personal property (movable property), not real property (immovable property.)
United Nations Convention on Contracts for the International Sale of Goods	The United Nations Convention on Contracts for the International Sale of Goods is a treaty offering a uniform international sales law that, as of July 2008, had been ratified by 71 countries that account for a significant proportion of world trade, making it one of the most successful international uniform laws. Japan is the most recent State to have ratified the Convention. It allows exporters to avoid choice of law issues as it offers "accepted substantive rules on which contracting parties, courts, and arbitrators may rely".
Oral contract	An Oral contract is a contract that terms of which have been agreed by spoken communication, in contrast to a written contract, where the contract is a written document. There may be written, or other physical evidence, of an Oral contract - for example where the parties write down what they have agreed - but the contract itself is not a written one. In general, Oral contract s are just as valid as written ones, but some jurisdictions either require a contract to be in writing in certain circumstances (for example where real property is being conveyed), or that a contract be evidenced in writing (though it may be oral.)
Subscription business model	The subscription business model is a business model where a customer must pay a subscription price to have access to the product/service. The model was pioneered by magazines and newspapers, but is now used by many businesses and websites. Rather than selling products individually, a subscription sells periodic (monthly or yearly or seasonal) use or access to a product or service, or, in the case of such non-profit organizations as opera companies or symphony orchestras, it sells tickets to the entire run of five to fifteen scheduled performances for an entire season.

United Nations Convention on Contracts for the International Sale of Goods	The United Nations Convention on Contracts for the International Sale of Goods is a treaty offering a uniform international sales law that, as of July 2008, had been ratified by 71 countries that account for a significant proportion of world trade, making it one of the most successful international uniform laws. Japan is the most recent State to have ratified the Convention. It allows exporters to avoid choice of law issues as it offers "accepted substantive rules on which contracting parties, courts, and arbitrators may rely".
Lease	A Lease is a contract conferring a right on one person to possess property belonging to another person (called a landlord or lessor) to the exclusion of the owner landlord, and all others except with the invitation of the tenant. It is a rental agreement between landlord and tenant. The relationship between the tenant and the landlord is called a tenancy, and the right to possession by the tenant is sometimes called a Leasehold interest.
Negotiable Instrument	A Negotiable instrument is a specialized type of "contract" for the payment of money that is unconditional and capable of transfer by negotiation. Common examples include cheques, banknotes (paper money), and commercial paper. A Negotiable instrument is not a contract, as contract formation requires an offer, acceptance, and consideration, none of which is an element of a Negotiable instrument.
Uniform Commercial Code	The Uniform Commercial Code is one of a number of uniform acts that have been promulgated in conjunction with efforts to harmonize the law of sales and other commercial transactions in all 50 states within the United States of America. This objective is deemed important because of the prevalence today of commercial transactions that extend beyond one state (for example, where the goods are manufactured in state A, warehoused in state B, sold from state C and delivered in state D.) The Uniform Commercial Code deals primarily with transactions involving personal property (movable property), not real property (immovable property.)
Consumer protection	Consumer protection laws are designed to ensure fair competition and the free flow of truthful information in the marketplace. The laws are designed to prevent businesses that engage in fraud or specified unfair practices from gaining an advantage over competitors and may provide additional protection for the weak and those unable to take care of themselves. Consumer protection laws are a form of government regulation which protects the interests of consumers.
Contract	Agreement is said to be reached when an offer capable of immediate acceptance is met with a "mirror image" acceptance (ie, an unqualified acceptance). The parties must have the necessary capacity to Contract and the Contract must not be either trifling, indeterminate, impossible or illegal. Contract law is based on the principle expressed in the Latin phrase pacta sunt servanda .
Good faith	Good faith is the mental and moral state of honesty, conviction as to the truth or falsehood of a proposition or body of opinion especially equitable matters. In contemporary English, "bona fides" is sometimes used as a synonym for credentials, background, or documentation of a person"s identity.

Damages

Damages for breach of contract is a common law remedy, available as of right. It is designed to compensate the victim for their actual loss as a result of the wrongdoer"s breach rather than to punish the wrongdoer. If no loss has been occasioned by the plaintiff, only nominal Damages will be awarded.

Lien

In law, a Lien is a form of security interest granted over an item of property to secure the payment of a debt or performance of some other obligation. The owner of the property, who grants the Lien, is referred to as the Lienor and the person who has the benefit of the Lien is referred to as the Lienee. The etymological root is Anglo-French Lien, loyen bond, restraint, from Latin ligamen, from ligare to bind.

Risk of loss

Risk of loss is a term used in the law of contracts to determine which party should bear the burden of risk for damage occurring to goods after the sale has been completed, but before delivery has occurred. Such considerations generally come into play after the contract is formed but before buyer receives goods, something bad happens.

There are four risk of loss rules, in order of application:

- Agreement - the agreement of the parties controls
- Breach - the breaching party is liable for any uninsured loss even though breach is unrelated to the problem. Hence, if the breach is the time of delivery, and the goods show up broken, then the breaching rule applies risk of loss on the seller.
- Delivery by common carrier other than by seller.
    - risk of loss shifts from seller to buyer at the time that seller completes its delivery obligations
    - If it is a destination contract (FOB (buyer"s city)), then risk of loss is on the seller.
    - If it is a delivery contract (standard, or FOB (seller"s city)), then the risk of loss is on the buyer.
- If the seller is a merchant, then the risk of loss shifts to the buyer upon buyer"s "receipt" of the goods. If the buyer never takes possession, then the seller still has the risk of loss.

Tangible

In law, tangibility is the attribute of being detectable with the senses.
In criminal law, one of the elements of an offense of larceny is that the stolen property must be tangible.
In the context of intellectual property, expression in tangible form is one of the requirements for copyright protection.

Parol evidence	The Parol evidence rule is the legal application of a rule of substantive law in contract cases that prevents a party to a written contract from contradicting (or sometimes adding to) the terms of the contract by seeking the admission of evidence "extrinsic" (outside) to the contract. For example, Carl agrees in writing to sell Betty a car for $1,000. Betty argues that Carl told her that she would only need to pay Carl $800.
Parol evidence rule	The Parol evidence rule is the legal application of a rule of substantive law in contract cases that prevents a party to a written contract from contradicting (or sometimes adding to) the terms of the contract by seeking the admission of evidence "extrinsic" (outside) to the contract. For example, Carl agrees in writing to sell Betty a car for $1,000. Betty argues that Carl told her that she would only need to pay Carl $800.
Statute	A statute is a formal written enactment of a legislative authority that governs a country, state, city, or county. Typically, statute s command or prohibit something, or declare policy. The word is often used to distinguish law made by legislative bodies from case law and the regulations issued by Government agencies.
Statute of Frauds	The Statute of Frauds refers to the requirement that certain kinds of contracts be made in writing and signed. Traditionally, the Statute of Frauds requires a writing signed by the defendant in the following circumstances: · Contracts in consideration of marriage. · Contracts which cannot be performed within one year. · Contracts for the transfer of an interest in land. · Contracts by the executor of a will to pay a debt of the estate with their own money. · Contracts for the sale of goods above a certain value. · Contracts in which one party becomes a surety (acts as guarantor) for another party"s debt or other obligation. This can be remembered by the mnemonic "MY LEGS": Marriage, one year, land, executor, goods, surety. The term Statute of Frauds comes from an English Act of Parliament passed in 1677 (authored by Sir Leoline Jenkins and passed by the Cavalier Parliament), and more properly called An Act for Prevention of Frauds and Perjuries. Many common law jurisdictions have made similar statutory provisions, while a number of civil law jurisdictions have equivalent legislation incorporated into their civil codes.
Consideration	Consideration is the legal concept of value in connection with contracts. It is anything of value in the common sense, promised to another when making a contract. It can take the form of money, physical objects, services, promised actions, or even abstinence from a future action.
Personal property	Personal property is a type of property. In the common law systems Personal property may also be called chattels or personalty. It is distinguished from real property, or real estate.

Personal property may be classified in a variety of ways. Tangible Personal property refers to any type of property that can generally be moved (i.e., it is not attached to real property or land), touched or felt. These generally include items such as furniture, clothing, jewelry, art, writings, or household goods. In some cases, there can be formal title documents that show the ownership and transfer rights of that property after a person"s death (for example, motor vehicles, boats, etc.) In many cases, however, tangible Personal property will not be "titled" in an owner"s name and is presumed to be whatever property he or she was in possession of at the time of his or her death.

Intangible Personal property or "intangibles" refers to Personal property that cannot actually be moved, touched or felt, but instead represents something of value such as negotiable instruments, securities, goods, and intangible assets including chose in action.

Writ

In law, a writ is a formal writ ten order issued by a body with administrative or judicial jurisdiction; in modern usage, this public body is generally a court. Warrants, prerogative writ s and subpoenas are types of writ s; there are many others.

Originally, a writ was a letter or command from the Sovereign, or from some person with appropriate jurisdiction.

Writ of attachment

A Writ of attachment is a court order to "attach" or seize an asset. It is issued by a court to a law enforcement officer or sheriff. The Writ of attachment is issued in order to satisfy a judgment issued by the court.

Job interview

A Job interview is a process in which a potential employee is evaluated by an employer for prospective employment in their company, organization and was established in the late 16th century.

A Job interview typically precedes the hiring decision, and is used to evaluate the candidate. The interview is usually preceded by the evaluation of submitted résumés from interested candidates, then selecting a small number of candidates for interviews.

Firm offer

In the United States, a Firm offer allows merchants to make offers to buy or sell irrevocable for up to three months provided that the offer be put down in writing or otherwise authenticated. Such offers are defined by UCC Â§ 2-205 of the Uniform Commercial Code of the United States.

A Firm offer in effect creates an option contract without requiring any consideration from the prospective buyer.

Option

In finance, an option is a contract between a buyer and a seller that gives the buyer the right--but not the obligation--to buy or to sell a particular asset (the underlying asset) at a later day at an agreed price. In return for granting the option, the seller collects a payment (the premium) from the buyer. A call option gives the buyer the right to buy the underlying asset; a put option gives the buyer of the option the right to sell the underlying asset.

Breach of Contract

Breach of contract is a legal concept in which a binding agreement or bargained-for exchange is not honored by one or more of the parties to the contract by non-performance or interference with the other party"s performance.

	A minor breach, a partial breach or an immaterial breach, occurs when the non-breaching party is unentitled to an order for performance of its obligations, but only to collect the actual amount of their damages. For example, suppose a homeowner hires a contractor to install new plumbing and insists that the pipes, which will ultimately be sealed behind the walls, be red.
Duty	Duty (from "due," that which is owing, O. Fr. deu, did, past participle of devoir; Lat. debere, debitum; cf.
Mirror image rule	In the law of contracts, the Mirror image rule, also referred to as an unequivocal and absolute acceptance requirement states that an offer must be accepted exactly without modifications. The offeror is the master of his own offer. An attempt to accept the offer on different terms instead creates a counter-offer, and this constitutes a rejection of the original offer.
Offeror	Offer and acceptance analysis is a traditional approach in contract law used to determine whether an agreement exists between two parties. As a contract is an agreement, an offer is an indication by one person (the "Offeror") to another (the "offeree") of the Offeror"s willingness to enter into a contract on certain terms without further negotiations. A contract is said to come into existence when acceptance of an offer (agreement to the terms in it) has been communicated to the Offeror by the offeree.
Liquidated damages	Liquidated damages (also referred to as liquidated and ascertained damages) are damages whose amount the parties designate during the formation of a contract for the injured party to collect as compensation upon a specific breach (e.g., late performance). When damages are not predetermined/assessed in advance, then the amount recoverable is said to be "at large" (to be agreed or determined by a court or tribunal in the event of breach). At common law, a Liquidated damages clause will not be enforced if its purpose is to punish the wrongdoer/party in breach rather than to compensate the injured party (in which case it is referred to as a penal or penalty clause).
Security interest	A Security interest is a property interest created by agreement or by operation of law over assets to secure the performance of an obligation, usually the payment of a debt. It gives the beneficiary of the Security interest certain preferential rights in the disposition of secured assets. Such rights vary according to the type of Security interest, but in most cases, a holder of the Security interest is entitled to seize, and usually sell, the property to discharge the debt that the Security interest secures.
Unconscionability	Unconscionability is a term used in contract law to describe a defense against the enforcement of a contract based on the presence of terms unfair to one party. Typically, such a contract is held to be unenforceable because the consideration offered is lacking or is so obviously inadequate that to enforce the contract would be unfair to the party seeking to escape the contract. In and of itself, inadequate consideration is likely not enough to make a contract unenforceable.

Constitution

· Apostolic Constitution (a class of Roman Catholic Church documents)
· Constitution of the Roman Republic
· Constitutional court
· Constitutionalism
· Corporate Constitution
· Judicial activism
· Judicial restraint
· Judicial review

Judicial philosophies of Constitutional interpretation (note: generally specific to United States Constitutional law)

· List of national Constitutions
· Originalism
· Strict constructionism
· Textualism
· Proposed European Union Constitution

· Treaty of Lisbon (adopts same changes, but without Constitutional name)
· United Nations Charter

Supremacy clause

The Supremacy clause is a clause in the United States Constitution, article VI, paragraph 2. The clause establishes the Constitution, Federal Statutes, and U.S. treaties as "the supreme law of the land". The text establishes these as the highest form of law in the American legal system, mandating that state judges uphold them, even if state laws or constitutions conflict.

United States

· History of competition law
· Monopoly

· Coercive monopoly
· Natural monopoly
· Barriers to entry
· Market power
· SSNIP test
· Relevant market
· Merger control

Anti-competitive practices

· Monopolization
· Collusion

· Formation of cartels
· Price fixing
· Bid rigging
· Product bundling and tying
· Refusal to deal

· Group boycott
· Exclusive dealing
· Dividing territories
· Conscious parallelism
· Predatory pricing
· Misuse of patents and copyrights

Laws and doctrines

United States

· Sherman Antitrust Act
· Clayton Antitrust Act
· Robinson-Patman Act
· FTC Act
· Hart-Scott-Rodino Act
· Merger guidelines
· Essential facilities doctrine
· Noerr-Pennington doctrine
· Parker immunity doctrine
· Rule of reason

Europe

· UK competition law
· Irish competition law

Australia

· Trade Practices Act 1974

Enforcement authorities and organizations

Competition law history refers to attempts by governments to regulate competitive markets for goods and services, leading up to the modern competition or antitrust laws around the world today. The earliest records traces back to the efforts of Roman legislators to control price fluctuations and unfair trade practices. Through the Middle Ages in Europe, Kings and Queens repeatedly cracked down on monopolies, including those created through state legislation.

· International Competition Network
· List of competition regulators

Business

There are many ways in which a business may be owned under the legal system of England and Wales.

Different types of ownership are suitable for organisations depending on the degree of control the owners wish to have over the business. The choice of ownership methor also relates to the organisations ability to raise funds for the business activities.

Force majeure

Force majeure is a common clause in contracts which essentially frees both parties from liability or obligation when an extraordinary event or circumstance beyond the control of the parties, such as a war, strike, riot, crime prevents one or both parties from fulfilling their obligations under the contract. However, Force majeure is not intended to excuse negligence or other malfeasance of a party, as where non-performance is caused by the usual and natural consequences of external forces either when they become likely or when they actually occur.

Bill of lading	A Bill of lading (sometimes referred to as a Bill of lading,or B/L) is a document issued by a carrier to a shipper, acknowledging that specified goods have been received on board as cargo for conveyance to a named place for delivery to the consignee who is usually identified. A through Bill of lading involves the use of at least two different modes of transport from road, rail, air, and sea. The term derives from the noun "bill", a schedule of costs for services supplied or to be supplied, and from the verb "to lade" which means to load a cargo onto a ship or other form of transport.
United Nations Convention on Contracts for the International Sale of Goods	The United Nations Convention on Contracts for the International Sale of Goods is a treaty offering a uniform international sales law that, as of July 2008, had been ratified by 71 countries that account for a significant proportion of world trade, making it one of the most successful international uniform laws. Japan is the most recent State to have ratified the Convention. It allows exporters to avoid choice of law issues as it offers "accepted substantive rules on which contracting parties, courts, and arbitrators may rely".
Lease	A Lease is a contract conferring a right on one person to possess property belonging to another person (called a landlord or lessor) to the exclusion of the owner landlord, and all others except with the invitation of the tenant. It is a rental agreement between landlord and tenant. The relationship between the tenant and the landlord is called a tenancy, and the right to possession by the tenant is sometimes called a Leasehold interest.
Statute	A statute is a formal written enactment of a legislative authority that governs a country, state, city, or county. Typically, statute s command or prohibit something, or declare policy. The word is often used to distinguish law made by legislative bodies from case law and the regulations issued by Government agencies.
Statute of Frauds	The Statute of Frauds refers to the requirement that certain kinds of contracts be made in writing and signed. Traditionally, the Statute of Frauds requires a writing signed by the defendant in the following circumstances: · Contracts in consideration of marriage. · Contracts which cannot be performed within one year. · Contracts for the transfer of an interest in land. · Contracts by the executor of a will to pay a debt of the estate with their own money. · Contracts for the sale of goods above a certain value. · Contracts in which one party becomes a surety (acts as guarantor) for another party"s debt or other obligation. This can be remembered by the mnemonic "MY LEGS": Marriage, one year, land, executor, goods, surety. The term Statute of Frauds comes from an English Act of Parliament passed in 1677 (authored by Sir Leoline Jenkins and passed by the Cavalier Parliament), and more properly called An Act for Prevention of Frauds and Perjuries. Many common law jurisdictions have made similar statutory provisions, while a number of civil law jurisdictions have equivalent legislation incorporated into their civil codes.

Warehouse receipt

A Warehouse receipt is a document that provides proof of ownership of commodities (e.g., bars of copper) that are stored in a warehouse, vault, or depository for safekeeping.

Warehouse receipt s may be negotiable or non-negotiable. Negotiable Warehouse receipt s allow transfer of ownership of that commodity without having to deliver the physical commodity.

Contract

Agreement is said to be reached when an offer capable of immediate acceptance is met with a "mirror image" acceptance (ie, an unqualified acceptance). The parties must have the necessary capacity to Contract and the Contract must not be either trifling, indeterminate, impossible or illegal. Contract law is based on the principle expressed in the Latin phrase pacta sunt servanda .

Estoppel

Estoppel is a legal doctrine at common law, where a party is barred from claiming or denying an argument on an equitable ground. Estoppel complements the requirement of consideration in contract law. In general, Estoppel protects an aggrieved party, if the counter-party induced an expectation from the aggrieved party, and the aggrieved party reasonably relied on the expectation and would suffer detriment if the expectation is not met.

Good faith

Good faith is the mental and moral state of honesty, conviction as to the truth or falsehood of a proposition or body of opinion especially equitable matters.

In contemporary English, "bona fides" is sometimes used as a synonym for credentials, background, or documentation of a person''s identity.

Insolvency

Insolvency means the inability to pay one''s debts as they fall due. Usually used in Business terms, Insolvency refers to the inability for a company to pay off its debts.

Business Insolvency is defined in two different ways:

Cash flow Insolvency

Unable to pay debts as they fall due.

Cash

Two primary accounting methods, cash and accrual basis, are used to calculate taxable income for U.S. federal income taxes. According to the Internal Revenue Code, a taxpayer may compute taxable income by:

· the cash receipts and disbursements method;
· an accrual method;
· any other method permitted by the chapter; or
· any combination of the foregoing methods permitted under regulations prescribed by the Secretary.

As a general rule, a taxpayer must compute taxable income using the same accounting method he uses to compute income in keeping his books.

Consumer protection	Consumer protection laws are designed to ensure fair competition and the free flow of truthful information in the marketplace. The laws are designed to prevent businesses that engage in fraud or specified unfair practices from gaining an advantage over competitors and may provide additional protection for the weak and those unable to take care of themselves. Consumer protection laws are a form of government regulation which protects the interests of consumers.
Voidable	In law, a transaction or action which is voidable is valid, but may be annulled by one of the parties to the transaction. voidable is usually used in distinction to void ab initio (or void from the outset) and unenforceable. The act of invalidating the contract by the party exercising its rights to anul the voidable contract is usually referred to either as voiding the contract (in the United States and Canada) or avoiding the contract (in the United Kingdom, Australia and other common law countries.)
Business	There are many ways in which a business may be owned under the legal system of England and Wales. Different types of ownership are suitable for organisations depending on the degree of control the owners wish to have over the business. The choice of ownership methor also relates to the organisations ability to raise funds for the business activities.
Ordinary course of business	In law, the Ordinary course of business covers the usual transactions, customs and practices of a certain business and of a certain firm. This term is used particularly to judge the validity of certain transactions. It is used in several different sections of the Uniform Commercial Code.
Risk of Loss	Risk of loss is a term used in the law of contracts to determine which party should bear the burden of risk for damage occurring to goods after the sale has been completed, but before delivery has occurred. Such considerations generally come into play after the contract is formed but before buyer receives goods, something bad happens. There are four risk of loss rules, in order of application: · Agreement - the agreement of the parties controls · Breach - the breaching party is liable for any uninsured loss even though breach is unrelated to the problem. Hence, if the breach is the time of delivery, and the goods show up broken, then the breaching rule applies risk of loss on the seller. · Delivery by common carrier other than by seller. · risk of loss shifts from seller to buyer at the time that seller completes its delivery obligations · If it is a destination contract (FOB (buyer"s city)), then risk of loss is on the seller. · If it is a delivery contract (standard, or FOB (seller"s city)), then the risk of loss is on the buyer. · If the seller is a merchant, then the risk of loss shifts to the buyer upon buyer"s "receipt" of the goods. If the buyer never takes possession, then the seller still has the risk of loss.

Damages	Damages for breach of contract is a common law remedy, available as of right. It is designed to compensate the victim for their actual loss as a result of the wrongdoer"s breach rather than to punish the wrongdoer. If no loss has been occasioned by the plaintiff, only nominal Damages will be awarded.

United Nations Convention on Contracts for the International Sale of Goods	The United Nations Convention on Contracts for the International Sale of Goods is a treaty offering a uniform international sales law that, as of July 2008, had been ratified by 71 countries that account for a significant proportion of world trade, making it one of the most successful international uniform laws. Japan is the most recent State to have ratified the Convention. It allows exporters to avoid choice of law issues as it offers "accepted substantive rules on which contracting parties, courts, and arbitrators may rely".
Damages	Damages for breach of contract is a common law remedy, available as of right. It is designed to compensate the victim for their actual loss as a result of the wrongdoer"s breach rather than to punish the wrongdoer. If no loss has been occasioned by the plaintiff, only nominal Damages will be awarded.
Duty	Duty (from "due," that which is owing, O. Fr. deu, did, past participle of devoir; Lat. debere, debitum; cf.
Good faith	Good faith is the mental and moral state of honesty, conviction as to the truth or falsehood of a proposition or body of opinion especially equitable matters. In contemporary English, "bona fides" is sometimes used as a synonym for credentials, background, or documentation of a person"s identity.
Obligation	An obligation is a requirement to take some course of action, whether legal or moral. There are also obligation s in other normative contexts, such as obligation s of etiquette, social obligation s, and possibly in terms of politics, where obligation s are requirements which must be fulfilled. These are generally legal obligation s, which can incur a penalty for unfulfilment, although certain people are obliged to carry out certain actions for other reasons as well, whether as a tradition or for social reasons.
Security interest	A Security interest is a property interest created by agreement or by operation of law over assets to secure the performance of an obligation, usually the payment of a debt. It gives the beneficiary of the Security interest certain preferential rights in the disposition of secured assets. Such rights vary according to the type of Security interest, but in most cases, a holder of the Security interest is entitled to seize, and usually sell, the property to discharge the debt that the Security interest secures.
Statute	A statute is a formal written enactment of a legislative authority that governs a country, state, city, or county. Typically, statute s command or prohibit something, or declare policy. The word is often used to distinguish law made by legislative bodies from case law and the regulations issued by Government agencies.
Statute of Frauds	The Statute of Frauds refers to the requirement that certain kinds of contracts be made in writing and signed. Traditionally, the Statute of Frauds requires a writing signed by the defendant in the following circumstances:

· Contracts in consideration of marriage.
· Contracts which cannot be performed within one year.
· Contracts for the transfer of an interest in land.
· Contracts by the executor of a will to pay a debt of the estate with their own money.
· Contracts for the sale of goods above a certain value.
· Contracts in which one party becomes a surety (acts as guarantor) for another party"s debt or other obligation.

This can be remembered by the mnemonic "MY LEGS": Marriage, one year, land, executor, goods, surety.

The term Statute of Frauds comes from an English Act of Parliament passed in 1677 (authored by Sir Leoline Jenkins and passed by the Cavalier Parliament), and more properly called An Act for Prevention of Frauds and Perjuries. Many common law jurisdictions have made similar statutory provisions, while a number of civil law jurisdictions have equivalent legislation incorporated into their civil codes.

Uniform Commercial Code

The Uniform Commercial Code is one of a number of uniform acts that have been promulgated in conjunction with efforts to harmonize the law of sales and other commercial transactions in all 50 states within the United States of America. This objective is deemed important because of the prevalence today of commercial transactions that extend beyond one state (for example, where the goods are manufactured in state A, warehoused in state B, sold from state C and delivered in state D.) The Uniform Commercial Code deals primarily with transactions involving personal property (movable property), not real property (immovable property.)

Contract

Agreement is said to be reached when an offer capable of immediate acceptance is met with a "mirror image" acceptance (ie, an unqualified acceptance). The parties must have the necessary capacity to Contract and the Contract must not be either trifling, indeterminate, impossible or illegal. Contract law is based on the principle expressed in the Latin phrase pacta sunt servanda .

Estoppel

Estoppel is a legal doctrine at common law, where a party is barred from claiming or denying an argument on an equitable ground. Estoppel complements the requirement of consideration in contract law. In general, Estoppel protects an aggrieved party, if the counter-party induced an expectation from the aggrieved party, and the aggrieved party reasonably relied on the expectation and would suffer detriment if the expectation is not met.

Risk of loss

Risk of loss is a term used in the law of contracts to determine which party should bear the burden of risk for damage occurring to goods after the sale has been completed, but before delivery has occurred. Such considerations generally come into play after the contract is formed but before buyer receives goods, something bad happens.

There are four risk of loss rules, in order of application:

· Agreement - the agreement of the parties controls
· Breach - the breaching party is liable for any uninsured loss even though breach is unrelated to the problem. Hence, if the breach is the time of delivery, and the goods show up broken, then the breaching rule applies risk of loss on the seller.
· Delivery by common carrier other than by seller.

· risk of loss shifts from seller to buyer at the time that seller completes its delivery obligations
· If it is a destination contract (FOB (buyer''s city)), then risk of loss is on the seller.
· If it is a delivery contract (standard, or FOB (seller''s city)), then the risk of loss is on the buyer.

· If the seller is a merchant, then the risk of loss shifts to the buyer upon buyer''s "receipt" of the goods. If the buyer never takes possession, then the seller still has the risk of loss.

Business

There are many ways in which a business may be owned under the legal system of England and Wales. Different types of ownership are suitable for organisations depending on the degree of control the owners wish to have over the business. The choice of ownership methor also relates to the organisations ability to raise funds for the business activities.

Lease

A Lease is a contract conferring a right on one person to possess property belonging to another person (called a landlord or lessor) to the exclusion of the owner landlord, and all others except with the invitation of the tenant. It is a rental agreement between landlord and tenant. The relationship between the tenant and the landlord is called a tenancy, and the right to possession by the tenant is sometimes called a Leasehold interest.

Perfect tender rule

The Perfect tender rule refers to the legal right for a buyer of goods to insist upon "perfect tender" by the seller. In a contract for the sale of goods, if the goods fail to conform exactly to the description in the contract (whether as to quality, quantity or manner of delivery) the buyer may reject the goods. (UCC 2-601.)

Terrorism

Terrorism is a policy or ideology of violence intended to intimidate or cause terror for the purpose of "exerting pressure on decision making by state bodies." The term "terror" is largely used to indicate clandestine, low-intensity violence that targets civilians and generates public fear. Thus "terror" is distinct from asymmetric warfare, and violates the concept of a common law of war in which civilian life is regarded. The term "-ism" is used to indicate an ideology --typically one that claims its attacks are in the domain of a "just war" concept, though most condemn such as crimes against humanity.

Parol evidence	The Parol evidence rule is the legal application of a rule of substantive law in contract cases that prevents a party to a written contract from contradicting (or sometimes adding to) the terms of the contract by seeking the admission of evidence "extrinsic" (outside) to the contract. For example, Carl agrees in writing to sell Betty a car for $1,000. Betty argues that Carl told her that she would only need to pay Carl $800.
Parol evidence rule	The Parol evidence rule is the legal application of a rule of substantive law in contract cases that prevents a party to a written contract from contradicting (or sometimes adding to) the terms of the contract by seeking the admission of evidence "extrinsic" (outside) to the contract. For example, Carl agrees in writing to sell Betty a car for $1,000. Betty argues that Carl told her that she would only need to pay Carl $800.
Consideration	Consideration is the legal concept of value in connection with contracts. It is anything of value in the common sense, promised to another when making a contract. It can take the form of money, physical objects, services, promised actions, or even abstinence from a future action.
Impracticability	The doctrine of Impracticability in the common law of contracts excuses performance of a duty, where that duty has become unfeasibly difficult or expensive for the party who was to perform. It is similar in some respects to the doctrine of impossibility because it is triggered by the occurrence of a condition, the nonoccurrence of which was a basic assumption of the contract. The major difference between impossibility and Impracticability, however, is that while impossibility excuses performance where the contractual duty cannot physically be performed, the doctrine of Impracticability comes into play where performance is still physically possible, but would be very burdensome for the party whose performance is due.
Ratification	Ratification is the act of approving and paying for supplies or services provided to and accepted by the government as a result of an unauthorized commitment. It gives official sanction or approval to a formal document such as a treaty or constitution. It includes the process of adopting an international treaty by the legislature, a constitution, or another nationally binding document (such as an amendment to a constitution) by the agreement of multiple sub-national entities.
Insolvency	Insolvency means the inability to pay one"s debts as they fall due. Usually used in Business terms, Insolvency refers to the inability for a company to pay off its debts. Business Insolvency is defined in two different ways: Cash flow Insolvency Unable to pay debts as they fall due.
Reseller	A reseller is a company or individual that purchases goods or services with the intention of reselling them rather than consuming or using them. This is usually done for profit (but could be resold at a loss.) One example can be found in the industry of telecommunications, where companies buy excess amounts of transmission capacity or call time from other carriers and resell it to smaller carriers.

Rescission	In contract law, rescission has been defined as the unmaking of a contract between parties. rescission is the unwinding of a transaction. This is done to bring the parties, as far as possible, back to the position in which they were before they entered into a contract (the "status quo ante".)
Breach of Contract	Breach of contract is a legal concept in which a binding agreement or bargained-for exchange is not honored by one or more of the parties to the contract by non-performance or interference with the other party"s performance. A minor breach, a partial breach or an immaterial breach, occurs when the non-breaching party is unentitled to an order for performance of its obligations, but only to collect the actual amount of their damages. For example, suppose a homeowner hires a contractor to install new plumbing and insists that the pipes, which will ultimately be sealed behind the walls, be red.
Specific performance	In the law of Remedy, an order of specific performance is an order of the court which requires a party to perform a specific act, usually what is stated in a contract. While specific performance can be in the form of any type of forced action, it is usually used to complete a previously established transaction, thus being the most effective remedy in protecting the expectation interest of the innocent party to a contract. It is usually the opposite of a prohibitory injunction but there are mandatory injunctions which have a similar effect to specific performance.
Replevin	In creditors" rights law, Replevin, sometimes known as "claim and delivery," is a legal remedy for a person to recover goods unlawfully withheld from his or her possession, by means of a special form of legal process in which a court may require a defendant to return specific goods to the plaintiff at the outset of the action (i.e. before judgment.) In other situations, a party seeking relief may elect to adjudicate the right to possession prior to obtaining immediate relief to obtain the property in question. In such cases, Replevin actions are still designed to afford the petitioning party a relatively speedy process for obtaining judgment, as compared to typical lawsuits.
Revocation	Revocation is the act of recall or annulment. It is the reversal of an act, the recalling of a grant, or the making void of some deed previously existing. In the law of contracts, revocation is a type of remedy for buyers when the buyer accepts a nonconforming good from the seller.
Unconscionability	Unconscionability is a term used in contract law to describe a defense against the enforcement of a contract based on the presence of terms unfair to one party. Typically, such a contract is held to be unenforceable because the consideration offered is lacking or is so obviously inadequate that to enforce the contract would be unfair to the party seeking to escape the contract. In and of itself, inadequate consideration is likely not enough to make a contract unenforceable.
Prima facie	Prima facie is a Latin expression meaning on its first appearance, or by first instance; at first sight. The literal translation would be "from first face", prima first, facie face, both in the ablative case. It is used in modern legal English to signify that on first examination, a matter appears to be self-evident from the facts.

Bill of lading	A Bill of lading (sometimes referred to as a Bill of lading,or B/L) is a document issued by a carrier to a shipper, acknowledging that specified goods have been received on board as cargo for conveyance to a named place for delivery to the consignee who is usually identified. A through Bill of lading involves the use of at least two different modes of transport from road, rail, air, and sea. The term derives from the noun "bill", a schedule of costs for services supplied or to be supplied, and from the verb "to lade" which means to load a cargo onto a ship or other form of transport.
Letter of credit	A standard, commercial Letter of credit is a document issued mostly by a financial institution, used primarily in trade finance, which usually provides an irrevocable payment undertaking. The LC can also be the source of payment for a transaction, meaning that redeeming the Letter of credit will pay an exporter. Letters of credit are used primarily in international trade transactions of significant value, for deals between a supplier in one country and a customer in another.

Lien

In law, a Lien is a form of security interest granted over an item of property to secure the payment of a debt or performance of some other obligation. The owner of the property, who grants the Lien, is referred to as the Lienor and the person who has the benefit of the Lien is referred to as the Lienee. The etymological root is Anglo-French Lien, loyen bond, restraint, from Latin ligamen, from ligare to bind.

Product liability

Product liability is the area of law in which manufacturers, distributors, suppliers, retailers, and others who make products available to the public are held responsible for the injuries those products cause. In the United States, the claims most commonly associated with Product liability are negligence, strict liability, breach of warranty, and various consumer protection claims. The majority of Product liability laws are determined at the state level and vary widely from state to state.

Rescission

In contract law, rescission has been defined as the unmaking of a contract between parties. rescission is the unwinding of a transaction. This is done to bring the parties, as far as possible, back to the position in which they were before they entered into a contract (the "status quo ante".)

Statute

A statute is a formal written enactment of a legislative authority that governs a country, state, city, or county. Typically, statute s command or prohibit something, or declare policy. The word is often used to distinguish law made by legislative bodies from case law and the regulations issued by Government agencies.

Statute of Frauds

The Statute of Frauds refers to the requirement that certain kinds of contracts be made in writing and signed.

Traditionally, the Statute of Frauds requires a writing signed by the defendant in the following circumstances:

· Contracts in consideration of marriage.
· Contracts which cannot be performed within one year.
· Contracts for the transfer of an interest in land.
· Contracts by the executor of a will to pay a debt of the estate with their own money.
· Contracts for the sale of goods above a certain value.
· Contracts in which one party becomes a surety (acts as guarantor) for another party"s debt or other obligation.

This can be remembered by the mnemonic "MY LEGS": Marriage, one year, land, executor, goods, surety.

The term Statute of Frauds comes from an English Act of Parliament passed in 1677 (authored by Sir Leoline Jenkins and passed by the Cavalier Parliament), and more properly called An Act for Prevention of Frauds and Perjuries. Many common law jurisdictions have made similar statutory provisions, while a number of civil law jurisdictions have equivalent legislation incorporated into their civil codes.

Warranty

In commercial and consumer transactions, a warranty is an obligation or guarantee that an article or service sold is as factually stated or legally implied by the seller, and that often provides for a specific remedy such as repair or replacement in the event the article or service fails to meet the warranty. A breach of warranty occurs when the promise is broken, i.e., a product is defective or not as should be expected by a reasonable buyer.

	In business and legal transactions, a warranty is an assurance by one party to the other party that certain facts or conditions are true or will happen; the other party is permitted to rely on that assurance and seek some type of remedy if it is not true or followed.
Contract	Agreement is said to be reached when an offer capable of immediate acceptance is met with a "mirror image" acceptance (ie, an unqualified acceptance). The parties must have the necessary capacity to Contract and the Contract must not be either trifling, indeterminate, impossible or illegal. Contract law is based on the principle expressed in the Latin phrase pacta sunt servanda .
Warranty of Title	Another implied warranty is the warranty of title, which implies that the seller of goods has the right to sell them (e.g., they are not stolen or already sold to someone else.) This theoretically saves a buyer from having to "pay twice" for a product, if it is confiscated by the rightful owner, but only if the seller can be found and makes restitution. An implied warranty of fitness for a particular purpose is a warranty implied by law that if a seller knows or has reason to know of a particular purpose for which some item is being purchased by the buyer, the seller is guaranteeing that the item is fit for that particular purpose.
Security interest	A Security interest is a property interest created by agreement or by operation of law over assets to secure the performance of an obligation, usually the payment of a debt. It gives the beneficiary of the Security interest certain preferential rights in the disposition of secured assets. Such rights vary according to the type of Security interest, but in most cases, a holder of the Security interest is entitled to seize, and usually sell, the property to discharge the debt that the Security interest secures.
Patent	A patent is a set of exclusive rights granted by a state to an inventor or his assignee for a limited period of time in exchange for a disclosure of an invention. The procedure for granting patent s, the requirements placed on the patent ee and the extent of the exclusive rights vary widely between countries according to national laws and international agreements. Typically, however, a patent application must include one or more claims defining the invention which must be new, inventive, and useful or industrially applicable.
Patent Infringement	Patent infringement is the performance of a prohibited act with respect to a patented invention without permission from the patent holder. Permission may typically be granted in the form of a licence. The acts may vary by jurisdiction, but typically include using or selling the patented invention.
Trademark	A trademark or trade mark is a distinctive sign or indicator used by an individual, business organization and to distinguish its products or services from those of other entities. A trademark is designated by the following symbols: · â„¢ (for an unregistered trademark that is, a mark used to promote or brand goods); · â„ (for an unregistered service mark, that is, a mark used to promote or brand services); and · Â® (for a registered trademark) A trademark is a type of intellectual property, and typically a name, word, phrase, logo, symbol, design, image, or a combination of these elements. There is also a range of non-conventional trademark s comprising marks which do not fall into these standard categories.

The owner of a registered trademark may commence legal proceedings for trademark infringement to prevent unauthorized use of that trademark

Trademark Infringement

Trademark infringement is a violation of the exclusive rights attaching to a trademark without the authorization of the trademark owner or any licensees (provided that such authorization was within the scope of the license.) Infringement may occur when one party, the "infringer", uses a trademark which is identical or confusingly similar to a trademark owned by another party, in relation to products or services which are identical or similar to the products or services which the registration covers. An owner of a trademark may commence legal proceedings against a party which infringes its registration.

Implied warranty

In common law jurisdictions, an Implied warranty is a contract law term for certain assurances that are presumed to be made in the sale of products or real property, due to the circumstances of the sale. These assurances are characterized as warranties irrespective of whether the seller has expressly promised them orally or in writing. They include an Implied warranty of fitness for a particular purpose, an Implied warranty of merchantability for products, Implied warranty of workmanlike quality for services, and an Implied warranty of habitability for a home.

Puffery

Puffery as a legal term refers to promotional statements and claims that express subjective rather than objective views, such that no reasonable person would take literally. Puffery is especially featured in testimonials.

In a legal context, the term originated in the English Court of Appeal case Carlill v Carbolic Smoke Ball Company, which centred on whether a monetary reimbursement should be paid when an influenza preventative device failed to work.

Cash

Two primary accounting methods, cash and accrual basis, are used to calculate taxable income for U.S. federal income taxes. According to the Internal Revenue Code, a taxpayer may compute taxable income by:

· the cash receipts and disbursements method;
· an accrual method;
· any other method permitted by the chapter; or
· any combination of the foregoing methods permitted under regulations prescribed by the Secretary.

As a general rule, a taxpayer must compute taxable income using the same accounting method he uses to compute income in keeping his books.

Warranty of merchantability

The Warranty of merchantability is implied, unless expressly disclaimed by name the goods must reasonably conform to an ordinary buyer"s expectations, i.e., they are what they say they are. For example, a fruit that looks and smells good but has hidden defects would violate the implied Warranty of merchantability if its quality does not meet the standards for such fruit "as passes ordinarily in the trade". In Massachusetts consumer protection law, it is illegal to disclaim this warranty on household goods sold to consumers etc.

Consumer protection	Consumer protection laws are designed to ensure fair competition and the free flow of truthful information in the marketplace. The laws are designed to prevent businesses that engage in fraud or specified unfair practices from gaining an advantage over competitors and may provide additional protection for the weak and those unable to take care of themselves. Consumer protection laws are a form of government regulation which protects the interests of consumers.
Privity	The doctrine of privity in contract law provides that a contract cannot confer rights or impose obligations arising under it on any person or agent except the parties to it. The premise is that only parties to contracts should be able to sue to enforce their rights or claim damages as such. However, the doctrine has proven problematic due to its implications upon contracts made for the benefit of third parties who are unable to enforce the obligations of the contracting parties.
Third party beneficiary	A third party beneficiary, in the law of contracts, is a person who may have the right to sue on a contract, despite not having originally been a party to the contract. This right arises where the third party is the intended beneficiary of the contract, as opposed to an incidental beneficiary. It vests when the third party relies on or assents to the relationship, and gives the third party the right to sue either the promisor or the promisee of the contract, depending on the circumstances under which the relationship was created.
Estoppel	Estoppel is a legal doctrine at common law, where a party is barred from claiming or denying an argument on an equitable ground. Estoppel complements the requirement of consideration in contract law. In general, Estoppel protects an aggrieved party, if the counter-party induced an expectation from the aggrieved party, and the aggrieved party reasonably relied on the expectation and would suffer detriment if the expectation is not met.
Uniform Commercial Code	The Uniform Commercial Code is one of a number of uniform acts that have been promulgated in conjunction with efforts to harmonize the law of sales and other commercial transactions in all 50 states within the United States of America. This objective is deemed important because of the prevalence today of commercial transactions that extend beyond one state (for example, where the goods are manufactured in state A, warehoused in state B, sold from state C and delivered in state D.) The Uniform Commercial Code deals primarily with transactions involving personal property (movable property), not real property (immovable property.)
Unconscionability	Unconscionability is a term used in contract law to describe a defense against the enforcement of a contract based on the presence of terms unfair to one party. Typically, such a contract is held to be unenforceable because the consideration offered is lacking or is so obviously inadequate that to enforce the contract would be unfair to the party seeking to escape the contract. In and of itself, inadequate consideration is likely not enough to make a contract unenforceable.
Statute of limitations	A statute of limitations is a statute in a common law legal system that sets forth the maximum period of time, after certain events, that legal proceedings based on those events may be initiated. In civil law systems, similar provisions are usually part of the civil code or criminal code and are often known collectively as "periods of prescription" or "prescriptive periods."

A common law legal system might have a statute limiting the time for prosecution of crimes called misdemeanors to two years after the offense occurred. In that statute, if a person is discovered to have committed a misdemeanor three years ago, the time has expired for the prosecution of the misdemeanor.

Public policy

Public policy can be generally defined as the course of action or inaction taken by governmental entities with regard to a particular issue or set of issues. Other scholars define it as a system of "courses of action, regulatory measures, laws, and funding priorities concerning a given topic promulgated by a governmental entity or its representatives." public policy is commonly embodied "in constitutions, legislative acts, and judicial decisions."

In the United States, this concept refers not only to the end result of policies, but more broadly to the decision-making and analysis of governmental decisions. public policy is also considered an academic discipline, as it is studied by professors and students at public policy schools of major universities throughout the country.

Restatements of the Law

The Restatements of the Law are treatises on U.S. legal topics published by the American Law Institute, an organization of legal academics and practitioners, as scholarly refinements of black-letter law, to "address uncertainty in the law through a restatement of basic legal subjects that would tell judges and lawyers what the law was."

As Harvard Law School describes the Restatements:

> The ALI"s aim is to distill the "black letter law" from cases, to indicate a trend in common law, and, occasionally, to recommend what a rule of law should be. In essence, they restate existing common law into a series of principles or rules.

While considered secondary authority (compare to primary authority), the authoritativeness of the Restatements of the Law is evidenced by their acceptance by courts throughout the United States.

Strict liability

Strict liability makes a person responsible for the damage and loss caused by his/her acts and omissions regardless of culpability .) Strict liability is important in torts (especially product liability), corporations law, and criminal law. For analysis of the pros and cons of Strict liability as applied to product liability, the most important Strict liability regime, see product liability.

Tort

Tort law is a body of law that addresses, and provides remedies for, civil wrongs not arising out of contractual obligations. A person who suffers legal damages may be able to use Tort law to receive compensation from someone who is legally responsible, or "liable," for those injuries. Generally speaking, Tort law defines what constitutes a legal injury and establishes the circumstances under which one person may be held liable for another"s injury.

Duty

Duty (from "due," that which is owing, O. Fr. deu, did, past participle of devoir; Lat. debere, debitum; cf.

Obligation

An obligation is a requirement to take some course of action, whether legal or moral. There are also obligation s in other normative contexts, such as obligation s of etiquette, social obligation s, and possibly in terms of politics, where obligation s are requirements which must be fulfilled. These are generally legal obligation s, which can incur a penalty for unfulfilment, although certain people are obliged to carry out certain actions for other reasons as well, whether as a tradition or for social reasons.

Arbitration

Arbitration, a form of alternative dispute resolution (ADR), is a legal technique for the resolution of disputes outside the courts, wherein the parties to a dispute refer it to one or more persons (the "arbitrators", "arbiters" or "arbitral tribunal"), by whose decision (the "award") they agree to be bound. It is a settlement technique in which a third party reviews the case and imposes a decision that is legally binding for both sides. Other forms of ADR include mediation (a form of settlement negotiation facilitated by a neutral third party) and non-binding resolution by experts.

Promissory note

A promissory note, referred to as a note payable in accounting, just a "note" is a contract where one party (the maker or issuer) makes an unconditional promise in writing to pay a sum of money to the other (the payee), either at a fixed or determinable future time or on demand of the payee, under specific terms. They differ from IOUs in that they contain a specific promise to pay, rather than simply acknowledging that a debt exists.

The terms of a note typically include the principal amount, the interest rate if any, the parties, the date, the terms of repayment (which could include interest) and the maturity date.

United Nations Convention on Contracts for the International Sale of Goods

The United Nations Convention on Contracts for the International Sale of Goods is a treaty offering a uniform international sales law that, as of July 2008, had been ratified by 71 countries that account for a significant proportion of world trade, making it one of the most successful international uniform laws. Japan is the most recent State to have ratified the Convention.

It allows exporters to avoid choice of law issues as it offers "accepted substantive rules on which contracting parties, courts, and arbitrators may rely".

Good faith

Good faith is the mental and moral state of honesty, conviction as to the truth or falsehood of a proposition or body of opinion especially equitable matters.

In contemporary English, "bona fides" is sometimes used as a synonym for credentials, background, or documentation of a person"s identity.

Freedom of contract

Freedom of contract or contractualism is the freedom of individuals to bargain among themselves the terms of their own contracts, without government interference. Anything more than minimal regulations and taxes may be seen as infringements. It is the underpinning of the theory of laissez-faire economics.

Misrepresentation

Misrepresentation is a contract law concept. It means a false statement of fact made by one party to another party, which has the effect of inducing that party into the contract. For example, under certain circumstances, false statements or promises made by a seller of goods regarding the quality or nature of the product that the seller has may constitute Misrepresentation.

Offeree	Offer and acceptance analysis is a traditional approach in contract law used to determine whether an agreement exists between two parties. As a contract is an agreement, an offer is an indication by one person (the "offeror") to another (the "Offeree") of the offeror"s willingness to enter into a contract on certain terms without further negotiations. A contract is said to come into existence when acceptance of an offer (agreement to the terms in it) has been communicated to the offeror by the Offeree.

Negotiable Instrument	A Negotiable instrument is a specialized type of "contract" for the payment of money that is unconditional and capable of transfer by negotiation. Common examples include cheques, banknotes (paper money), and commercial paper. A Negotiable instrument is not a contract, as contract formation requires an offer, acceptance, and consideration, none of which is an element of a Negotiable instrument.
Uniform Electronic Transactions Act	The Uniform Electronic Transactions Act is one of the several United States Uniform Acts proposed by the National Conference of Commissioners on Uniform State Laws (NCCUSL.) Since then 46 States, the District of Columbia, Puerto Rico, and the U.S. Virgin Islands have adopted it into their own laws. Its overarching purpose is to bring into line the differing State laws over such areas as retention of paper records (checks in particular), and the validity of electronic signatures, thereby supporting the validity of electronic contracts as a viable medium of agreement.
Sight draft	A draft can require immediate payment by the second party to the third upon presentation of the draft. This is called a Sight draft Cheques are Sight draft s.
Promissory Note	A promissory note, referred to as a note payable in accounting, just a "note" is a contract where one party (the maker or issuer) makes an unconditional promise in writing to pay a sum of money to the other (the payee), either at a fixed or determinable future time or on demand of the payee, under specific terms. They differ from IOUs in that they contain a specific promise to pay, rather than simply acknowledging that a debt exists. The terms of a note typically include the principal amount, the interest rate if any, the parties, the date, the terms of repayment (which could include interest) and the maturity date.
Installment Note	An Installment Note is a form of promissory note calling for payment of both principal and interest in specified amounts at specific time intervals. This periodic reduction of principal amortizes the loan.
Writ	In law, a writ is a formal writ ten order issued by a body with administrative or judicial jurisdiction; in modern usage, this public body is generally a court. Warrants, prerogative writ s and subpoenas are types of writ s; there are many others. Originally, a writ was a letter or command from the Sovereign, or from some person with appropriate jurisdiction.
Writ of attachment	A Writ of attachment is a court order to "attach" or seize an asset. It is issued by a court to a law enforcement officer or sheriff. The Writ of attachment is issued in order to satisfy a judgment issued by the court.
Mortgage note	In the US a Mortgage note is a promissory note associated with specified mortgage loan; it is a written promise to repay a specified sum of money plus interest at a specified rate and length of time to fulfill the promise. While the mortgage itself pledges the title to real property as security for a loan, the Mortgage note states the amount of debt and the rate of interest, and makes the borrower who signs the note personally responsible for repayment. In foreclosure proceedings in certain jurisdictions, borrowers may require the foreclosing party to produce the note as evidence that they are the true owners of the debt.

Blank endorsement	Blank endorsement of a financial instrument such as a check is only a signature, not indicating the payee. The effect of this is that it is payable only to the bearer. It is "an endorsement consisting of nothing but a signature and allowing any party in possession of the endorsed item to execute a claim." A Blank endorsement is commonly known and accepted in the legal and business worlds.
Acceleration clause	An Acceleration clause, in the law of contracts, is a term that fully matures the performance due from a party upon a breach of the contract. Such clauses are most prevalent in mortgages and similar contracts to purchase real estate in installments. Suppose, for example, the contract was for A to purchase Blackacre from B for $100,000, to be paid in 5 monthly installments of $20,000.
Obligation	An obligation is a requirement to take some course of action, whether legal or moral. There are also obligation s in other normative contexts, such as obligation s of etiquette, social obligation s, and possibly in terms of politics, where obligation s are requirements which must be fulfilled. These are generally legal obligation s, which can incur a penalty for unfulfilment, although certain people are obliged to carry out certain actions for other reasons as well, whether as a tradition or for social reasons.

Holder in due course	To facilitate a freely transferable substitute for cash, a central theme of the Negotiable Instrument Article (Article 3) is the Holder in due course rule. A Holder in due course (HDC) is a person who takes a negotiable instrument, such as a promissory note, for value without knowledge of any apparent defect in the instrument nor any notice of dishonor. (Black"s Law Dictionary 2nd Pocket ed.
Negotiable instrument	A Negotiable instrument is a specialized type of "contract" for the payment of money that is unconditional and capable of transfer by negotiation. Common examples include cheques, banknotes (paper money), and commercial paper. A Negotiable instrument is not a contract, as contract formation requires an offer, acceptance, and consideration, none of which is an element of a Negotiable instrument.
Cash	Two primary accounting methods, cash and accrual basis, are used to calculate taxable income for U.S. federal income taxes. According to the Internal Revenue Code, a taxpayer may compute taxable income by: · the cash receipts and disbursements method; · an accrual method; · any other method permitted by the chapter; or · any combination of the foregoing methods permitted under regulations prescribed by the Secretary. As a general rule, a taxpayer must compute taxable income using the same accounting method he uses to compute income in keeping his books.
Good faith	Good faith is the mental and moral state of honesty, conviction as to the truth or falsehood of a proposition or body of opinion especially equitable matters. In contemporary English, "bona fides" is sometimes used as a synonym for credentials, background, or documentation of a person"s identity.
Chief brand officer	A Chief brand officer is a relatively new executive level position at a corporation, company, organization typically reporting directly to the CEO or board of directors. The Chief brand officer is responsible for a brand"s image, experience, and promise, and propagating it throughout all aspects of the company. The brand officer oversees marketing, advertising, design, public relations and customer service departments.
Duty	Duty (from "due," that which is owing, O. Fr. deu, did, past participle of devoir; Lat. debere, debitum; cf.
Trust	In common law legal systems, a trust is an arrangement whereby property (including real, tangible and intangible) is managed by one person (or persons, or organizations) for the benefit of another. A trust is created by a settlor, who entrusts some or all of his or her property to people of his choice (the trustees.) The trustees hold legal title to the trust property (or trust corpus), but they are obliged to hold the property for the benefit of one or more individuals or organizations (the beneficiary, a.k.a. cestui que use or cestui que trust), usually specified by the settlor, who hold equitable title.

Obligation	An obligation is a requirement to take some course of action, whether legal or moral. There are also obligation s in other normative contexts, such as obligation s of etiquette, social obligation s, and possibly in terms of politics, where obligation s are requirements which must be fulfilled. These are generally legal obligation s, which can incur a penalty for unfulfilment, although certain people are obliged to carry out certain actions for other reasons as well, whether as a tradition or for social reasons.
Consideration	Consideration is the legal concept of value in connection with contracts. It is anything of value in the common sense, promised to another when making a contract. It can take the form of money, physical objects, services, promised actions, or even abstinence from a future action.
Contract	Agreement is said to be reached when an offer capable of immediate acceptance is met with a "mirror image" acceptance (ie, an unqualified acceptance). The parties must have the necessary capacity to Contract and the Contract must not be either trifling, indeterminate, impossible or illegal. Contract law is based on the principle expressed in the Latin phrase pacta sunt servanda .
United Nations Convention on Contracts for the International Sale of Goods	The United Nations Convention on Contracts for the International Sale of Goods is a treaty offering a uniform international sales law that, as of July 2008, had been ratified by 71 countries that account for a significant proportion of world trade, making it one of the most successful international uniform laws. Japan is the most recent State to have ratified the Convention. It allows exporters to avoid choice of law issues as it offers "accepted substantive rules on which contracting parties, courts, and arbitrators may rely".
Uniform Commercial Code	The Uniform Commercial Code is one of a number of uniform acts that have been promulgated in conjunction with efforts to harmonize the law of sales and other commercial transactions in all 50 states within the United States of America. This objective is deemed important because of the prevalence today of commercial transactions that extend beyond one state (for example, where the goods are manufactured in state A, warehoused in state B, sold from state C and delivered in state D.) The Uniform Commercial Code deals primarily with transactions involving personal property (movable property), not real property (immovable property.)

Duty	Duty (from "due," that which is owing, O. Fr. deu, did, past participle of devoir; Lat. debere, debitum; cf.
Obligation	An obligation is a requirement to take some course of action, whether legal or moral. There are also obligation s in other normative contexts, such as obligation s of etiquette, social obligation s, and possibly in terms of politics, where obligation s are requirements which must be fulfilled. These are generally legal obligation s, which can incur a penalty for unfulfilment, although certain people are obliged to carry out certain actions for other reasons as well, whether as a tradition or for social reasons.
Negotiable instrument	A Negotiable instrument is a specialized type of "contract" for the payment of money that is unconditional and capable of transfer by negotiation. Common examples include cheques, banknotes (paper money), and commercial paper. A Negotiable instrument is not a contract, as contract formation requires an offer, acceptance, and consideration, none of which is an element of a Negotiable instrument.
Warranty	In commercial and consumer transactions, a warranty is an obligation or guarantee that an article or service sold is as factually stated or legally implied by the seller, and that often provides for a specific remedy such as repair or replacement in the event the article or service fails to meet the warranty. A breach of warranty occurs when the promise is broken, i.e., a product is defective or not as should be expected by a reasonable buyer. In business and legal transactions, a warranty is an assurance by one party to the other party that certain facts or conditions are true or will happen; the other party is permitted to rely on that assurance and seek some type of remedy if it is not true or followed.
Product Liability	Product liability is the area of law in which manufacturers, distributors, suppliers, retailers, and others who make products available to the public are held responsible for the injuries those products cause. In the United States, the claims most commonly associated with Product liability are negligence, strict liability, breach of warranty, and various consumer protection claims. The majority of Product liability laws are determined at the state level and vary widely from state to state.
Chief brand officer	A Chief brand officer is a relatively new executive level position at a corporation, company, organization typically reporting directly to the CEO or board of directors. The Chief brand officer is responsible for a brand"s image, experience, and promise, and propagating it throughout all aspects of the company. The brand officer oversees marketing, advertising, design, public relations and customer service departments.
Holder in due course	To facilitate a freely transferable substitute for cash, a central theme of the Negotiable Instrument Article (Article 3) is the Holder in due course rule. A Holder in due course (HDC) is a person who takes a negotiable instrument, such as a promissory note, for value without knowledge of any apparent defect in the instrument nor any notice of dishonor. (Black"s Law Dictionary 2nd Pocket ed.

Ratification	Ratification is the act of approving and paying for supplies or services provided to and accepted by the government as a result of an unauthorized commitment. It gives official sanction or approval to a formal document such as a treaty or constitution. It includes the process of adopting an international treaty by the legislature, a constitution, or another nationally binding document (such as an amendment to a constitution) by the agreement of multiple sub-national entities.
United Nations Convention on Contracts for the International Sale of Goods	The United Nations Convention on Contracts for the International Sale of Goods is a treaty offering a uniform international sales law that, as of July 2008, had been ratified by 71 countries that account for a significant proportion of world trade, making it one of the most successful international uniform laws. Japan is the most recent State to have ratified the Convention. It allows exporters to avoid choice of law issues as it offers "accepted substantive rules on which contracting parties, courts, and arbitrators may rely".
Misrepresentation	Misrepresentation is a contract law concept. It means a false statement of fact made by one party to another party, which has the effect of inducing that party into the contract. For example, under certain circumstances, false statements or promises made by a seller of goods regarding the quality or nature of the product that the seller has may constitute Misrepresentation.
Contract	Agreement is said to be reached when an offer capable of immediate acceptance is met with a "mirror image" acceptance (ie, an unqualified acceptance). The parties must have the necessary capacity to Contract and the Contract must not be either trifling, indeterminate, impossible or illegal. Contract law is based on the principle expressed in the Latin phrase pacta sunt servanda .
Bank Secrecy Act	The Bank Secrecy Act of 1970 (or Bank Secrecy Act, or otherwise known as the Currency and Foreign Transactions Reporting Act) requires financial institutions in the United States to assist U.S. government agencies to detect and prevent money laundering. Specifically, the act requires financial institutions to keep records of [cash purchases of negotiable instruments, and file reports of cash purchases of these negotiable instruments of $3,000 or more (daily aggregate amount), and to report suspicious activity that might signify money laundering, tax evasion, or other criminal activities. Many banks will no longer sell negotiable instruments when purchased with cash, requiring the purchase to be withdrawn from an account at that institution.
Bankruptcy	Bankruptcy is a legally declared inability or impairment of ability of an individual or organization to pay its creditors. Creditors may file a Bankruptcy petition against a debtor ("involuntary Bankruptcy") in an effort to recoup a portion of what they are owed or initiate a restructuring. In the majority of cases, however, Bankruptcy is initiated by the debtor (a "voluntary Bankruptcy" that is filed by the insolvent individual or organization).
Duress	Duress or coercion (as a term of jurisprudence) is a possible legal defense, one of four of the most important justification defenses, by which defendants argue that they should not be held liable because the actions that broke the law were only performed out of an immediate fear of injury. Black"s Law Dictionary (6th ed). defines Duress as "any unlawful threat or coercion used...

Lease	A Lease is a contract conferring a right on one person to possess property belonging to another person (called a landlord or lessor) to the exclusion of the owner landlord, and all others except with the invitation of the tenant. It is a rental agreement between landlord and tenant. The relationship between the tenant and the landlord is called a tenancy, and the right to possession by the tenant is sometimes called a Leasehold interest.
Consideration	Consideration is the legal concept of value in connection with contracts. It is anything of value in the common sense, promised to another when making a contract. It can take the form of money, physical objects, services, promised actions, or even abstinence from a future action.
Rescission	In contract law, rescission has been defined as the unmaking of a contract between parties. rescission is the unwinding of a transaction. This is done to bring the parties, as far as possible, back to the position in which they were before they entered into a contract (the "status quo ante".)
Undue influence	Undue influence is an equitable doctrine that involves one person taking advantage of a position of power over another person. It is where free will to bargain is not possible. If undue influence is proved in a contract, in USA law, the contract is voidable by the innocent party, and the remedy is rescission.
Voidable	In law, a transaction or action which is voidable is valid, but may be annulled by one of the parties to the transaction. voidable is usually used in distinction to void ab initio (or void from the outset) and unenforceable. The act of invalidating the contract by the party exercising its rights to anul the voidable contract is usually referred to either as voiding the contract (in the United States and Canada) or avoiding the contract (in the United Kingdom, Australia and other common law countries.)
Expedited Funds Availability Act	The Expedited Funds Availability Act (EFA or Expedited Funds Availability Act) was enacted in 1987 by the United States Congress for the purpose of standardizing hold periods on deposits made to commercial banks and to regulate institutions" use of deposit holds. It is also referred to as Regulation CC or Reg CC, after the Federal Reserve regulation that implements the act. The law is codified in Title 12, Chapter 41 of the US Code and Title 12, Part 229 of the Code of Federal Regulations.
Regulation CC	The Expedited Funds Availability Act (EFA or EFAA) was enacted in 1987 by the United States Congress for the purpose of standardizing hold periods on deposits made to commercial banks and to regulate institutions" use of deposit holds. It is also referred to as Regulation CC after the Federal Reserve regulation that implements the act. The law is codified in Title 12, Chapter 41 of the US Code and Title 12, Part 229 of the Code of Federal Regulations.
Statute	A statute is a formal written enactment of a legislative authority that governs a country, state, city, or county. Typically, statute s command or prohibit something, or declare policy. The word is often used to distinguish law made by legislative bodies from case law and the regulations issued by Government agencies.

Damages

Damages for breach of contract is a common law remedy, available as of right. It is designed to compensate the victim for their actual loss as a result of the wrongdoer"s breach rather than to punish the wrongdoer. If no loss has been occasioned by the plaintiff, only nominal Damages will be awarded.

Cash

Two primary accounting methods, cash and accrual basis, are used to calculate taxable income for U.S. federal income taxes. According to the Internal Revenue Code, a taxpayer may compute taxable income by:

· the cash receipts and disbursements method;
· an accrual method;
· any other method permitted by the chapter; or
· any combination of the foregoing methods permitted under regulations prescribed by the Secretary.

As a general rule, a taxpayer must compute taxable income using the same accounting method he uses to compute income in keeping his books.

Punitive Damages

Punitive Damages are damages not awarded in order to compensate the plaintiff, but in order to reform or deter the defendant and similar persons from pursuing a course of action such as that which damaged the plaintiff.

punitive Damages are often awarded where compensatory damages are deemed an inadequate remedy. The court may impose them to prevent under-compensation of plaintiffs, to allow redress for undetectable torts and taking some strain away from the criminal justice system.

United States

· History of competition law
· Monopoly

  · Coercive monopoly
  · Natural monopoly
  · Barriers to entry
  · Market power
  · SSNIP test
  · Relevant market
  · Merger control

Anti-competitive practices

· Monopolization
· Collusion

· Formation of cartels
· Price fixing
· Bid rigging
· Product bundling and tying
· Refusal to deal

- Group boycott
- Exclusive dealing
- Dividing territories
- Conscious parallelism
- Predatory pricing
- Misuse of patents and copyrights

Laws and doctrines

United States

- Sherman Antitrust Act
- Clayton Antitrust Act
- Robinson-Patman Act
- FTC Act
- Hart-Scott-Rodino Act
- Merger guidelines
- Essential facilities doctrine
- Noerr-Pennington doctrine
- Parker immunity doctrine
- Rule of reason

Europe

- UK competition law
- Irish competition law

Australia

- Trade Practices Act 1974

Enforcement authorities and organizations

Competition law history refers to attempts by governments to regulate competitive markets for goods and services, leading up to the modern competition or antitrust laws around the world today. The earliest records traces back to the efforts of Roman legislators to control price fluctuations and unfair trade practices. Through the Middle Ages in Europe, Kings and Queens repeatedly cracked down on monopolies, including those created through state legislation.

- International Competition Network
- List of competition regulators

Terrorism

Terrorism is a policy or ideology of violence intended to intimidate or cause terror for the purpose of "exerting pressure on decision making by state bodies." The term "terror" is largely used to indicate clandestine, low-intensity violence that targets civilians and generates public fear. Thus "terror" is distinct from asymmetric warfare, and violates the concept of a common law of war in which civilian life is regarded. The term "-ism" is used to indicate an ideology --typically one that claims its attacks are in the domain of a "just war" concept, though most condemn such as crimes against humanity.

Constitution	· Apostolic Constitution (a class of Roman Catholic Church documents) · Constitution of the Roman Republic · Constitutional court · Constitutionalism · Corporate Constitution · Judicial activism · Judicial restraint · Judicial review Judicial philosophies of Constitutional interpretation (note: generally specific to United States Constitutional law) · List of national Constitutions · Originalism · Strict constructionism · Textualism · Proposed European Union Constitution · Treaty of Lisbon (adopts same changes, but without Constitutional name) · United Nations Charter
Privacy	Privacy is the ability of an individual or group to seclude themselves or information about themselves and thereby reveal themselves selectively. The boundaries and content of what is considered private differ among cultures and individuals, but share basic common themes. Privacy is sometimes related to anonymity, the wish to remain unnoticed or unidentified in the public realm.
Regulatory	Regulation refers to "controlling human or societal behaviour by rules or restrictions." Regulation can take many forms: legal restrictions promulgated by a government authority, self-regulation, social regulation (e.g. norms), co-regulation and market regulation. One can consider regulation as actions of conduct imposing sanctions (such as a fine.) This action of administrative law, or implementing regulatory law, may be contrasted with statutory or case law.
Regulatory compliance	Regulatory compliance describes the goal that corporations or public agencies aspire to in their efforts to ensure that personnel are aware of and take steps to comply with relevant laws and regulations. The International Organisation for Standardisation (ISO) produces international standards such as ISO17799. The International Electrotechnical Commission (IEC) produces international standards in the electrotechnology area.
Right to Financial Privacy Act	The Right to Financial Privacy Act, also known as the RFPA is a United States Act that gives the customers of financial institutions the right to some level of privacy from government searches. Before the Act was passed, the United States government did not have to tell customers that they were accessing their records, and customers did not have the right to prevent such actions.

Good faith	Good faith is the mental and moral state of honesty, conviction as to the truth or falsehood of a proposition or body of opinion especially equitable matters. In contemporary English, "bona fides" is sometimes used as a synonym for credentials, background, or documentation of a person"s identity.
Uniform Commercial Code	The Uniform Commercial Code is one of a number of uniform acts that have been promulgated in conjunction with efforts to harmonize the law of sales and other commercial transactions in all 50 states within the United States of America. This objective is deemed important because of the prevalence today of commercial transactions that extend beyond one state (for example, where the goods are manufactured in state A, warehoused in state B, sold from state C and delivered in state D.) The Uniform Commercial Code deals primarily with transactions involving personal property (movable property), not real property (immovable property.)
Arbitration	Arbitration, a form of alternative dispute resolution (ADR), is a legal technique for the resolution of disputes outside the courts, wherein the parties to a dispute refer it to one or more persons (the "arbitrators", "arbiters" or "arbitral tribunal"), by whose decision (the "award") they agree to be bound. It is a settlement technique in which a third party reviews the case and imposes a decision that is legally binding for both sides. Other forms of ADR include mediation (a form of settlement negotiation facilitated by a neutral third party) and non-binding resolution by experts.

Foreclosure	Foreclosure is the legal and professional proceeding in which a mortgagee usually a lender, obtains a court ordered termination of a mortgagor"s equitable right of redemption. Usually a lender obtains a security interest from a borrower who mortgages or pledges an asset like a house to secure the loan. If the borrower defaults and the lender tries to repossess the property, courts of equity can grant the borrower the equitable right of redemption if the borrower repays the debt.
Lien	In law, a Lien is a form of security interest granted over an item of property to secure the payment of a debt or performance of some other obligation. The owner of the property, who grants the Lien, is referred to as the Lienor and the person who has the benefit of the Lien is referred to as the Lienee. The etymological root is Anglo-French Lien, loyen bond, restraint, from Latin ligamen, from ligare to bind.
Bankruptcy	Bankruptcy is a legally declared inability or impairment of ability of an individual or organization to pay its creditors. Creditors may file a Bankruptcy petition against a debtor ("involuntary Bankruptcy") in an effort to recoup a portion of what they are owed or initiate a restructuring. In the majority of cases, however, Bankruptcy is initiated by the debtor (a "voluntary Bankruptcy" that is filed by the insolvent individual or organization).
Consumer protection	Consumer protection laws are designed to ensure fair competition and the free flow of truthful information in the marketplace. The laws are designed to prevent businesses that engage in fraud or specified unfair practices from gaining an advantage over competitors and may provide additional protection for the weak and those unable to take care of themselves. Consumer protection laws are a form of government regulation which protects the interests of consumers.
Security interest	A Security interest is a property interest created by agreement or by operation of law over assets to secure the performance of an obligation, usually the payment of a debt. It gives the beneficiary of the Security interest certain preferential rights in the disposition of secured assets. Such rights vary according to the type of Security interest, but in most cases, a holder of the Security interest is entitled to seize, and usually sell, the property to discharge the debt that the Security interest secures.
Writ	In law, a writ is a formal writ ten order issued by a body with administrative or judicial jurisdiction; in modern usage, this public body is generally a court. Warrants, prerogative writ s and subpoenas are types of writ s; there are many others. Originally, a writ was a letter or command from the Sovereign, or from some person with appropriate jurisdiction.
Writ of attachment	A Writ of attachment is a court order to "attach" or seize an asset. It is issued by a court to a law enforcement officer or sheriff. The Writ of attachment is issued in order to satisfy a judgment issued by the court.
Contract	Agreement is said to be reached when an offer capable of immediate acceptance is met with a "mirror image" acceptance (ie, an unqualified acceptance). The parties must have the necessary capacity to Contract and the Contract must not be either trifling, indeterminate, impossible or illegal. Contract law is based on the principle expressed in the Latin phrase pacta sunt servanda .

Guarantee	The act of becoming a surety is also called a Guarantee. Traditionally a Guarantee was distinguished from a surety in that the surety"s liability was joint and primary with the principal, whereas the guaranty"s liability was ancillary and derivative, but many jurisdictions have abolished this distinction
Garnishment	A Garnishment is a means of collecting a monetary judgment against a defendant by ordering a third party (the garnishee) to pay money, otherwise owed to the defendant, directly to the plaintiff. In the case of collecting for taxes, the law of a jurisdiction may allow for collection without a judgment or other court order. Wage Garnishment, the most common type of Garnishment, is the process of deducting money from an employee"s monetary compensation (including salary), sometimes as a result of a court order.
Chief brand officer	A Chief brand officer is a relatively new executive level position at a corporation, company, organization typically reporting directly to the CEO or board of directors. The Chief brand officer is responsible for a brand"s image, experience, and promise, and propagating it throughout all aspects of the company. The brand officer oversees marketing, advertising, design, public relations and customer service departments.
Surety	A surety is a person who agrees to be responsible for the debt or obligation of another. Furthermore, a surety is also a "security against loss or damage or for the fulfillment of an obligation, the payment of a debt, etc.; a pledge, guaranty, or bond." The situation in which a surety is most typically required is when the ability of the primary obligor or principal to perform its obligations under a contract is in question, or when there is some public or private interest which requires protection from the consequences of the principal"s default or delinquency. In most common law jurisdictions, a contract of surety ship is subject to the statute of frauds (or its equivalent local laws) and is only enforceable if recorded in writing and signed by the surety and the principal.
Suretyship	A surety is a person who agrees to be responsible for the debt or obligation of another. Furthermore, a surety is also a "security against loss or damage or for the fulfillment of an obligation, the payment of a debt, etc.; a pledge, guaranty, or bond." The situation in which a surety is most typically required is when the ability of the primary obligor or principal to perform its obligations under a contract is in question, or when there is some public or private interest which requires protection from the consequences of the principal"s default or delinquency. In most common law jurisdictions, a contract of Suretyship is subject to the statute of frauds (or its equivalent local laws) and is only enforceable if recorded in writing and signed by the surety and the principal.
Deficiency Judgment	A Deficiency judgment is a judgment lien against a debtor, defendant or borrower whose foreclosure sale did not produce sufficient funds to pay the mortgage in full. This option may or may not be available to the lender, depending on whether they have made a recourse or nonrecourse loan. The fuller, New York statutory definition is this: "the whole residue, or so much thereof as the court may determine to be just and equitable, of the debt remaining unsatisfied, after a sale of the mortgaged property and the application of the proceeds, pursuant to the directions contained in such judgment, the amount thereof to be determined by the court as herein provided.

United Nations Convention on Contracts for the International Sale of Goods	The United Nations Convention on Contracts for the International Sale of Goods is a treaty offering a uniform international sales law that, as of July 2008, had been ratified by 71 countries that account for a significant proportion of world trade, making it one of the most successful international uniform laws. Japan is the most recent State to have ratified the Convention. It allows exporters to avoid choice of law issues as it offers "accepted substantive rules on which contracting parties, courts, and arbitrators may rely".
Duty	Duty (from "due," that which is owing, O. Fr. deu, did, past participle of devoir; Lat. debere, debitum; cf.
Obligation	An obligation is a requirement to take some course of action, whether legal or moral. There are also obligation s in other normative contexts, such as obligation s of etiquette, social obligation s, and possibly in terms of politics, where obligation s are requirements which must be fulfilled. These are generally legal obligation s, which can incur a penalty for unfulfilment, although certain people are obliged to carry out certain actions for other reasons as well, whether as a tradition or for social reasons.
Statute	A statute is a formal written enactment of a legislative authority that governs a country, state, city, or county. Typically, statute s command or prohibit something, or declare policy. The word is often used to distinguish law made by legislative bodies from case law and the regulations issued by Government agencies.
Statute of Frauds	The Statute of Frauds refers to the requirement that certain kinds of contracts be made in writing and signed. Traditionally, the Statute of Frauds requires a writing signed by the defendant in the following circumstances: · Contracts in consideration of marriage. · Contracts which cannot be performed within one year. · Contracts for the transfer of an interest in land. · Contracts by the executor of a will to pay a debt of the estate with their own money. · Contracts for the sale of goods above a certain value. · Contracts in which one party becomes a surety (acts as guarantor) for another party"s debt or other obligation. This can be remembered by the mnemonic "MY LEGS": Marriage, one year, land, executor, goods, surety. The term Statute of Frauds comes from an English Act of Parliament passed in 1677 (authored by Sir Leoline Jenkins and passed by the Cavalier Parliament), and more properly called An Act for Prevention of Frauds and Perjuries. Many common law jurisdictions have made similar statutory provisions, while a number of civil law jurisdictions have equivalent legislation incorporated into their civil codes.

Estoppel

Estoppel is a legal doctrine at common law, where a party is barred from claiming or denying an argument on an equitable ground. Estoppel complements the requirement of consideration in contract law. In general, Estoppel protects an aggrieved party, if the counter-party induced an expectation from the aggrieved party, and the aggrieved party reasonably relied on the expectation and would suffer detriment if the expectation is not met.

Product Liability

Product liability is the area of law in which manufacturers, distributors, suppliers, retailers, and others who make products available to the public are held responsible for the injuries those products cause.
In the United States, the claims most commonly associated with Product liability are negligence, strict liability, breach of warranty, and various consumer protection claims. The majority of Product liability laws are determined at the state level and vary widely from state to state.

Subrogation

Subrogation is the legal technique under the common law by which one party, commonly an insurer (I-X) of another party (X), steps into X"s shoes, so as to have the benefit of X"s rights and remedies against a third party such as a defendant (D.) Subrogation is similar in effect to assignment, but unlike assignment, Subrogation can occur without any agreement between I-X and X to transfer X"s rights. Subrogation most commonly arises in relation to policies of insurance, but the legal technique is of more general application.

Bank Secrecy Act

The Bank Secrecy Act of 1970 (or Bank Secrecy Act, or otherwise known as the Currency and Foreign Transactions Reporting Act) requires financial institutions in the United States to assist U.S. government agencies to detect and prevent money laundering. Specifically, the act requires financial institutions to keep records of [cash purchases of negotiable instruments, and file reports of cash purchases of these negotiable instruments of $3,000 or more (daily aggregate amount), and to report suspicious activity that might signify money laundering, tax evasion, or other criminal activities. Many banks will no longer sell negotiable instruments when purchased with cash, requiring the purchase to be withdrawn from an account at that institution.

Personal property

Personal property is a type of property. In the common law systems Personal property may also be called chattels or personalty. It is distinguished from real property, or real estate.
Personal property may be classified in a variety of ways. Tangible Personal property refers to any type of property that can generally be moved (i.e., it is not attached to real property or land), touched or felt. These generally include items such as furniture, clothing, jewelry, art, writings, or household goods. In some cases, there can be formal title documents that show the ownership and transfer rights of that property after a person"s death (for example, motor vehicles, boats, etc.) In many cases, however, tangible Personal property will not be "titled" in an owner"s name and is presumed to be whatever property he or she was in possession of at the time of his or her death.
Intangible Personal property or "intangibles" refers to Personal property that cannot actually be moved, touched or felt, but instead represents something of value such as negotiable instruments, securities, goods, and intangible assets including chose in action.

Bank Secrecy Act

The Bank Secrecy Act of 1970 (or Bank Secrecy Act, or otherwise known as the Currency and Foreign Transactions Reporting Act) requires financial institutions in the United States to assist U.S. government agencies to detect and prevent money laundering. Specifically, the act requires financial institutions to keep records of [cash purchases of negotiable instruments, and file reports of cash purchases of these negotiable instruments of $3,000 or more (daily aggregate amount), and to report suspicious activity that might signify money laundering, tax evasion, or other criminal activities. Many banks will no longer sell negotiable instruments when purchased with cash, requiring the purchase to be withdrawn from an account at that institution.

Bankruptcy

Bankruptcy is a legally declared inability or impairment of ability of an individual or organization to pay its creditors. Creditors may file a Bankruptcy petition against a debtor ("involuntary Bankruptcy") in an effort to recoup a portion of what they are owed or initiate a restructuring. In the majority of cases, however, Bankruptcy is initiated by the debtor (a "voluntary Bankruptcy" that is filed by the insolvent individual or organization).

Constitution

· Apostolic Constitution (a class of Roman Catholic Church documents)
· Constitution of the Roman Republic
· Constitutional court
· Constitutionalism
· Corporate Constitution
· Judicial activism
· Judicial restraint
· Judicial review

Judicial philosophies of Constitutional interpretation (note: generally specific to United States Constitutional law)

· List of national Constitutions
· Originalism
· Strict constructionism
· Textualism
· Proposed European Union Constitution

· Treaty of Lisbon (adopts same changes, but without Constitutional name)
· United Nations Charter

Liquidation

In law, Liquidation refers to the process by which a company (or part of a company) is brought to an end, and the assets and property of the company redistributed. Liquidation can also be referred to as winding-up or dissolution, although dissolution technically refers to the last stage of Liquidation. The process of Liquidation also arises when customs, an authority or agency in a country responsible for collecting and safeguarding customs duties, determines the final computation or ascertainment of the duties or drawback accruing on an entry.

United States

· History of competition law
· Monopoly

- Coercive monopoly
- Natural monopoly
- Barriers to entry
- Market power
- SSNIP test
- Relevant market
- Merger control

Anti-competitive practices

- Monopolization
- Collusion

- Formation of cartels
- Price fixing
- Bid rigging
- Product bundling and tying
- Refusal to deal

- Group boycott
- Exclusive dealing
- Dividing territories
- Conscious parallelism
- Predatory pricing
- Misuse of patents and copyrights

Laws and doctrines

United States

- Sherman Antitrust Act
- Clayton Antitrust Act
- Robinson-Patman Act
- FTC Act
- Hart-Scott-Rodino Act
- Merger guidelines
- Essential facilities doctrine
- Noerr-Pennington doctrine
- Parker immunity doctrine
- Rule of reason

Europe

- UK competition law
- Irish competition law

Australia

· Trade Practices Act 1974

Enforcement authorities and organizations

Competition law history refers to attempts by governments to regulate competitive markets for goods and services, leading up to the modern competition or antitrust laws around the world today. The earliest records traces back to the efforts of Roman legislators to control price fluctuations and unfair trade practices. Through the Middle Ages in Europe, Kings and Queens repeatedly cracked down on monopolies, including those created through state legislation.

· International Competition Network
· List of competition regulators

Business

There are many ways in which a business may be owned under the legal system of England and Wales. Different types of ownership are suitable for organisations depending on the degree of control the owners wish to have over the business. The choice of ownership methor also relates to the organisations ability to raise funds for the business activities.

Insolvency

Insolvency means the inability to pay one"s debts as they fall due. Usually used in Business terms, Insolvency refers to the inability for a company to pay off its debts.
Business Insolvency is defined in two different ways:

Cash flow Insolvency
Unable to pay debts as they fall due.

Trust

In common law legal systems, a trust is an arrangement whereby property (including real, tangible and intangible) is managed by one person (or persons, or organizations) for the benefit of another. A trust is created by a settlor, who entrusts some or all of his or her property to people of his choice (the trustees.) The trustees hold legal title to the trust property (or trust corpus), but they are obliged to hold the property for the benefit of one or more individuals or organizations (the beneficiary, a.k.a. cestui que use or cestui que trust), usually specified by the settlor, who hold equitable title.

Trustee

Trustee is a legal term that refers to a holder of property on behalf of a beneficiary. A trust can be set up either to benefit particular persons, or for any charitable purposes (but not generally for non-charitable purposes): typical examples are a will trust for the testator"s children and family, a pension trust (to confer benefits on employees and their families), and a charitable trust. In all cases, the Trustee may be a person or company, whether or not they are a prospective beneficiary.

Petition

A petition is a request to change something, most commonly made to a government official or public entity. petition s to a deity are a form of prayer.
In the colloquial sense, a petition is a document addressed to some official and signed by numerous individuals.

Automatic stay

In bankruptcy law, an Automatic stay is an automatic injunction which halts actions by creditors, with certain exceptions, to collect debts from a debtor who has declared bankruptcy. Under section 362 of the United States Bankruptcy Code, 11 U.S.C. Â§ 362, the stay begins at the moment the bankruptcy petition is filed. Secured creditors may, however, petition the bankruptcy court for relief from the Automatic stay upon a showing of cause.

Statute

A statute is a formal written enactment of a legislative authority that governs a country, state, city, or county. Typically, statute s command or prohibit something, or declare policy. The word is often used to distinguish law made by legislative bodies from case law and the regulations issued by Government agencies.

Statute of limitations

A statute of limitations is a statute in a common law legal system that sets forth the maximum period of time, after certain events, that legal proceedings based on those events may be initiated. In civil law systems, similar provisions are usually part of the civil code or criminal code and are often known collectively as "periods of prescription" or "prescriptive periods."

A common law legal system might have a statute limiting the time for prosecution of crimes called misdemeanors to two years after the offense occurred. In that statute, if a person is discovered to have committed a misdemeanor three years ago, the time has expired for the prosecution of the misdemeanor.

Personal property

Personal property is a type of property. In the common law systems Personal property may also be called chattels or personalty. It is distinguished from real property, or real estate.

Personal property may be classified in a variety of ways. Tangible Personal property refers to any type of property that can generally be moved (i.e., it is not attached to real property or land), touched or felt. These generally include items such as furniture, clothing, jewelry, art, writings, or household goods. In some cases, there can be formal title documents that show the ownership and transfer rights of that property after a person''s death (for example, motor vehicles, boats, etc.) In many cases, however, tangible Personal property will not be "titled" in an owner''s name and is presumed to be whatever property he or she was in possession of at the time of his or her death.

Intangible Personal property or "intangibles" refers to Personal property that cannot actually be moved, touched or felt, but instead represents something of value such as negotiable instruments, securities, goods, and intangible assets including chose in action.

Lien

In law, a Lien is a form of security interest granted over an item of property to secure the payment of a debt or performance of some other obligation. The owner of the property, who grants the Lien, is referred to as the Lienor and the person who has the benefit of the Lien is referred to as the Lienee.

The etymological root is Anglo-French Lien, loyen bond, restraint, from Latin ligamen, from ligare to bind.

Voidable

In law, a transaction or action which is voidable is valid, but may be annulled by one of the parties to the transaction. voidable is usually used in distinction to void ab initio (or void from the outset) and unenforceable.

The act of invalidating the contract by the party exercising its rights to anul the voidable contract is usually referred to either as voiding the contract (in the United States and Canada) or avoiding the contract (in the United Kingdom, Australia and other common law countries.)

Secured Creditor

A Secured creditor is a creditor which has the benefit of a security interest over some or all of the assets of the debtor.

In the event of the bankruptcy of the debtor, the Secured creditor can enforce their security against the assets of the debtor, and avoid competing for a distribution on liquidation together with the un Secured creditor s.

In most legal systems, Secured creditor s also have the option of releasing their security and proving in the liquidation, although in practice they would rarely do so.

Contract

Agreement is said to be reached when an offer capable of immediate acceptance is met with a "mirror image" acceptance (ie, an unqualified acceptance). The parties must have the necessary capacity to Contract and the Contract must not be either trifling, indeterminate, impossible or illegal. Contract law is based on the principle expressed in the Latin phrase pacta sunt servanda .

Revocation

Revocation is the act of recall or annulment. It is the reversal of an act, the recalling of a grant, or the making void of some deed previously existing.

In the law of contracts, revocation is a type of remedy for buyers when the buyer accepts a nonconforming good from the seller.

Chief brand officer

A Chief brand officer is a relatively new executive level position at a corporation, company, organization typically reporting directly to the CEO or board of directors. The Chief brand officer is responsible for a brand"s image, experience, and promise, and propagating it throughout all aspects of the company. The brand officer oversees marketing, advertising, design, public relations and customer service departments.

Reaffirmation Agreement

A Reaffirmation agreement in United States bankruptcy law refers to an agreement made between a creditor and the debtor that waives discharge of a debt that would otherwise be discharged in the pending bankruptcy proceeding. A properly executed, timely filed Reaffirmation agreement modifies the discharge such that it is rendered inoperable against the subject debt. Most statutory authority for Reaffirmation agreements is codified at 11 U.S.C. Â§ 524(c).

Debtor in Possession

A Debtor in possession in United States bankruptcy law is a person or corporation who has filed a bankruptcy petition, but remains in possession of property upon which a creditor has a lien or similar security interest. A corporation which continues to operate its business under Chapter 11 bankruptcy proceedings is a Debtor in possession.

Under certain circumstances, the Debtor in possession may be able to keep the property by paying the creditor the fair market value, as opposed to the contract price.

Security interest

A Security interest is a property interest created by agreement or by operation of law over assets to secure the performance of an obligation, usually the payment of a debt. It gives the beneficiary of the Security interest certain preferential rights in the disposition of secured assets. Such rights vary according to the type of Security interest, but in most cases, a holder of the Security interest is entitled to seize, and usually sell, the property to discharge the debt that the Security interest secures.

Limited liability

Limited liability is a concept whereby a person"s financial liability is limited to a fixed sum, most commonly the value of a person"s investment in a company or partnership with Limited liability. In other words, if a company with Limited liability is sued, then the plaintiffs are suing the company, not its owners or investors. A shareholder in a limited company is not personally liable for any of the debts of the company, other than for the value of his investment in that company.

Partnership

A Partnership is a type of business entity in which partners (owners) share with each other the profits or losses of the business. Partnership s are often favored over corporations for taxation purposes, as the Partnership structure does not generally incur a tax on profits before it is distributed to the partners (i.e. there is no dividend tax levied.) However, depending on the Partnership structure and the jurisdiction in which it operates, owners of a Partnership may be exposed to greater personal liability than they would as shareholders of a corporation.

Breach of contract

Breach of contract is a legal concept in which a binding agreement or bargained-for exchange is not honored by one or more of the parties to the contract by non-performance or interference with the other party"s performance.
A minor breach, a partial breach or an immaterial breach, occurs when the non-breaching party is unentitled to an order for performance of its obligations, but only to collect the actual amount of their damages. For example, suppose a homeowner hires a contractor to install new plumbing and insists that the pipes, which will ultimately be sealed behind the walls, be red.

Arbitration

Arbitration, a form of alternative dispute resolution (ADR), is a legal technique for the resolution of disputes outside the courts, wherein the parties to a dispute refer it to one or more persons (the "arbitrators", "arbiters" or "arbitral tribunal"), by whose decision (the "award") they agree to be bound. It is a settlement technique in which a third party reviews the case and imposes a decision that is legally binding for both sides. Other forms of ADR include mediation (a form of settlement negotiation facilitated by a neutral third party) and non-binding resolution by experts.

Chief brand officer	A Chief brand officer is a relatively new executive level position at a corporation, company, organization typically reporting directly to the CEO or board of directors. The Chief brand officer is responsible for a brand''s image, experience, and promise, and propagating it throughout all aspects of the company. The brand officer oversees marketing, advertising, design, public relations and customer service departments.
Employment	Employment is a contract between two parties, one being the employer and the other being the employee. An employee may be defined as: "A person in the service of another under any contract of hire, express or implied, oral or written, where the employer has the power or right to control and direct the employee in the material details of how the work is to be performed." Black''s Law Dictionary page 471 (5th ed. 1979).
Employment discrimination	Employment discrimination (or workplace discrimination) is discrimination in hiring, promotion, job assignment, termination, and compensation. It includes various types of harassment. Many jurisdictions prohibit some types of Employment discrimination, often by forbidding discrimination based on certain traits ("protected categories").
Lease	A Lease is a contract conferring a right on one person to possess property belonging to another person (called a landlord or lessor) to the exclusion of the owner landlord, and all others except with the invitation of the tenant. It is a rental agreement between landlord and tenant. The relationship between the tenant and the landlord is called a tenancy, and the right to possession by the tenant is sometimes called a Leasehold interest.
Unemployment	Unemployment occurs when a person is available to work and seeking work but currently without work. The prevalence of Unemployment is usually measured using the Unemployment rate, which is defined as the percentage of those in the labor force who are unemployed. The Unemployment rate is also used in economic studies and economic indexes such as the United States'' Conference Board''s Index of Leading Indicators as a measure of the state of the macroeconomics.
Unemployment Compensation	Unemployment compensation is money received by an unemployed worker from the United States or a state. In the United States, this compensation is classified as a type of social welfare benefit. According to the Internal Revenue Code, these types of benefits are to be included in a taxpayer''s gross income.
Withholding	Withholding, in general, usually refers to a deduction of money (as "withholding tax") from an employee''s wages or salary by an employer, for projected or actual Income tax liabilities, see: · PAYE (United Kingdom, Ireland, Australia and New Zealand) · Tax withholding in the United States .
Independent contractor	An Independent contractor is a natural person, business, or corporation which provides goods or services to another entity under terms specified in a contract or within a verbal agreement. Unlike an employee, an Independent contractor does not work regularly for an employer but works as and when required, during which time she or he may be subject to the Law of Agency. Independent contractors are usually paid on a freelance basis.

Work made for hire	A work made for hire is an exception to the general rule that the person who actually creates a work is the legally-recognized author of that work. According to copyright law in the United States and certain other copyright jurisdictions, if a work is "made for hire", the employer--not the employee--is considered the legal author. In some countries, this is known as corporate authorship.
Contract	Agreement is said to be reached when an offer capable of immediate acceptance is met with a "mirror image" acceptance (ie, an unqualified acceptance). The parties must have the necessary capacity to Contract and the Contract must not be either trifling, indeterminate, impossible or illegal. Contract law is based on the principle expressed in the Latin phrase pacta sunt servanda .
Ratification	Ratification is the act of approving and paying for supplies or services provided to and accepted by the government as a result of an unauthorized commitment. It gives official sanction or approval to a formal document such as a treaty or constitution. It includes the process of adopting an international treaty by the legislature, a constitution, or another nationally binding document (such as an amendment to a constitution) by the agreement of multiple sub-national entities.
Estoppel	Estoppel is a legal doctrine at common law, where a party is barred from claiming or denying an argument on an equitable ground. Estoppel complements the requirement of consideration in contract law. In general, Estoppel protects an aggrieved party, if the counter-party induced an expectation from the aggrieved party, and the aggrieved party reasonably relied on the expectation and would suffer detriment if the expectation is not met.
Operation of law	The phrase "by Operation of law" is a legal term that indicates that a right or liability has been created for a party, irrespective of the intent of that party, because it is dictated by existing legal principles. For example, if a person dies without a will, his heirs are determined by Operation of law. Similarly, if a person marries or has a child after his or her will has been executed, the law writes this pretermitted spouse or pretermitted heir into the will if no provision for this situation was specifically included.
Reasonable person standard	The reasonable person is a legal fiction of the common law representing an objective standard against which any individual"s conduct can be measured. It is used to determine if a breach of the standard of care has occurred, provided a duty of care can be proven. The Reasonable person standard holds: each person owes a duty to behave as a reasonable person would under the same or similar circumstances.
Security interest	A Security interest is a property interest created by agreement or by operation of law over assets to secure the performance of an obligation, usually the payment of a debt. It gives the beneficiary of the Security interest certain preferential rights in the disposition of secured assets. Such rights vary according to the type of Security interest, but in most cases, a holder of the Security interest is entitled to seize, and usually sell, the property to discharge the debt that the Security interest secures.
Duty	Duty (from "due," that which is owing, O. Fr. deu, did, past participle of devoir; Lat. debere, debitum; cf.

Perfect tender rule	The Perfect tender rule refers to the legal right for a buyer of goods to insist upon "perfect tender" by the seller. In a contract for the sale of goods, if the goods fail to conform exactly to the description in the contract (whether as to quality, quantity or manner of delivery) the buyer may reject the goods. (UCC 2-601.)
Specific performance	In the law of Remedy, an order of specific performance is an order of the court which requires a party to perform a specific act, usually what is stated in a contract. While specific performance can be in the form of any type of forced action, it is usually used to complete a previously established transaction, thus being the most effective remedy in protecting the expectation interest of the innocent party to a contract. It is usually the opposite of a prohibitory injunction but there are mandatory injunctions which have a similar effect to specific performance.
Tort	Tort law is a body of law that addresses, and provides remedies for, civil wrongs not arising out of contractual obligations. A person who suffers legal damages may be able to use Tort law to receive compensation from someone who is legally responsible, or "liable," for those injuries. Generally speaking, Tort law defines what constitutes a legal injury and establishes the circumstances under which one person may be held liable for another"s injury.
Trust	In common law legal systems, a trust is an arrangement whereby property (including real, tangible and intangible) is managed by one person (or persons, or organizations) for the benefit of another. A trust is created by a settlor, who entrusts some or all of his or her property to people of his choice (the trustees.) The trustees hold legal title to the trust property (or trust corpus), but they are obliged to hold the property for the benefit of one or more individuals or organizations (the beneficiary, a.k.a. cestui que use or cestui que trust), usually specified by the settlor, who hold equitable title.
Bankruptcy	Bankruptcy is a legally declared inability or impairment of ability of an individual or organization to pay its creditors. Creditors may file a Bankruptcy petition against a debtor ("involuntary Bankruptcy") in an effort to recoup a portion of what they are owed or initiate a restructuring. In the majority of cases, however, Bankruptcy is initiated by the debtor (a "voluntary Bankruptcy" that is filed by the insolvent individual or organization).
Breach of contract	Breach of contract is a legal concept in which a binding agreement or bargained-for exchange is not honored by one or more of the parties to the contract by non-performance or interference with the other party"s performance. A minor breach, a partial breach or an immaterial breach, occurs when the non-breaching party is unentitled to an order for performance of its obligations, but only to collect the actual amount of their damages. For example, suppose a homeowner hires a contractor to install new plumbing and insists that the pipes, which will ultimately be sealed behind the walls, be red.

Notary public	A Notary public is a public officer constituted by law to serve the public in non-contentious matters usually concerned with estates, deeds, powers-of-attorney, and foreign and international business. A notary"s main functions are to administer oaths and affirmations, take affidavits and statutory declarations, witness and authenticate the execution of certain classes of documents, take acknowledgements of deeds and other conveyances, protest notes and bills of exchange, provide notice of foreign drafts, prepare marine protests in cases of damage, provide exemplifications and notarial copies, and perform certain other official acts depending on the jurisdiction. Any such act is known as a notarization.
Power of attorney	A power of attorney or letter of attorney in common law systems or mandate in civil law systems is an authorization to act on someone else"s behalf in a legal or business matter. The person authorizing the other to act is the principal, granter or donor (of the power), and the one authorized to act is the agent, the attorney-in-fact, or in many Common Law jurisdictions, simply the attorney. The term attorney-in-fact is commonly used in the United States, to make a distinction from the term Attorney at law.
Statute	A statute is a formal written enactment of a legislative authority that governs a country, state, city, or county. Typically, statute s command or prohibit something, or declare policy. The word is often used to distinguish law made by legislative bodies from case law and the regulations issued by Government agencies.
Statute of Frauds	The Statute of Frauds refers to the requirement that certain kinds of contracts be made in writing and signed. Traditionally, the Statute of Frauds requires a writing signed by the defendant in the following circumstances: · Contracts in consideration of marriage. · Contracts which cannot be performed within one year. · Contracts for the transfer of an interest in land. · Contracts by the executor of a will to pay a debt of the estate with their own money. · Contracts for the sale of goods above a certain value. · Contracts in which one party becomes a surety (acts as guarantor) for another party"s debt or other obligation. This can be remembered by the mnemonic "MY LEGS": Marriage, one year, land, executor, goods, surety. The term Statute of Frauds comes from an English Act of Parliament passed in 1677 (authored by Sir Leoline Jenkins and passed by the Cavalier Parliament), and more properly called An Act for Prevention of Frauds and Perjuries. Many common law jurisdictions have made similar statutory provisions, while a number of civil law jurisdictions have equivalent legislation incorporated into their civil codes.

Apparent Authority	Apparent authority is a term used in the law of agency to describe a situation in which a principal leads a third party to believe that an agent has authority to bind the principal, even where the agent lacks the actual authority to bind the principal. In such circumstances, the law will hold the principal liable for the acts of the agent, out of fairness to the third party. There must be some act or some knowing omission on the part of the principal - if the agent alone acts to give the third party this false impression, then the principal is not bound.
Implied Authority	Implied authority of Contract is a legal term. In contract law, it is the implied ability of an individual to make a legally binding contract on behalf of an organization, by way of uniform or interaction with the public on behalf of that organization. When a person is wearing a uniform or nametag bearing the logo or trademark of a business or organization; or if that person is functioning in an obviously authorized capacity on behalf of a business or organization, that person carries an Implied authority of Contract.
Voidable	In law, a transaction or action which is voidable is valid, but may be annulled by one of the parties to the transaction. voidable is usually used in distinction to void ab initio (or void from the outset) and unenforceable. The act of invalidating the contract by the party exercising its rights to anul the voidable contract is usually referred to either as voiding the contract (in the United States and Canada) or avoiding the contract (in the United Kingdom, Australia and other common law countries.)
Estoppel	Estoppel is a legal doctrine at common law, where a party is barred from claiming or denying an argument on an equitable ground. Estoppel complements the requirement of consideration in contract law. In general, Estoppel protects an aggrieved party, if the counter-party induced an expectation from the aggrieved party, and the aggrieved party reasonably relied on the expectation and would suffer detriment if the expectation is not met.
Chief brand officer	A Chief brand officer is a relatively new executive level position at a corporation, company, organization typically reporting directly to the CEO or board of directors. The Chief brand officer is responsible for a brand"s image, experience, and promise, and propagating it throughout all aspects of the company. The brand officer oversees marketing, advertising, design, public relations and customer service departments.
Ratification	Ratification is the act of approving and paying for supplies or services provided to and accepted by the government as a result of an unauthorized commitment. It gives official sanction or approval to a formal document such as a treaty or constitution. It includes the process of adopting an international treaty by the legislature, a constitution, or another nationally binding document (such as an amendment to a constitution) by the agreement of multiple sub-national entities.
Contract	Agreement is said to be reached when an offer capable of immediate acceptance is met with a "mirror image" acceptance (ie, an unqualified acceptance). The parties must have the necessary capacity to Contract and the Contract must not be either trifling, indeterminate, impossible or illegal. Contract law is based on the principle expressed in the Latin phrase pacta sunt servanda .

Partially disclosed Principal	A Partially disclosed principal is one whose agent reveals that he has a principal, but does not reveal the principal"s identity. This concept has important implications in liability law. It is in contrast to a disclosed principal and undisclosed principal.
Rescission	In contract law, rescission has been defined as the unmaking of a contract between parties. rescission is the unwinding of a transaction. This is done to bring the parties, as far as possible, back to the position in which they were before they entered into a contract (the "status quo ante".)
Undisclosed Principal	In the field of law, the term Undisclosed principal relates mainly to the liability of an agent for obligations incurred on behalf of a principal. If the agent does not disclose the nature of his agency (the fact that he acts on behalf of another), and thus does not disclose the name of the principal, the agent may be held personally liable for his actions. If however, the agent disclosed his agency and the name of the principal (disclosed principal), he will normally not be held liable for commitments undertaken within his authorized agency.
Duty	Duty (from "due," that which is owing, O. Fr. deu, did, past participle of devoir; Lat. debere, debitum; cf.
Implied warranty	In common law jurisdictions, an Implied warranty is a contract law term for certain assurances that are presumed to be made in the sale of products or real property, due to the circumstances of the sale. These assurances are characterized as warranties irrespective of whether the seller has expressly promised them orally or in writing. They include an Implied warranty of fitness for a particular purpose, an Implied warranty of merchantability for products, Implied warranty of workmanlike quality for services, and an Implied warranty of habitability for a home.
Uniform Electronic Transactions Act	The Uniform Electronic Transactions Act is one of the several United States Uniform Acts proposed by the National Conference of Commissioners on Uniform State Laws (NCCUSL.) Since then 46 States, the District of Columbia, Puerto Rico, and the U.S. Virgin Islands have adopted it into their own laws. Its overarching purpose is to bring into line the differing State laws over such areas as retention of paper records (checks in particular), and the validity of electronic signatures, thereby supporting the validity of electronic contracts as a viable medium of agreement.
Tort	Tort law is a body of law that addresses, and provides remedies for, civil wrongs not arising out of contractual obligations. A person who suffers legal damages may be able to use Tort law to receive compensation from someone who is legally responsible, or "liable," for those injuries. Generally speaking, Tort law defines what constitutes a legal injury and establishes the circumstances under which one person may be held liable for another"s injury.
Misrepresentation	Misrepresentation is a contract law concept. It means a false statement of fact made by one party to another party, which has the effect of inducing that party into the contract. For example, under certain circumstances, false statements or promises made by a seller of goods regarding the quality or nature of the product that the seller has may constitute Misrepresentation.

Obligation

An obligation is a requirement to take some course of action, whether legal or moral. There are also obligation s in other normative contexts, such as obligation s of etiquette, social obligation s, and possibly in terms of politics, where obligation s are requirements which must be fulfilled. These are generally legal obligation s, which can incur a penalty for unfulfilment, although certain people are obliged to carry out certain actions for other reasons as well, whether as a tradition or for social reasons.

Partnership

A Partnership is a type of business entity in which partners (owners) share with each other the profits or losses of the business. Partnership s are often favored over corporations for taxation purposes, as the Partnership structure does not generally incur a tax on profits before it is distributed to the partners (i.e. there is no dividend tax levied.) However, depending on the Partnership structure and the jurisdiction in which it operates, owners of a Partnership may be exposed to greater personal liability than they would as shareholders of a corporation.

Several Liability

Several liability is where the parties are liable for only their respective obligations. A common example of Several liability is in syndicated loan agreements, which will normally provide that each bank is severally liable for its own part of the loan. If one bank fails to advance its agreed part of the loan to the borrower, then the borrower can only sue that bank, and the other banks in the syndicate have no liability.

Employment

Employment is a contract between two parties, one being the employer and the other being the employee. An employee may be defined as: "A person in the service of another under any contract of hire, express or implied, oral or written, where the employer has the power or right to control and direct the employee in the material details of how the work is to be performed." Black"s Law Dictionary page 471 (5th ed. 1979).

Employment discrimination

Employment discrimination (or workplace discrimination) is discrimination in hiring, promotion, job assignment, termination, and compensation. It includes various types of harassment.

Many jurisdictions prohibit some types of Employment discrimination, often by forbidding discrimination based on certain traits ("protected categories").

Respondeat superior

"respondeat superior" is a legal doctrine which states that, in many circumstances, an employer is responsible for the actions of employees performed within the course of their employment. This rule is also called the "Master-Servant Rule". It is recognized in both common law and civil law jurisdictions.

Vicarious Liability

Vicarious liability is a form of strict, secondary liability that arises under the common law doctrine of agency - respondeat superior - the responsibility of the superior for the acts of their subordinate, or, in a broader sense, the responsibility of any third party that had the "right, ability or duty to control" the activities of a violator. It can be distinguished from contributory liability, another form of secondary liability, which is rooted in the tort theory of enterprise liability.

Employers are vicariously liable, under the respondeat superior doctrine, for negligent acts or omissions by their employees in the course of employment.

Negotiable instrument

A Negotiable instrument is a specialized type of "contract" for the payment of money that is unconditional and capable of transfer by negotiation. Common examples include cheques, banknotes (paper money), and commercial paper.

A Negotiable instrument is not a contract, as contract formation requires an offer, acceptance, and consideration, none of which is an element of a Negotiable instrument.

Revocation

Revocation is the act of recall or annulment. It is the reversal of an act, the recalling of a grant, or the making void of some deed previously existing.

In the law of contracts, revocation is a type of remedy for buyers when the buyer accepts a nonconforming good from the seller.

Impossibility

In contract law, Impossibility is an excuse for the nonperformance of duties under a contract, based on a change in circumstances (or the discovery of preexisting circumstances), the nonoccurrence of which was an underlying assumption of the contract, that makes performance of the contract literally impossible. For such a defense to be raised, performance must not merely be difficult or unexpectedly costly for one party; there must be no way for it to actually be accomplished.

For example, if Rachel contracts to pay Joey $1000 to paint her house on October 1, but the house burns to the ground before the end of September, Rachel is excused from her duty to pay Joey the $1000, and he is excused from his duty to paint her house; however, Joey may still be able to sue for the unjust enrichment of any benefit conferred on Rachel before her house burned down.

Operation of law

The phrase "by Operation of law" is a legal term that indicates that a right or liability has been created for a party, irrespective of the intent of that party, because it is dictated by existing legal principles. For example, if a person dies without a will, his heirs are determined by Operation of law. Similarly, if a person marries or has a child after his or her will has been executed, the law writes this pretermitted spouse or pretermitted heir into the will if no provision for this situation was specifically included.

Bank Secrecy Act

The Bank Secrecy Act of 1970 (or Bank Secrecy Act, or otherwise known as the Currency and Foreign Transactions Reporting Act) requires financial institutions in the United States to assist U.S. government agencies to detect and prevent money laundering. Specifically, the act requires financial institutions to keep records of [cash purchases of negotiable instruments, and file reports of cash purchases of these negotiable instruments of $3,000 or more (daily aggregate amount), and to report suspicious activity that might signify money laundering, tax evasion, or other criminal activities. Many banks will no longer sell negotiable instruments when purchased with cash, requiring the purchase to be withdrawn from an account at that institution.

Bankruptcy

Bankruptcy is a legally declared inability or impairment of ability of an individual or organization to pay its creditors. Creditors may file a Bankruptcy petition against a debtor ("involuntary Bankruptcy") in an effort to recoup a portion of what they are owed or initiate a restructuring. In the majority of cases, however, Bankruptcy is initiated by the debtor (a "voluntary Bankruptcy" that is filed by the insolvent individual or organization).

Insolvency

Insolvency means the inability to pay one''s debts as they fall due. Usually used in Business terms, Insolvency refers to the inability for a company to pay off its debts.

Business Insolvency is defined in two different ways:

Cash flow Insolvency

Unable to pay debts as they fall due.

Employment

Employment is a contract between two parties, one being the employer and the other being the employee. An employee may be defined as: "A person in the service of another under any contract of hire, express or implied, oral or written, where the employer has the power or right to control and direct the employee in the material details of how the work is to be performed." Black"s Law Dictionary page 471 (5th ed. 1979).

Employment discrimination

Employment discrimination (or workplace discrimination) is discrimination in hiring, promotion, job assignment, termination, and compensation. It includes various types of harassment.

Many jurisdictions prohibit some types of Employment discrimination, often by forbidding discrimination based on certain traits ("protected categories").

Parol evidence

The Parol evidence rule is the legal application of a rule of substantive law in contract cases that prevents a party to a written contract from contradicting (or sometimes adding to) the terms of the contract by seeking the admission of evidence "extrinsic" (outside) to the contract. For example, Carl agrees in writing to sell Betty a car for $1,000. Betty argues that Carl told her that she would only need to pay Carl $800.

Parol evidence rule

The Parol evidence rule is the legal application of a rule of substantive law in contract cases that prevents a party to a written contract from contradicting (or sometimes adding to) the terms of the contract by seeking the admission of evidence "extrinsic" (outside) to the contract. For example, Carl agrees in writing to sell Betty a car for $1,000. Betty argues that Carl told her that she would only need to pay Carl $800.

Statute

A statute is a formal written enactment of a legislative authority that governs a country, state, city, or county. Typically, statute s command or prohibit something, or declare policy. The word is often used to distinguish law made by legislative bodies from case law and the regulations issued by Government agencies.

Statute of Frauds

The Statute of Frauds refers to the requirement that certain kinds of contracts be made in writing and signed.

Traditionally, the Statute of Frauds requires a writing signed by the defendant in the following circumstances:

· Contracts in consideration of marriage.
· Contracts which cannot be performed within one year.
· Contracts for the transfer of an interest in land.
· Contracts by the executor of a will to pay a debt of the estate with their own money.
· Contracts for the sale of goods above a certain value.
· Contracts in which one party becomes a surety (acts as guarantor) for another party"s debt or other obligation.

This can be remembered by the mnemonic "MY LEGS": Marriage, one year, land, executor, goods, surety.

The term Statute of Frauds comes from an English Act of Parliament passed in 1677 (authored by Sir Leoline Jenkins and passed by the Cavalier Parliament), and more properly called An Act for Prevention of Frauds and Perjuries. Many common law jurisdictions have made similar statutory provisions, while a number of civil law jurisdictions have equivalent legislation incorporated into their civil codes.

Consideration

Consideration is the legal concept of value in connection with contracts. It is anything of value in the common sense, promised to another when making a contract. It can take the form of money, physical objects, services, promised actions, or even abstinence from a future action.

Contract

Agreement is said to be reached when an offer capable of immediate acceptance is met with a "mirror image" acceptance (ie, an unqualified acceptance). The parties must have the necessary capacity to Contract and the Contract must not be either trifling, indeterminate, impossible or illegal. Contract law is based on the principle expressed in the Latin phrase pacta sunt servanda .

Labor law

Labor law (or employment law) is the body of laws, administrative rulings, and precedents which address the legal rights of, and restrictions on, working people and their organizations. As such, it mediates many aspects of the relationship between trade unions, employers and employees. In Canada, employment laws related to unionized workplaces are differentiated from those relating to particular individuals.

Public policy

Public policy can be generally defined as the course of action or inaction taken by governmental entities with regard to a particular issue or set of issues. Other scholars define it as a system of "courses of action, regulatory measures, laws, and funding priorities concerning a given topic promulgated by a governmental entity or its representatives." public policy is commonly embodied "in constitutions, legislative acts, and judicial decisions."

In the United States, this concept refers not only to the end result of policies, but more broadly to the decision-making and analysis of governmental decisions. public policy is also considered an academic discipline, as it is studied by professors and students at public policy schools of major universities throughout the country.

Tort

Tort law is a body of law that addresses, and provides remedies for, civil wrongs not arising out of contractual obligations. A person who suffers legal damages may be able to use Tort law to receive compensation from someone who is legally responsible, or "liable," for those injuries. Generally speaking, Tort law defines what constitutes a legal injury and establishes the circumstances under which one person may be held liable for another"s injury.

Walsh-Healey Act

The Walsh-Healey Act or Walsh-Healey Public Contracts Act, passed in 1936 as part of the New Deal, is a United States federal law which protects employees of government contractors whose contracts exceed USD 10,000. For these employees, it establishes overtime as hours worked in excess of 8 hours per day or 40 hours per week, sets the minimum wage equal to the prevailing wage in an area, and sets standards for child and convict labor, as well as job sanitation and safety standards.

Whistleblower

A Whistleblower is a person who alleges misconduct. More complex definitions may be used, but the issue is that the Whistleblower usually faces reprisal. The misconduct may be classified in many ways; for example, a violation of a law, rule, regulation and/or a direct threat to public interest, such as fraud, health/safety violations, and corruption.

United States

- History of competition law
- Monopoly
  - Coercive monopoly
  - Natural monopoly
  - Barriers to entry
  - Market power
  - SSNIP test
  - Relevant market
  - Merger control

Anti-competitive practices

- Monopolization
- Collusion
- Formation of cartels
- Price fixing
- Bid rigging
- Product bundling and tying
- Refusal to deal
  - Group boycott
  - Exclusive dealing
  - Dividing territories
  - Conscious parallelism
  - Predatory pricing
  - Misuse of patents and copyrights

Laws and doctrines

United States

- Sherman Antitrust Act
- Clayton Antitrust Act
- Robinson-Patman Act
- FTC Act
- Hart-Scott-Rodino Act
- Merger guidelines
- Essential facilities doctrine
- Noerr-Pennington doctrine
- Parker immunity doctrine
- Rule of reason

Europe

- UK competition law
- Irish competition law

Australia

- Trade Practices Act 1974

Enforcement authorities and organizations

Competition law history refers to attempts by governments to regulate competitive markets for goods and services, leading up to the modern competition or antitrust laws around the world today. The earliest records traces back to the efforts of Roman legislators to control price fluctuations and unfair trade practices. Through the Middle Ages in Europe, Kings and Queens repeatedly cracked down on monopolies, including those created through state legislation.

- International Competition Network
- List of competition regulators

United States Department of Justice

The United States Department of Justice is a Cabinet department in the United States government designed to enforce the law and defend the interests of the United States according to the law and to ensure fair and impartial administration of justice for all Americans The DOJ is administered by the United States Attorney General (see 28 U.S.C.

Child labour

Child labour refers to the employment of children at regular and sustained labour. This practice is considered exploitative by many international organizations and is illegal in many countries. Child labour was utilized to varying extents through most of history, but entered public dispute with the advent of universal schooling, with changes in working conditions during the industrial revolution, and with the emergence of the concepts of workers" and children"s rights.

Overtime

Overtime is the amount of time someone works beyond normal working hours. Normal hours may be determined in several ways:

· by custom (what is considered healthy or reasonable by society),
· by practices of a given trade or profession,
· by legislation,
· by agreement between employers and workers or their representatives.

Most nations have Overtime laws designed to dissuade or prevent employers from forcing their employees to work excessively long hours. These laws may take into account other considerations than the humanitarian, such as increasing the overall level of employment in the economy. One common approach to regulating Overtime is to require employers to pay workers at a higher hourly rate for Overtime work.

Wage

A Wage is a compensation, usually financial, received by a worker in exchange for their labor. Compensation in terms of Wage s is given to worker and compensation in terms of salary is given to employees. Compensation is a monetary benefits given to employees in returns of the services provided by them.

Telecommuters

Telecommuters spend at least part of their workday at home or a telecottage, using computers or other telecommunications equipment. Most Telecommuters live on the fringe of large cities and in the suburbs and exurbs, in what is known as the "two-hour telecommuting ring". Nowadays, they are being used by almost every office and organization.

Closed shop

A Closed shop is a form of union security agreement under which the employer agrees to only hire union members, and employees must remain a member of the union at all times in order to remain employed. International Labour Organization covenants do not address the legality of Closed shop provisions, leaving the question up to each individual nation. The legal status of closed shp agreements varies widely from country to country, ranging from bans on the agreement to extensive regulation of the agrement to not mentioning it at all.

Sexual harassment

Sexual harassment is unwelcome harassment of a sexual nature, or based upon the receiving party"s sex or gender. In some contexts or circumstances, Sexual harassment may be illegal. It includes a range of behavior from seemingly mild transgressions and annoyances to actual sexual abuse or sexual assault.

Trust

In common law legal systems, a trust is an arrangement whereby property (including real, tangible and intangible) is managed by one person (or persons, or organizations) for the benefit of another. A trust is created by a settlor, who entrusts some or all of his or her property to people of his choice (the trustees.) The trustees hold legal title to the trust property (or trust corpus), but they are obliged to hold the property for the benefit of one or more individuals or organizations (the beneficiary, a.k.a. cestui que use or cestui que trust), usually specified by the settlor, who hold equitable title.

Union shop	In the United States of America, a union shop is a place of employment, government agency or company whereby the employer may hire either labor union members or nonmembers but where nonmembers must become union members within a specified period of time or lose their jobs. Under the National Labor Relations Act, the union may only require that employees either join the union or pay the equivalent of union dues. Nonmembers who object to that requirement may only be compelled to pay that portion of union dues that is attributable to the cost of representing employees in collective bargaining and in providing services to all represented employees, but not, with certain exceptions, to the union"s political activities or organizing employees of other employers.
Chief brand officer	A Chief brand officer is a relatively new executive level position at a corporation, company, organization typically reporting directly to the CEO or board of directors. The Chief brand officer is responsible for a brand"s image, experience, and promise, and propagating it throughout all aspects of the company. The brand officer oversees marketing, advertising, design, public relations and customer service departments.
Secondary Boycott	A Secondary boycott is an attempt by labor to convince others to stop doing business with a particular firm because that firm does business with another firm that is the subject of a strike and/or a primary boycott. This type of action is illegal in many countries. In the U.S. it is banned by the interpretation of the Sherman Antitrust Act, by the Taft-Hartley Act, which amends the National Labor Relations Act of 1935, also known as the Wagner Act.
Good faith	Good faith is the mental and moral state of honesty, conviction as to the truth or falsehood of a proposition or body of opinion especially equitable matters. In contemporary English, "bona fides" is sometimes used as a synonym for credentials, background, or documentation of a person"s identity.
Consumer protection	Consumer protection laws are designed to ensure fair competition and the free flow of truthful information in the marketplace. The laws are designed to prevent businesses that engage in fraud or specified unfair practices from gaining an advantage over competitors and may provide additional protection for the weak and those unable to take care of themselves. Consumer protection laws are a form of government regulation which protects the interests of consumers.
Occupational Safety and Health Act	The Occupational Safety and Health Act is the primary federal law which governs occupational health and safety in the private sector and federal government in the United States. It was enacted by Congress in 1970 and was signed by President Richard Nixon on December 29, 1970. Its main goal is to ensure that employers provide employees with an environment free from recognized hazards, such as exposure to toxic chemicals, excessive noise levels, mechanical dangers, heat or cold stress, or unsanitary conditions.

Occupational Safety and Health Administration

The United States Occupational Safety and Health Administration is an agency of the United States Department of Labor. It was created by Congress under the Occupational Safety and Health Act, signed by President Richard M. Nixon, on December 29, 1970. Its mission is to prevent work-related injuries, illnesses, and deaths by issuing and enforcing rules (called standards) for workplace safety and health.

Social Security Administration

The United States Social Security Administration is an independent agency of the United States federal government that administers Social Security, a social insurance program consisting of retirement, disability, and survivors" benefits. To qualify for these benefits, most American workers pay Social Security taxes on their earnings; future benefits are based on the employees" contributions.
The Social Security Administration was established by a law currently codified at 42 U.S.C.

Federal Unemployment Tax Act

The Federal Unemployment Tax Act (or Federal Unemployment Tax Act, 26 U.S.C. ch.23) is a United States federal law that imposes a federal employer tax used to fund state workforce agencies. Employers report this tax by filing an annual Form 940 with the Internal Revenue Service. In some cases, the employer is required to pay the tax in installments during the tax year.

Retirement

Retirement is the point where a person stops employment completely. A person may also semi-retire and keep some sort of Retirement job, out of choice rather than necessity. This usually happens upon reaching a determined age, when physical conditions don"t allow the person to work any more (by illness or accident), or even for personal choice (usually in the presence of an adequate pension or personal savings.)

Unemployment

Unemployment occurs when a person is available to work and seeking work but currently without work. The prevalence of Unemployment is usually measured using the Unemployment rate, which is defined as the percentage of those in the labor force who are unemployed. The Unemployment rate is also used in economic studies and economic indexes such as the United States" Conference Board"s Index of Leading Indicators as a measure of the state of the macroeconomics.

Pension

In general, a Pension is an arrangement to provide people with an income when they are no longer earning a regular income from employment.
The terms retirement plan or superannuation refer to a Pension granted upon retirement . Retirement plans may be set up by employers, insurance companies, the government or other institutions such as employer associations or trade unions.

Unemployment Compensation

Unemployment compensation is money received by an unemployed worker from the United States or a state. In the United States, this compensation is classified as a type of social welfare benefit. According to the Internal Revenue Code, these types of benefits are to be included in a taxpayer"s gross income.

Constitution

- Apostolic Constitution (a class of Roman Catholic Church documents)
- Constitution of the Roman Republic
- Constitutional court
- Constitutionalism
- Corporate Constitution
- Judicial activism
- Judicial restraint
- Judicial review

Judicial philosophies of Constitutional interpretation (note: generally specific to United States Constitutional law)

- List of national Constitutions
- Originalism
- Strict constructionism
- Textualism
- Proposed European Union Constitution

- Treaty of Lisbon (adopts same changes, but without Constitutional name)
- United Nations Charter

Privacy

Privacy is the ability of an individual or group to seclude themselves or information about themselves and thereby reveal themselves selectively. The boundaries and content of what is considered private differ among cultures and individuals, but share basic common themes. Privacy is sometimes related to anonymity, the wish to remain unnoticed or unidentified in the public realm.

Freedom of contract

Freedom of contract or contractualism is the freedom of individuals to bargain among themselves the terms of their own contracts, without government interference. Anything more than minimal regulations and taxes may be seen as infringements. It is the underpinning of the theory of laissez-faire economics.

Misrepresentation

Misrepresentation is a contract law concept. It means a false statement of fact made by one party to another party, which has the effect of inducing that party into the contract. For example, under certain circumstances, false statements or promises made by a seller of goods regarding the quality or nature of the product that the seller has may constitute Misrepresentation.

Business

There are many ways in which a business may be owned under the legal system of England and Wales. Different types of ownership are suitable for organisations depending on the degree of control the owners wish to have over the business. The choice of ownership methor also relates to the organisations ability to raise funds for the business activities.

Employee Polygraph Protection Act	The U.S. Employee Polygraph Protection Act of 1988 () generally prevents employers from using lie detector tests, either for pre-employment screening or during the course of employment, with certain exemptions. Employers generally may not require or request any employee or job applicant to take a lie detector test, or discharge, discipline, or discriminate against an employee or job applicant for refusing to take a test or for exercising other rights under the Act. In addition, employers are required to display a poster in the workplace explaining the Employee Polygraph Protection Act for their employees.

Chapter 33. Employment Discrimination

Age Discrimination in Employment Act	The Age Discrimination in Employment Act of 1967, Pub. L. No. 90-202, 81 Stat. 602 (Dec.
Employment	Employment is a contract between two parties, one being the employer and the other being the employee. An employee may be defined as: "A person in the service of another under any contract of hire, express or implied, oral or written, where the employer has the power or right to control and direct the employee in the material details of how the work is to be performed." Black"s Law Dictionary page 471 (5th ed. 1979).
Employment discrimination	Employment discrimination (or workplace discrimination) is discrimination in hiring, promotion, job assignment, termination, and compensation. It includes various types of harassment. Many jurisdictions prohibit some types of Employment discrimination, often by forbidding discrimination based on certain traits ("protected categories").
Protected class	Protected class is a term used in United States anti-discrimination law. The term describes groups of people who are protected from discrimination and harassment. The following characteristics are considered " Protected class es" and persons cannot be discriminated against based on these characteristics: · Race - Federal: Civil Rights Act of 1964 and The Civil Rights Act of 1866 · Ethnicity · Religion or sect - Federal: Civil Rights Act of 1964 · Color - Federal: Civil Rights Act of 1964 · National origin - Federal: Civil Rights Act of 1964 · Age (40 and over) - Federal: Age Discrimination in Employment Act of 1967 · Sex - Federal: Equal Pay Act of 1963 ' Civil Rights Act of 1964 · Familial status (Housing, cannot discriminate for having children, exception for senior housing) · Sexual orientation (in some jurisdictions and not in others) · Disability status - Federal: Vocational Rehabilitation and Other Rehabilitation Services of 1973 ' Americans with Disabilities Act of 1990 · Veteran status - Federal Vietnam Era Veterans Readjustment Assistance Act of 1974 · Genetic Information - Federal: Genetic Information Nondiscrimination Act .
Sexual harassment	Sexual harassment is unwelcome harassment of a sexual nature, or based upon the receiving party"s sex or gender. In some contexts or circumstances, Sexual harassment may be illegal. It includes a range of behavior from seemingly mild transgressions and annoyances to actual sexual abuse or sexual assault.
Prima facie	Prima facie is a Latin expression meaning on its first appearance, or by first instance; at first sight. The literal translation would be "from first face", prima first, facie face, both in the ablative case. It is used in modern legal English to signify that on first examination, a matter appears to be self-evident from the facts.

Seniority	Seniority is the concept of a person or group of people being in charge or in command of another person or group. This control is often granted to the senior person(s) due to experience or length of service in a given position, but it is not uncommon for a senior person(s) to have less experience or length of service than their subordinates. More generally, "Seniority" can be a description of an individual"s experience or length of service, and can thus be used to differentiate between individuals of otherwise equivalent status without placing them in a hierarchy of direct authority.
Wage	A Wage is a compensation, usually financial, received by a worker in exchange for their labor. Compensation in terms of Wage s is given to worker and compensation in terms of salary is given to employees. Compensation is a monetary benefits given to employees in returns of the services provided by them.
Reasonable accommodation	Reasonable accommodation is a term used in Canada to refer to the theory that equality rights set out in section 15 of the Canadian Charter of Rights and Freedoms demand that accommodation be made to various ethnic minorities. The concept is especially applied with reference to the anti-discrimination laws in Québec"s Charter of Human Rights and Freedoms. (The origin of the term "Reasonable accommodation" is found in labour law jurisprudence, specifically Central Okanagan School District No.
Reverse Discrimination	Reverse discrimination is, in its simplest form, the practice of favoring members of a historically disadvantaged group at the expense of members of a historically advantaged group. In the United States, the terms "Reverse discrimination" and "reverse racism" have been used in past discussions of racial quotas or gender quotas for collegiate admission to government-run educational institutions. Such policies were held to be unconstitutional in the United States, while non-quota programs such as affirmative action (whether based on race, ethnic minorities, and physical, mental, or learning disabiities) are legal.
Undue hardship	Undue hardship is a legalistic term used to design an accommodation to employee that would either alter the nature of the enterprise or affect its viability. It is used in the employment discrimination law in the USA, Canada, and other countries.
Pregnancy Discrimination	Pregnancy discrimination occurs when expectant women are fired, not hired, or otherwise discriminated against due to their pregnancy or intention to become pregnant. Common forms of Pregnancy discrimination include not being hired due to visible pregnancy or likelihood of becoming pregnant, being fired after informing an employer of one"s pregnancy, being fired after maternity leave, and receiving a pay dock due to pregnancy. In the United States, since 1978, employers are legally bound to provide what insurance, leave pay, and additional support that would be bestowed upon any employee with medical leave or disability.
Quid pro quo	Quid pro quo indicates a more-or-less equal exchange or substitution of goods or services. English speakers often use the term to mean "a favour for a favour" and the phrases with almost identical meaning include: "what for what," "give and take," "tit for tat", "this for that", and "you scratch my back, and I"ll scratch yours".

In legal usage, Quid pro quo indicates that an item or a service has been traded in return for something of value, usually when the propriety or equity of the transaction is in question.

Bankruptcy

Bankruptcy is a legally declared inability or impairment of ability of an individual or organization to pay its creditors. Creditors may file a Bankruptcy petition against a debtor ("involuntary Bankruptcy") in an effort to recoup a portion of what they are owed or initiate a restructuring. In the majority of cases, however, Bankruptcy is initiated by the debtor (a "voluntary Bankruptcy" that is filed by the insolvent individual or organization).

Constructive dismissal

In employment law, Constructive dismissal is where an employee resigns because of their employer"s behaviour. The employee must prove that the behaviour was unlawful -- that the employer"s actions amounted to a fundamental breach of contract but generally a Constructive dismissal leads to the employee"s obligations ending and the employee acquiring the right to make claims against the employer.

Supreme Court

A supreme court is in some jurisdictions the highest judicial body within that jurisdiction"s court system, whose rulings are not subject to further review by another court. The designations for such courts differ among jurisdictions. Courts of last resort typically function primarily as appellate courts, hearing appeals from the lower trial courts or intermediate-level appellate courts.

Tangible

In law, tangibility is the attribute of being detectable with the senses.

In criminal law, one of the elements of an offense of larceny is that the stolen property must be tangible.

In the context of intellectual property, expression in tangible form is one of the requirements for copyright protection.

United States

· History of competition law
· Monopoly

  · Coercive monopoly
  · Natural monopoly
  · Barriers to entry
  · Market power
  · SSNIP test
  · Relevant market
  · Merger control

Anti-competitive practices

· Monopolization
· Collusion

- Formation of cartels
- Price fixing
- Bid rigging
- Product bundling and tying
- Refusal to deal
  - Group boycott
  - Exclusive dealing
  - Dividing territories
  - Conscious parallelism
  - Predatory pricing
  - Misuse of patents and copyrights

Laws and doctrines

United States

- Sherman Antitrust Act
- Clayton Antitrust Act
- Robinson-Patman Act
- FTC Act
- Hart-Scott-Rodino Act
- Merger guidelines
- Essential facilities doctrine
- Noerr-Pennington doctrine
- Parker immunity doctrine
- Rule of reason

Europe

- UK competition law
- Irish competition law

Australia

- Trade Practices Act 1974

Enforcement authorities and organizations

Competition law history refers to attempts by governments to regulate competitive markets for goods and services, leading up to the modern competition or antitrust laws around the world today. The earliest records traces back to the efforts of Roman legislators to control price fluctuations and unfair trade practices. Through the Middle Ages in Europe, Kings and Queens repeatedly cracked down on monopolies, including those created through state legislation.

- International Competition Network
- List of competition regulators

Constitution	· Apostolic Constitution (a class of Roman Catholic Church documents) · Constitution of the Roman Republic · Constitutional court · Constitutionalism · Corporate Constitution · Judicial activism · Judicial restraint · Judicial review Judicial philosophies of Constitutional interpretation (note: generally specific to United States Constitutional law) · List of national Constitutions · Originalism · Strict constructionism · Textualism · Proposed European Union Constitution · Treaty of Lisbon (adopts same changes, but without Constitutional name) · United Nations Charter
Pornography	Pornography or porn is the depiction of explicit sexual subject matter for the purpose of sexually exciting the viewer. Pornography makes no claim to artistic merit, unlike erotica which does. Over the past few decades, an immense industry for the production and consumption of Pornography has grown, with the increasing use of the VCR, the DVD, and the Internet, as well as the emergence of social attitudes more tolerant of sexual portrayals.
Privacy	Privacy is the ability of an individual or group to seclude themselves or information about themselves and thereby reveal themselves selectively. The boundaries and content of what is considered private differ among cultures and individuals, but share basic common themes. Privacy is sometimes related to anonymity, the wish to remain unnoticed or unidentified in the public realm.
Business	There are many ways in which a business may be owned under the legal system of England and Wales. Different types of ownership are suitable for organisations depending on the degree of control the owners wish to have over the business. The choice of ownership methor also relates to the organisations ability to raise funds for the business activities.
Child labour	Child labour refers to the employment of children at regular and sustained labour. This practice is considered exploitative by many international organizations and is illegal in many countries. Child labour was utilized to varying extents through most of history, but entered public dispute with the advent of universal schooling, with changes in working conditions during the industrial revolution, and with the emergence of the concepts of workers" and children"s rights.

Service provider	A service provider is an entity that provides services to other entities. Usually this refers to a business that provides subscription or web service to other businesses or individuals. Examples of these services include Internet access, Mobile phone operator, and web application hosting.
Sovereign Immunity	Sovereign immunity is a type of immunity that in common law jurisdictions traces its origins from early English law. Generally speaking it is the doctrine that the sovereign or state cannot commit a legal wrong and is immune from civil suit or criminal prosecution; hence the saying, the king (or queen) can do no wrong. In many cases, governments have waived this immunity to allow for suits; in some cases, an individual may technically appear as defendant on the state"s behalf.
Rehabilitation Act	The U.S. Rehabilitation Act of 1973 prohibits discrimination on the basis of disability in programs conducted by Federal agencies, in programs receiving Federal financial assistance, in Federal employment, and in the employment practices of Federal contractors. The standards for determining employment discrimination under the Rehabilitation Act are the same as those used in title I of the Americans with Disabilities Act. There are four key sections of the Act.
United States Department of Transportation	The United States Department of Transportation is a federal Cabinet department of the United States government concerned with transportation. It was established by an act of Congress on October 15, 1966 and began operation on April 1, 1967. It is administered by the United States Secretary of Transportation.
Chief brand officer	A Chief brand officer is a relatively new executive level position at a corporation, company, organization typically reporting directly to the CEO or board of directors. The Chief brand officer is responsible for a brand"s image, experience, and promise, and propagating it throughout all aspects of the company. The brand officer oversees marketing, advertising, design, public relations and customer service departments.
Trade secret	A trade secret is a formula, practice, process, design, instrument, pattern by which a business can obtain an economic advantage over competitors or customers. In some jurisdictions, such secrets are referred to as "confidential information" or "classified information". The precise language by which a trade secret is defined varies by jurisdiction (as do the particular types of information that are subject to trade secret protection.)
Duty	Duty (from "due," that which is owing, O. Fr. deu, did, past participle of devoir; Lat. debere, debitum; cf.
Estoppel	Estoppel is a legal doctrine at common law, where a party is barred from claiming or denying an argument on an equitable ground. Estoppel complements the requirement of consideration in contract law. In general, Estoppel protects an aggrieved party, if the counter-party induced an expectation from the aggrieved party, and the aggrieved party reasonably relied on the expectation and would suffer detriment if the expectation is not met.

Apparent Authority

Apparent authority is a term used in the law of agency to describe a situation in which a principal leads a third party to believe that an agent has authority to bind the principal, even where the agent lacks the actual authority to bind the principal. In such circumstances, the law will hold the principal liable for the acts of the agent, out of fairness to the third party. There must be some act or some knowing omission on the part of the principal - if the agent alone acts to give the third party this false impression, then the principal is not bound.

Respondeat superior

"respondeat superior" is a legal doctrine which states that, in many circumstances, an employer is responsible for the actions of employees performed within the course of their employment. This rule is also called the "Master-Servant Rule". It is recognized in both common law and civil law jurisdictions.

Tort

Tort law is a body of law that addresses, and provides remedies for, civil wrongs not arising out of contractual obligations. A person who suffers legal damages may be able to use Tort law to receive compensation from someone who is legally responsible, or "liable," for those injuries. Generally speaking, Tort law defines what constitutes a legal injury and establishes the circumstances under which one person may be held liable for another"s injury.

Business

There are many ways in which a business may be owned under the legal system of England and Wales. Different types of ownership are suitable for organisations depending on the degree of control the owners wish to have over the business. The choice of ownership methor also relates to the organisations ability to raise funds for the business activities.

Proprietorship

A sole Proprietorship). All assets of the business are owned by the proprietor and all debts of the business are his debts and he must pay them from his personal resources.

Sole proprietorship

A Sole proprietorship, or simply proprietorship is a type of business entity which legally has no separate existence from its owner. Hence, the limitations of liability enjoyed by a corporation and limited liability partnerships do not apply to sole proprietors. All debts of the business are debts of the owner.

Duty

Duty (from "due," that which is owing, O. Fr. deu, did, past participle of devoir; Lat. debere, debitum; cf.

Obligation

An obligation is a requirement to take some course of action, whether legal or moral. There are also obligation s in other normative contexts, such as obligation s of etiquette, social obligation s, and possibly in terms of politics, where obligation s are requirements which must be fulfilled. These are generally legal obligation s, which can incur a penalty for unfulfilment, although certain people are obliged to carry out certain actions for other reasons as well, whether as a tradition or for social reasons.

Parol evidence

The Parol evidence rule is the legal application of a rule of substantive law in contract cases that prevents a party to a written contract from contradicting (or sometimes adding to) the terms of the contract by seeking the admission of evidence "extrinsic" (outside) to the contract. For example, Carl agrees in writing to sell Betty a car for $1,000. Betty argues that Carl told her that she would only need to pay Carl $800.

Parol evidence rule

The Parol evidence rule is the legal application of a rule of substantive law in contract cases that prevents a party to a written contract from contradicting (or sometimes adding to) the terms of the contract by seeking the admission of evidence "extrinsic" (outside) to the contract. For example, Carl agrees in writing to sell Betty a car for $1,000. Betty argues that Carl told her that she would only need to pay Carl $800.

Statute

A statute is a formal written enactment of a legislative authority that governs a country, state, city, or county. Typically, statute s command or prohibit something, or declare policy. The word is often used to distinguish law made by legislative bodies from case law and the regulations issued by Government agencies.

Statute of Frauds

The Statute of Frauds refers to the requirement that certain kinds of contracts be made in writing and signed.

Traditionally, the Statute of Frauds requires a writing signed by the defendant in the following circumstances:

· Contracts in consideration of marriage.
· Contracts which cannot be performed within one year.
· Contracts for the transfer of an interest in land.
· Contracts by the executor of a will to pay a debt of the estate with their own money.
· Contracts for the sale of goods above a certain value.
· Contracts in which one party becomes a surety (acts as guarantor) for another party''s debt or other obligation.

This can be remembered by the mnemonic "MY LEGS": Marriage, one year, land, executor, goods, surety.

The term Statute of Frauds comes from an English Act of Parliament passed in 1677 (authored by Sir Leoline Jenkins and passed by the Cavalier Parliament), and more properly called An Act for Prevention of Frauds and Perjuries. Many common law jurisdictions have made similar statutory provisions, while a number of civil law jurisdictions have equivalent legislation incorporated into their civil codes.

Consideration

Consideration is the legal concept of value in connection with contracts. It is anything of value in the common sense, promised to another when making a contract. It can take the form of money, physical objects, services, promised actions, or even abstinence from a future action.

Vicarious Liability

Vicarious liability is a form of strict, secondary liability that arises under the common law doctrine of agency - respondeat superior - the responsibility of the superior for the acts of their subordinate, or, in a broader sense, the responsibility of any third party that had the "right, ability or duty to control" the activities of a violator. It can be distinguished from contributory liability, another form of secondary liability, which is rooted in the tort theory of enterprise liability.

Employers are vicariously liable, under the respondeat superior doctrine, for negligent acts or omissions by their employees in the course of employment.

Good faith

Good faith is the mental and moral state of honesty, conviction as to the truth or falsehood of a proposition or body of opinion especially equitable matters.

In contemporary English, "bona fides" is sometimes used as a synonym for credentials, background, or documentation of a person''s identity.

Partnership

A Partnership is a type of business entity in which partners (owners) share with each other the profits or losses of the business. Partnership s are often favored over corporations for taxation purposes, as the Partnership structure does not generally incur a tax on profits before it is distributed to the partners (i.e. there is no dividend tax levied.) However, depending on the Partnership structure and the jurisdiction in which it operates, owners of a Partnership may be exposed to greater personal liability than they would as shareholders of a corporation.

Uniform Partnership Act

The Uniform Partnership Act , which includes revisions that are sometimes called the Revised Uniform Partnership Act, is a uniform act (similar to a model statute), proposed by the National Conference of Commissioners on Uniform State Laws ("NCCUSL") for the governance of business partnerships by U.S. States. Several versions of Uniform Partnership Act have been promulgated by the NCCUSL, the earliest having been put forth in 1914, and the most recent in 1997.

The NCCUSL"s first revision of Uniform Partnership Act was promulgated in 1992 and amended in 1993 and 1994.

Chief brand officer

A Chief brand officer is a relatively new executive level position at a corporation, company, organization typically reporting directly to the CEO or board of directors. The Chief brand officer is responsible for a brand"s image, experience, and promise, and propagating it throughout all aspects of the company. The brand officer oversees marketing, advertising, design, public relations and customer service departments.

Tenancy

Leasehold is a form of property tenure where one party buys the right to occupy land or a building for a given length of time. As lease is a legal estate, leasehold estate can be bought and sold on the open market. A leasehold thus differs from a freehold where the ownership of a property is purchased outright and thereafter held for an indeterminate length of time, and also differs from a tenancy where a property is let on a periodic basis such as weekly or monthly.

Business

There are many ways in which a business may be owned under the legal system of England and Wales. Different types of ownership are suitable for organisations depending on the degree of control the owners wish to have over the business. The choice of ownership methor also relates to the organisations ability to raise funds for the business activities.

United Nations Convention on Contracts for the International Sale of Goods

The United Nations Convention on Contracts for the International Sale of Goods is a treaty offering a uniform international sales law that, as of July 2008, had been ratified by 71 countries that account for a significant proportion of world trade, making it one of the most successful international uniform laws. Japan is the most recent State to have ratified the Convention.

It allows exporters to avoid choice of law issues as it offers "accepted substantive rules on which contracting parties, courts, and arbitrators may rely".

Contract

Agreement is said to be reached when an offer capable of immediate acceptance is met with a "mirror image" acceptance (ie, an unqualified acceptance). The parties must have the necessary capacity to Contract and the Contract must not be either trifling, indeterminate, impossible or illegal. Contract law is based on the principle expressed in the Latin phrase pacta sunt servanda .

Estoppel	Estoppel is a legal doctrine at common law, where a party is barred from claiming or denying an argument on an equitable ground. Estoppel complements the requirement of consideration in contract law. In general, Estoppel protects an aggrieved party, if the counter-party induced an expectation from the aggrieved party, and the aggrieved party reasonably relied on the expectation and would suffer detriment if the expectation is not met.
Statute	A statute is a formal written enactment of a legislative authority that governs a country, state, city, or county. Typically, statute s command or prohibit something, or declare policy. The word is often used to distinguish law made by legislative bodies from case law and the regulations issued by Government agencies.
Statute of Frauds	The Statute of Frauds refers to the requirement that certain kinds of contracts be made in writing and signed. Traditionally, the Statute of Frauds requires a writing signed by the defendant in the following circumstances: · Contracts in consideration of marriage. · Contracts which cannot be performed within one year. · Contracts for the transfer of an interest in land. · Contracts by the executor of a will to pay a debt of the estate with their own money. · Contracts for the sale of goods above a certain value. · Contracts in which one party becomes a surety (acts as guarantor) for another party"s debt or other obligation. This can be remembered by the mnemonic "MY LEGS": Marriage, one year, land, executor, goods, surety. The term Statute of Frauds comes from an English Act of Parliament passed in 1677 (authored by Sir Leoline Jenkins and passed by the Cavalier Parliament), and more properly called An Act for Prevention of Frauds and Perjuries. Many common law jurisdictions have made similar statutory provisions, while a number of civil law jurisdictions have equivalent legislation incorporated into their civil codes.
Writ	In law, a writ is a formal writ ten order issued by a body with administrative or judicial jurisdiction; in modern usage, this public body is generally a court. Warrants, prerogative writ s and subpoenas are types of writ s; there are many others. Originally, a writ was a letter or command from the Sovereign, or from some person with appropriate jurisdiction.
Writ of attachment	A Writ of attachment is a court order to "attach" or seize an asset. It is issued by a court to a law enforcement officer or sheriff. The Writ of attachment is issued in order to satisfy a judgment issued by the court.
Business judgment rule	The Business judgment rule is an American case law-derived concept in corporations law whereby the "directors of a corporation .

Partnership Agreement	Articles of Partnership is a voluntary contract between two or among more than two persons to place their capital, labor, and skills, and corporation in business with the understanding that there will be a sharing of the profits and losses between/among partners. Outside of North America, it is normally referred to simply as a Partnership agreement. There are also multiple sections which are often included as well in articles of partnership, based on the circumstance.
Limited partnership	A Limited partnership is a form of partnership similar to a general partnership, except that in addition to one or more general partners (GPs), there are one or more limited partners (Limited partnerships). It is a partnership in which only one partner is required to be a general partner. The GPs are, in all major respects, in the same legal position as partners in a conventional firm, i.e. they have management control, share the right to use partnership property, share the profits of the firm in predefined proportions, and have joint and several liability for the debts of the partnership.
Implied Authority	Implied authority of Contract is a legal term. In contract law, it is the implied ability of an individual to make a legally binding contract on behalf of an organization, by way of uniform or interaction with the public on behalf of that organization. When a person is wearing a uniform or nametag bearing the logo or trademark of a business or organization; or if that person is functioning in an obviously authorized capacity on behalf of a business or organization, that person carries an Implied authority of Contract.
Duty	Duty (from "due," that which is owing, O. Fr. deu, did, past participle of devoir; Lat. debere, debitum; cf.
Obligation	An obligation is a requirement to take some course of action, whether legal or moral. There are also obligation s in other normative contexts, such as obligation s of etiquette, social obligation s, and possibly in terms of politics, where obligation s are requirements which must be fulfilled. These are generally legal obligation s, which can incur a penalty for unfulfilment, although certain people are obliged to carry out certain actions for other reasons as well, whether as a tradition or for social reasons.
Several Liability	Several liability is where the parties are liable for only their respective obligations. A common example of Several liability is in syndicated loan agreements, which will normally provide that each bank is severally liable for its own part of the loan. If one bank fails to advance its agreed part of the loan to the borrower, then the borrower can only sue that bank, and the other banks in the syndicate have no liability.
Buy-sell Agreement	A Buy-sell agreement may be thought of as a sort of "premarital agreement" between business partners/shareholders. It is sometimes called a "business will". An insured Buy-sell agreement (agreement funded with life insurance on the participating owner"s lives) is often recommended by business succession specialists and financial planners to ensure the buy-sell arrangement is well-funded and also to guarantee there will be money when the buy-sell event is triggered.

Limited liability	Limited liability is a concept whereby a person"s financial liability is limited to a fixed sum, most commonly the value of a person"s investment in a company or partnership with Limited liability. In other words, if a company with Limited liability is sued, then the plaintiffs are suing the company, not its owners or investors. A shareholder in a limited company is not personally liable for any of the debts of the company, other than for the value of his investment in that company.
Revised Uniform Limited Partnership Act	The Uniform Limited Partnership Act (ULPA), which includes its 1976 revision called the Revised Uniform Limited Partnership Act , is a uniform act (similar to a model statute), proposed by the National Conference of Commissioners on Uniform State Laws ("NCCUSL") for the governance of business partnerships by U.S. States. The NCCUSL promulgated the original ULPA in 1916 and the most recent revision in 2001. The NCCUSL promulgated the original ULPA in 1916, which is now called the Uniform Limited Partnership Act (1916) or ULPA (1916); a 1976 revision named the Revised Uniform Limited Partnership Act which is also now called the Uniform Limited Partnership Act (1976), ULPA (1976) or Revised Uniform Limited Partnership Act; a 1985 revision named Uniform Limited Partnership Act (1976) with 1985 Amendments, which is also now called ULPA (1985) or Revised Uniform Limited Partnership Act (1985); and a 2001 revision that was colloquially called Re-Revised Uniform Limited Partnership Act during the drafting process but then was officially named the Uniform Limited Partnership Act (2001) or ULPA (2001.)
Limited liability limited partnership	The Limited liability limited partnership is a relatively new modification of the limited partnership, a form of business entity recognized under U.S. commercial law. An Limited liability limited partnership is a limited partnership and as such consists of one or more general partners and one or more limited partners. The general partners manage the Limited liability limited partnership, while typically the limited partners only have a financial interest.
Limited liability company	A Limited liability company in the law of the vast majority of United States jurisdictions is a legal form of business company that provides limited liability to its owners. Often incorrectly called a "limited liability corporation" (instead of company), it is a hybrid business entity having certain characteristics of both a corporation and a partnership or sole proprietorship (depending on how many owners there are). An Limited liability company, although a business entity, is a type of unincorporated association and is not a corporation.

Limited Liability	Limited liability is a concept whereby a person"s financial liability is limited to a fixed sum, most commonly the value of a person"s investment in a company or partnership with Limited liability. In other words, if a company with Limited liability is sued, then the plaintiffs are suing the company, not its owners or investors. A shareholder in a limited company is not personally liable for any of the debts of the company, other than for the value of his investment in that company.
Limited Liability Company	A Limited liability company in the law of the vast majority of United States jurisdictions is a legal form of business company that provides limited liability to its owners. Often incorrectly called a "limited liability corporation" (instead of company), it is a hybrid business entity having certain characteristics of both a corporation and a partnership or sole proprietorship (depending on how many owners there are). An Limited liability company, although a business entity, is a type of unincorporated association and is not a corporation.
Numerary	Numerary is a civil designation for persons who are incorporated in a fixed or permanent way to a society or group: regular member of the working staff, permanent staff distinguished from a super Numerary . The term Numerary and its counterpart, "super Numerary ," originated in Spanish and Latin American academy and government; it is now also used in countries all over the world, such as France, the U.S., England, Italy, etc. There are Numerary members of surgical organizations, of universities, of gastronomical associations, etc.
Company formation	In the UK the process of incorporation is called Company formation, it is also sometimes referred to as company registration. Under UK and most international law a company or corporation is considered a separate entity to the people who own or operate the business. Today the majority of UK companies are formed electronically.
Contract	Agreement is said to be reached when an offer capable of immediate acceptance is met with a "mirror image" acceptance (ie, an unqualified acceptance). The parties must have the necessary capacity to Contract and the Contract must not be either trifling, indeterminate, impossible or illegal. Contract law is based on the principle expressed in the Latin phrase pacta sunt servanda .
Duty	Duty (from "due," that which is owing, O. Fr. deu, did, past participle of devoir; Lat. debere, debitum; cf.
Obligation	An obligation is a requirement to take some course of action, whether legal or moral. There are also obligation s in other normative contexts, such as obligation s of etiquette, social obligation s, and possibly in terms of politics, where obligation s are requirements which must be fulfilled. These are generally legal obligation s, which can incur a penalty for unfulfilment, although certain people are obliged to carry out certain actions for other reasons as well, whether as a tradition or for social reasons.

Chief brand officer	A Chief brand officer is a relatively new executive level position at a corporation, company, organization typically reporting directly to the CEO or board of directors. The Chief brand officer is responsible for a brand"s image, experience, and promise, and propagating it throughout all aspects of the company. The brand officer oversees marketing, advertising, design, public relations and customer service departments.
Operating Agreement	An operating agreement is an agreement among limited liability company ("LLC") Members governing the LLC"s business, and Member"s financial and managerial rights and duties. Many states require an LLC to have an operating agreement. LLCs operating without an operating agreement are governed by the State"s default rules contained in the relevant statute and developed through state court decisions.
Business	There are many ways in which a business may be owned under the legal system of England and Wales. Different types of ownership are suitable for organisations depending on the degree of control the owners wish to have over the business. The choice of ownership methor also relates to the organisations ability to raise funds for the business activities.
Joint venture	A Joint venture is an entity formed between two or more parties to undertake economic activity together. The parties agree to create a new entity by both contributing equity, and they then share in the revenues, expenses, and control of the enterprise. The venture can be for one specific project only, or a continuing business relationship such as the Fuji Xerox Joint venture.
Proprietorship	A sole Proprietorship). All assets of the business are owned by the proprietor and all debts of the business are his debts and he must pay them from his personal resources.
Sole proprietorship	A Sole proprietorship, or simply proprietorship is a type of business entity which legally has no separate existence from its owner. Hence, the limitations of liability enjoyed by a corporation and limited liability partnerships do not apply to sole proprietors. All debts of the business are debts of the owner.
Trust	In common law legal systems, a trust is an arrangement whereby property (including real, tangible and intangible) is managed by one person (or persons, or organizations) for the benefit of another. A trust is created by a settlor, who entrusts some or all of his or her property to people of his choice (the trustees.) The trustees hold legal title to the trust property (or trust corpus), but they are obliged to hold the property for the benefit of one or more individuals or organizations (the beneficiary, a.k.a. cestui que use or cestui que trust), usually specified by the settlor, who hold equitable title.

Business

There are many ways in which a business may be owned under the legal system of England and Wales. Different types of ownership are suitable for organisations depending on the degree of control the owners wish to have over the business. The choice of ownership methor also relates to the organisations ability to raise funds for the business activities.

Shareholder

A mutual shareholder or stockholder is an individual or company (including a corporation) that legally owns one or more shares of stock in a joint stock company. A company"s shareholder s collectively own that company. Thus, the typical goal of such companies is to enhance shareholder value.

Business judgment rule

The Business judgment rule is an American case law-derived concept in corporations law whereby the "directors of a corporation .

Piercing the corporate veil

Piercing the corporate veil describes a legal decision to treat the rights or duties of a corporation as the rights or liabilities of its shareholders or directors. Usually a corporation is treated as a separate legal person, which is solely responsible for the debts it incurs and the sole beneficiary of the credit it is owed. Common law countries usually uphold this principle of seperate personhood, but in exceptional situations may "pierce" or "lift" the corporate veil.

Constitution

· Apostolic Constitution (a class of Roman Catholic Church documents)
· Constitution of the Roman Republic
· Constitutional court
· Constitutionalism
· Corporate Constitution
· Judicial activism
· Judicial restraint
· Judicial review
Judicial philosophies of Constitutional interpretation (note: generally specific to United States Constitutional law)

· List of national Constitutions
· Originalism
· Strict constructionism
· Textualism
· Proposed European Union Constitution

· Treaty of Lisbon (adopts same changes, but without Constitutional name)
· United Nations Charter

Employment

Employment is a contract between two parties, one being the employer and the other being the employee. An employee may be defined as: "A person in the service of another under any contract of hire, express or implied, oral or written, where the employer has the power or right to control and direct the employee in the material details of how the work is to be performed." Black"s Law Dictionary page 471 (5th ed. 1979).

Employment discrimination

Employment discrimination (or workplace discrimination) is discrimination in hiring, promotion, job assignment, termination, and compensation. It includes various types of harassment.

Many jurisdictions prohibit some types of Employment discrimination, often by forbidding discrimination based on certain traits ("protected categories").

Freedom of contract

Freedom of contract or contractualism is the freedom of individuals to bargain among themselves the terms of their own contracts, without government interference. Anything more than minimal regulations and taxes may be seen as infringements. It is the underpinning of the theory of laissez-faire economics.

Misrepresentation

Misrepresentation is a contract law concept. It means a false statement of fact made by one party to another party, which has the effect of inducing that party into the contract. For example, under certain circumstances, false statements or promises made by a seller of goods regarding the quality or nature of the product that the seller has may constitute Misrepresentation.

Self-incrimination

Self-incrimination is the act of accusing oneself of a crime for which a person can then be prosecuted. self-incrimination can occur either directly or indirectly: directly, by means of interrogation where information of a self-incriminatory nature is disclosed; indirectly, when information of a self-incriminatory nature is disclosed voluntarily without pressure from another person.

The Fifth Amendment to the United States Constitution protects witnesses from being forced to incriminate themselves.

United States

- History of competition law
- Monopoly
  - Coercive monopoly
  - Natural monopoly
  - Barriers to entry
  - Market power
  - SSNIP test
  - Relevant market
  - Merger control

Anti-competitive practices

- Monopolization
- Collusion

- Formation of cartels
- Price fixing
- Bid rigging
- Product bundling and tying
- Refusal to deal

- Group boycott
- Exclusive dealing
- Dividing territories
- Conscious parallelism
- Predatory pricing
- Misuse of patents and copyrights

Laws and doctrines

United States

- Sherman Antitrust Act
- Clayton Antitrust Act
- Robinson-Patman Act
- FTC Act
- Hart-Scott-Rodino Act
- Merger guidelines
- Essential facilities doctrine
- Noerr-Pennington doctrine
- Parker immunity doctrine
- Rule of reason

Europe

- UK competition law
- Irish competition law

Australia

- Trade Practices Act 1974

Enforcement authorities and organizations

Competition law history refers to attempts by governments to regulate competitive markets for goods and services, leading up to the modern competition or antitrust laws around the world today. The earliest records traces back to the efforts of Roman legislators to control price fluctuations and unfair trade practices. Through the Middle Ages in Europe, Kings and Queens repeatedly cracked down on monopolies, including those created through state legislation.

- International Competition Network
- List of competition regulators

Chief brand officer

A Chief brand officer is a relatively new executive level position at a corporation, company, organization typically reporting directly to the CEO or board of directors. The Chief brand officer is responsible for a brand''s image, experience, and promise, and propagating it throughout all aspects of the company. The brand officer oversees marketing, advertising, design, public relations and customer service departments.

Guarantee	The act of becoming a surety is also called a Guarantee. Traditionally a Guarantee was distinguished from a surety in that the surety"s liability was joint and primary with the principal, whereas the guaranty"s liability was ancillary and derivative, but many jurisdictions have abolished this distinction
Privileges and immunities clause	The privileges and immunities clause (U.S The clause also embraces a right to travel, so that a citizen of one state can go and enjoy privileges and immunities in any other state. The text of the clause reads: The privileges and immunities clause is similar to a provision that was contained in the Articles of Confederation.
Respondeat superior	"respondeat superior" is a legal doctrine which states that, in many circumstances, an employer is responsible for the actions of employees performed within the course of their employment. This rule is also called the "Master-Servant Rule". It is recognized in both common law and civil law jurisdictions.
Tort	Tort law is a body of law that addresses, and provides remedies for, civil wrongs not arising out of contractual obligations. A person who suffers legal damages may be able to use Tort law to receive compensation from someone who is legally responsible, or "liable," for those injuries. Generally speaking, Tort law defines what constitutes a legal injury and establishes the circumstances under which one person may be held liable for another"s injury.
Sentencing guidelines	The Federal Sentencing guidelines are rules that set out a uniform sentencing policy for convicted felons in the United States federal courts system. The Guidelines are the product of the United States Sentencing Commission and are part of an overall federal sentencing reform package that took effect in the mid-1960s. The implementation of this reform package was the result of bipartisan cooperation, led chiefly by Senator Edward Kennedy, as Chair of the Senate Judiciary Committee, and Attorney General Edwin Meese.
United States Sentencing Commission	The United States Sentencing Commission is an independent agency of the judicial branch of the federal government of the United States. It is responsible for articulating the sentencing guidelines for the United States federal courts. The Commission promulgates the Federal Sentencing Guidelines, which replaced the prior system of indeterminate sentencing that allowed trial judges to give sentences ranging from probation to the maximum statutory punishment for the offense.
Sarbanes-Oxley Act	The Sarbanes-Oxley Act of 2002 (Pub.L. 107-204, 116 Stat. 745, enacted July 30, 2002), also known as the Public Company Accounting Reform and Investor Protection Act of 2002 and commonly called Sarbanes-Oxley, Sarbox or SOX, is a United States federal law enacted on July 30, 2002, as a reaction to a number of major corporate and accounting scandals including those affecting Enron, Tyco International, Adelphia, Peregrine Systems and WorldCom.

Contract

Agreement is said to be reached when an offer capable of immediate acceptance is met with a "mirror image" acceptance (ie, an unqualified acceptance). The parties must have the necessary capacity to Contract and the Contract must not be either trifling, indeterminate, impossible or illegal. Contract law is based on the principle expressed in the Latin phrase pacta sunt servanda .

Share

In business and finance, a share of stock (also referred to as equity share) means a share of ownership in a corporation (company.) In the plural, stocks is often used as a synonym for shares especially in the United States, but it is less commonly used that way outside of North America.

In the United Kingdom, South Africa, and Australia, stock can also refer to completely different financial instruments such as government bonds or, less commonly, to all kinds of marketable securities.

S corporation

An S corporation for United States federal income tax purposes, is a corporation that makes a valid election to be taxed under Subchapter S of Chapter 1 of the Internal Revenue Code.

In general, S corporation s do not pay any income taxes. Instead, the corporation"s income or losses are divided among and passed through to its shareholders.

Novation

Novation is a term used in contract law and business law to describe the act of either replacing an obligation to perform with a new obligation, or replacing a party to an agreement with a new party. In contrast to an assignment, which is valid so long as the obligee (person receiving the benefit of the bargain) is given notice, a Novation is valid only with the consent of all parties to the original agreement: the obligee must consent to the replacement of the original obligor with the new obligor. A contract transferred by the Novation process transfers all duties and obligations from the original obligor to the new obligor.

Board of directors

A Board of directors is a body of elected or appointed members who jointly oversee the activities of a company or organization. The body sometimes has a different name, such as board of trustees, board of governors, board of managers, or executive board. It is often simply referred to as "the board."

A board"s activities are determined by the powers, duties, and responsibilities delegated to it or conferred on it by an authority outside itself.

Charter

A Charter is the grant of authority or rights, stating that the granter formally recognizes the prerogative of the recipient to exercise the rights specified. It is implicit that the granter retains superiority (or sovereignty), and that the recipient admits a limited (or inferior) status within the relationship, and it is within that sense that Charters were historically granted, and that sense is retained in modern usage of the term. Also, Charter can simply be a document giving royal permission to start a colony.

Registered Agent

In the US, a Registered agent is a business or individual designated to receive service of process (SOP) when a business entity is a party in a legal action such as a lawsuit or summons. In some states the agent is also referred to as a resident agent or statutory agent, but most states have changed their statutes and now call this function "Registered agent". The Registered agent for a business entity may be an individual member of the company, or (more often) a third party, such as the organization"s lawyer or a service company.

Estoppel	Estoppel is a legal doctrine at common law, where a party is barred from claiming or denying an argument on an equitable ground. Estoppel complements the requirement of consideration in contract law. In general, Estoppel protects an aggrieved party, if the counter-party induced an expectation from the aggrieved party, and the aggrieved party reasonably relied on the expectation and would suffer detriment if the expectation is not met.
Power of attorney	A power of attorney or letter of attorney in common law systems or mandate in civil law systems is an authorization to act on someone else"s behalf in a legal or business matter. The person authorizing the other to act is the principal, granter or donor (of the power), and the one authorized to act is the agent, the attorney-in-fact, or in many Common Law jurisdictions, simply the attorney. The term attorney-in-fact is commonly used in the United States, to make a distinction from the term Attorney at law.
Ultra vires	Ultra vires is a Latin phrase that literally means "beyond the powers". Its inverse is called intra vires, meaning "within the powers". It is used as a legal term in a number of common law contexts.
Ownership equity	In accounting terms, after all liabilities are paid, ownership equity is the remaining interest in assets. If valuations placed on assets do not exceed liabilities, negative equity exists. Shareholders" equity (or stockholders" equity, shareholders" funds, shareholders" capital employed) is this interest in remaining assets, spread among individual shareholders of common or preferred stock.

Quorum	In law, a Quorum is the minimum number of members of a deliberative body necessary to conduct the business of that group. Ordinarily, this is a majority of the people expected to be there, although bodies may have a lower or higher Quorum. When Quorum is not met, a legislative body cannot hold a vote, and cannot change the status quo.
Audit committee	In a publicly-held company, an Audit committee is an operating committee of the Board of Directors, typically charged with oversight of financial reporting and disclosure. Committee members are drawn from members of the Company"s board of directors, with a Chairperson selected from among the members. An Audit committee of a publicly-traded company in the United States is composed of independent and outside directors referred to as non-executive directors, at least one of which is typically a financial expert.
Chief brand officer	A Chief brand officer is a relatively new executive level position at a corporation, company, organization typically reporting directly to the CEO or board of directors. The Chief brand officer is responsible for a brand"s image, experience, and promise, and propagating it throughout all aspects of the company. The brand officer oversees marketing, advertising, design, public relations and customer service departments.
Business	There are many ways in which a business may be owned under the legal system of England and Wales. Different types of ownership are suitable for organisations depending on the degree of control the owners wish to have over the business. The choice of ownership methor also relates to the organisations ability to raise funds for the business activities.
Business judgment rule	The Business judgment rule is an American case law-derived concept in corporations law whereby the "directors of a corporation .
Shareholder	A mutual shareholder or stockholder is an individual or company (including a corporation) that legally owns one or more shares of stock in a joint stock company. A company"s shareholder s collectively own that company. Thus, the typical goal of such companies is to enhance shareholder value.
Contract	Agreement is said to be reached when an offer capable of immediate acceptance is met with a "mirror image" acceptance (ie, an unqualified acceptance). The parties must have the necessary capacity to Contract and the Contract must not be either trifling, indeterminate, impossible or illegal. Contract law is based on the principle expressed in the Latin phrase pacta sunt servanda .
Trust	In common law legal systems, a trust is an arrangement whereby property (including real, tangible and intangible) is managed by one person (or persons, or organizations) for the benefit of another. A trust is created by a settlor, who entrusts some or all of his or her property to people of his choice (the trustees.) The trustees hold legal title to the trust property (or trust corpus), but they are obliged to hold the property for the benefit of one or more individuals or organizations (the beneficiary, a.k.a. cestui que use or cestui que trust), usually specified by the settlor, who hold equitable title.

Voting trust	A Voting trust is a trust whereby the shares in a company of one or more shareholders and the voting rights attached thereto are legally transferred to a trustee, usually for a specified period of time (the "trust period".) In some Voting trust s, the trustee may also be granted additional powers (such as to sell or redeem the shares.) At the end of the trust period, the shares would ordinarily be re-transferred to the beneficiary(ies), although in practice many Voting trust s contain provisions for them to re-vested on the Voting trust s with identical terms.
Sarbanes-Oxley Act	The Sarbanes-Oxley Act of 2002 (Pub.L. 107-204, 116 Stat. 745, enacted July 30, 2002), also known as the Public Company Accounting Reform and Investor Protection Act of 2002 and commonly called Sarbanes-Oxley, Sarbox or SOX, is a United States federal law enacted on July 30, 2002, as a reaction to a number of major corporate and accounting scandals including those affecting Enron, Tyco International, Adelphia, Peregrine Systems and WorldCom.
Share	In business and finance, a share of stock (also referred to as equity share) means a share of ownership in a corporation (company.) In the plural, stocks is often used as a synonym for shares especially in the United States, but it is less commonly used that way outside of North America. In the United Kingdom, South Africa, and Australia, stock can also refer to completely different financial instruments such as government bonds or, less commonly, to all kinds of marketable securities.
Stock Certificate	In corporate law, a Stock certificate is a legal document that certifies ownership of a specific number of stock shares in a corporation. In large corporations, buying shares does not always lead to a Stock certificate In at least one unspecified country, usually only shareholders with Stock certificate s can vote in a shareholders" general meeting.

Business
There are many ways in which a business may be owned under the legal system of England and Wales. Different types of ownership are suitable for organisations depending on the degree of control the owners wish to have over the business. The choice of ownership methor also relates to the organisations ability to raise funds for the business activities.

Business judgment rule
The Business judgment rule is an American case law-derived concept in corporations law whereby the "directors of a corporation .

Share
In business and finance, a share of stock (also referred to as equity share) means a share of ownership in a corporation (company.) In the plural, stocks is often used as a synonym for shares especially in the United States, but it is less commonly used that way outside of North America.

In the United Kingdom, South Africa, and Australia, stock can also refer to completely different financial instruments such as government bonds or, less commonly, to all kinds of marketable securities.

Shareholder
A mutual shareholder or stockholder is an individual or company (including a corporation) that legally owns one or more shares of stock in a joint stock company. A company"s shareholder s collectively own that company. Thus, the typical goal of such companies is to enhance shareholder value.

Subsidiary
A subsidiary, in business matters, is an entity that is controlled by a bigger and more powerful entity. The controlled entity is called a company, corporation, or limited liability company and in some cases can be a government or state-owned enterprise, and the controlling entity is called its parent (or the parent company.) The reason for this distinction is that a lone company cannot be a subsidiary of any organization; only an entity representing a legal fiction as a separate entity can be a subsidiary.

Duty
Duty (from "due," that which is owing, O. Fr. deu, did, past participle of devoir; Lat. debere, debitum; cf.

Obligation
An obligation is a requirement to take some course of action, whether legal or moral. There are also obligation s in other normative contexts, such as obligation s of etiquette, social obligation s, and possibly in terms of politics, where obligation s are requirements which must be fulfilled. These are generally legal obligation s, which can incur a penalty for unfulfilment, although certain people are obliged to carry out certain actions for other reasons as well, whether as a tradition or for social reasons.

Warranty
In commercial and consumer transactions, a warranty is an obligation or guarantee that an article or service sold is as factually stated or legally implied by the seller, and that often provides for a specific remedy such as repair or replacement in the event the article or service fails to meet the warranty. A breach of warranty occurs when the promise is broken, i.e., a product is defective or not as should be expected by a reasonable buyer.

In business and legal transactions, a warranty is an assurance by one party to the other party that certain facts or conditions are true or will happen; the other party is permitted to rely on that assurance and seek some type of remedy if it is not true or followed.

Constitution

· Apostolic Constitution (a class of Roman Catholic Church documents)
· Constitution of the Roman Republic
· Constitutional court
· Constitutionalism
· Corporate Constitution
· Judicial activism
· Judicial restraint
· Judicial review

Judicial philosophies of Constitutional interpretation (note: generally specific to United States Constitutional law)

· List of national Constitutions
· Originalism
· Strict constructionism
· Textualism
· Proposed European Union Constitution

· Treaty of Lisbon (adopts same changes, but without Constitutional name)
· United Nations Charter

Poison pill

Poison pill is a term referring to any strategy, generally in business or politics, to increase the likelihood of negative results over positive ones for a party that attempts any kind of takeover. It derives from its original meaning of a literal Poison pill carried by various spies throughout history, taken when discovered to eliminate the possibility of being interrogated for the enemy"s gain.

In publicly held companies, various methods to deter coercive takeover bids are called " Poison pill s".

Securities and Exchange Commission

The U.S. Securities and Exchange Commission is an independent agency of the United States government which holds primary responsibility for enforcing the federal securities laws and regulating the securities industry, the nation"s stock and options exchanges, and other electronic securities markets. The SEC was created by section 4 of the Securities Exchange Act of 1934 (now codified as 15 U.S.C. Â§ 78d and commonly referred to as the 1934 Act.)

Takeovers

Takeovers in the UK (meaning acquisitions of public companies only) are governed by the City Code on Takeovers and Mergers, also known as the "City Code" or "Takeover Code". The rules for a takeover, can be found what is primarily known as "The Blue Book". The Code used to be a non-statutory set of rules that was controlled by City institutions on a theoretically voluntary basis.

Tender offer

Tender offer is a corporate finance term denoting a type of takeover bid. The Tender offer is a public, open offer or invitation (usually announced in a newspaper advertisement) by a prospective acquirer to all stockholders of a publicly traded corporation (the target corporation) to tender their stock for sale at a specified price during a specified time, subject to the tendering of a minimum and maximum number of shares. In a Tender offer, the bidder contacts shareholders directly; the directors of the company may or may not have endorsed the Tender offer proposal.

United States

- History of competition law
- Monopoly
  - Coercive monopoly
  - Natural monopoly
  - Barriers to entry
  - Market power
  - SSNIP test
  - Relevant market
  - Merger control

Anti-competitive practices

- Monopolization
- Collusion
- Formation of cartels
- Price fixing
- Bid rigging
- Product bundling and tying
- Refusal to deal
  - Group boycott
  - Exclusive dealing
  - Dividing territories
  - Conscious parallelism
  - Predatory pricing
  - Misuse of patents and copyrights

Laws and doctrines

United States

- Sherman Antitrust Act
- Clayton Antitrust Act
- Robinson-Patman Act
- FTC Act
- Hart-Scott-Rodino Act
- Merger guidelines
- Essential facilities doctrine
- Noerr-Pennington doctrine
- Parker immunity doctrine
- Rule of reason

Europe

- UK competition law
- Irish competition law

Australia

· Trade Practices Act 1974

Enforcement authorities and organizations

Competition law history refers to attempts by governments to regulate competitive markets for goods and services, leading up to the modern competition or antitrust laws around the world today. The earliest records traces back to the efforts of Roman legislators to control price fluctuations and unfair trade practices. Through the Middle Ages in Europe, Kings and Queens repeatedly cracked down on monopolies, including those created through state legislation.

· International Competition Network
· List of competition regulators

Golden parachute

A Golden parachute is an agreement between a company and an employee (usually upper executive) specifying that the employee will receive certain significant benefits if employment is terminated. Sometimes, certain conditions, typically a change in company ownership, must be met, but often the cause of termination is unspecified. These benefits may include severance pay, cash bonuses, stock options, or other benefits.

Greenmail

Greenmail or Greenmailing is the practice of purchasing enough shares in a firm to threaten a takeover and thereby forcing the target firm to buy those shares back at a premium in order to suspend the takeover.

The term is a neologism derived from blackmail and greenback as commentators and journalists saw the practice of said corporate raiders as attempts by well-financed individuals to blackmail a company into handing over money by using the threat of a takeover.

Corporate raids aim to generate large amounts of money by hostile takeovers of large, often undervalued or inefficient companies, by either asset stripping and/or replacing management and employees.

Chief brand officer

A Chief brand officer is a relatively new executive level position at a corporation, company, organization typically reporting directly to the CEO or board of directors. The Chief brand officer is responsible for a brand''s image, experience, and promise, and propagating it throughout all aspects of the company. The brand officer oversees marketing, advertising, design, public relations and customer service departments.

Liquidation

In law, Liquidation refers to the process by which a company (or part of a company) is brought to an end, and the assets and property of the company redistributed. Liquidation can also be referred to as winding-up or dissolution, although dissolution technically refers to the last stage of Liquidation. The process of Liquidation also arises when customs, an authority or agency in a country responsible for collecting and safeguarding customs duties, determines the final computation or ascertainment of the duties or drawback accruing on an entry.

Ultra vires	Ultra vires is a Latin phrase that literally means "beyond the powers". Its inverse is called intra vires, meaning "within the powers". It is used as a legal term in a number of common law contexts.
Bankruptcy	Bankruptcy is a legally declared inability or impairment of ability of an individual or organization to pay its creditors. Creditors may file a Bankruptcy petition against a debtor ("involuntary Bankruptcy") in an effort to recoup a portion of what they are owed or initiate a restructuring. In the majority of cases, however, Bankruptcy is initiated by the debtor (a "voluntary Bankruptcy" that is filed by the insolvent individual or organization).
Limited liability	Limited liability is a concept whereby a person"s financial liability is limited to a fixed sum, most commonly the value of a person"s investment in a company or partnership with Limited liability. In other words, if a company with Limited liability is sued, then the plaintiffs are suing the company, not its owners or investors. A shareholder in a limited company is not personally liable for any of the debts of the company, other than for the value of his investment in that company.
Limited liability company	A Limited liability company in the law of the vast majority of United States jurisdictions is a legal form of business company that provides limited liability to its owners. Often incorrectly called a "limited liability corporation" (instead of company), it is a hybrid business entity having certain characteristics of both a corporation and a partnership or sole proprietorship (depending on how many owners there are). An Limited liability company, although a business entity, is a type of unincorporated association and is not a corporation.
Limited partnership	A Limited partnership is a form of partnership similar to a general partnership, except that in addition to one or more general partners (GPs), there are one or more limited partners (Limited partnerships). It is a partnership in which only one partner is required to be a general partner. The GPs are, in all major respects, in the same legal position as partners in a conventional firm, i.e. they have management control, share the right to use partnership property, share the profits of the firm in predefined proportions, and have joint and several liability for the debts of the partnership.
Proprietorship	A sole Proprietorship). All assets of the business are owned by the proprietor and all debts of the business are his debts and he must pay them from his personal resources.
Sole proprietorship	A Sole proprietorship, or simply proprietorship is a type of business entity which legally has no separate existence from its owner. Hence, the limitations of liability enjoyed by a corporation and limited liability partnerships do not apply to sole proprietors. All debts of the business are debts of the owner.

Sarbanes-Oxley Act	The Sarbanes-Oxley Act of 2002 (Pub.L. 107-204, 116 Stat. 745, enacted July 30, 2002), also known as the Public Company Accounting Reform and Investor Protection Act of 2002 and commonly called Sarbanes-Oxley, Sarbox or SOX, is a United States federal law enacted on July 30, 2002, as a reaction to a number of major corporate and accounting scandals including those affecting Enron, Tyco International, Adelphia, Peregrine Systems and WorldCom.
Securities Act	Congress enacted the Securities Act of 1933 (the "1933 Act," the "Truth in Securities Act" or the "Federal Securities Act", 48 Stat. 74, enacted 1933-05-27, codified at 15 U.S.C. Â§ 77a et seq.), in the aftermath of the stock market crash of 1929 and during the ensuing Great Depression.
Securities Exchange Act	The Securities Exchange Act of 1934 is a law governing the secondary trading of securities (stocks, bonds, and debentures) in the United States of America. The Act, 48 Stat. 881 (enacted June 6, 1934), codified at 15 U.S.C.
Securities and Exchange Commission	The U.S. Securities and Exchange Commission is an independent agency of the United States government which holds primary responsibility for enforcing the federal securities laws and regulating the securities industry, the nation"s stock and options exchanges, and other electronic securities markets. The SEC was created by section 4 of the Securities Exchange Act of 1934 (now codified as 15 U.S.C. Â§ 78d and commonly referred to as the 1934 Act.)
Job description	A Job description is a list of the general tasks and responsibilities of a position. Typically, it also includes to whom the position reports, specifications such as the qualifications needed by the person in the job, salary range for the position, etc. A Job description is usually developed by conducting a job analysis, which includes examining the tasks and sequences of tasks necessary to perform the job.
Parol evidence	The Parol evidence rule is the legal application of a rule of substantive law in contract cases that prevents a party to a written contract from contradicting (or sometimes adding to) the terms of the contract by seeking the admission of evidence "extrinsic" (outside) to the contract. For example, Carl agrees in writing to sell Betty a car for $1,000. Betty argues that Carl told her that she would only need to pay Carl $800.
Parol evidence rule	The Parol evidence rule is the legal application of a rule of substantive law in contract cases that prevents a party to a written contract from contradicting (or sometimes adding to) the terms of the contract by seeking the admission of evidence "extrinsic" (outside) to the contract. For example, Carl agrees in writing to sell Betty a car for $1,000. Betty argues that Carl told her that she would only need to pay Carl $800.
Statute	A statute is a formal written enactment of a legislative authority that governs a country, state, city, or county. Typically, statute s command or prohibit something, or declare policy. The word is often used to distinguish law made by legislative bodies from case law and the regulations issued by Government agencies.
Statute of Frauds	The Statute of Frauds refers to the requirement that certain kinds of contracts be made in writing and signed. Traditionally, the Statute of Frauds requires a writing signed by the defendant in the following circumstances:

· Contracts in consideration of marriage.
· Contracts which cannot be performed within one year.
· Contracts for the transfer of an interest in land.
· Contracts by the executor of a will to pay a debt of the estate with their own money.
· Contracts for the sale of goods above a certain value.
· Contracts in which one party becomes a surety (acts as guarantor) for another party"s debt or other obligation.

This can be remembered by the mnemonic "MY LEGS": Marriage, one year, land, executor, goods, surety.

The term Statute of Frauds comes from an English Act of Parliament passed in 1677 (authored by Sir Leoline Jenkins and passed by the Cavalier Parliament), and more properly called An Act for Prevention of Frauds and Perjuries. Many common law jurisdictions have made similar statutory provisions, while a number of civil law jurisdictions have equivalent legislation incorporated into their civil codes.

Consideration

Consideration is the legal concept of value in connection with contracts. It is anything of value in the common sense, promised to another when making a contract. It can take the form of money, physical objects, services, promised actions, or even abstinence from a future action.

Personal Property

Personal property is a type of property. In the common law systems Personal property may also be called chattels or personalty. It is distinguished from real property, or real estate.

Personal property may be classified in a variety of ways. Tangible Personal property refers to any type of property that can generally be moved (i.e., it is not attached to real property or land), touched or felt. These generally include items such as furniture, clothing, jewelry, art, writings, or household goods. In some cases, there can be formal title documents that show the ownership and transfer rights of that property after a person"s death (for example, motor vehicles, boats, etc.) In many cases, however, tangible Personal property will not be "titled" in an owner"s name and is presumed to be whatever property he or she was in possession of at the time of his or her death.

Intangible Personal property or "intangibles" refers to Personal property that cannot actually be moved, touched or felt, but instead represents something of value such as negotiable instruments, securities, goods, and intangible assets including chose in action.

Regulation D

Under the Securities Act of 1933, any offer to sell securities must either be registered with the SEC or meet an exemption. Regulation D contains three rules providing exemptions from the registration requirements, allowing some companies to offer and sell their securities without having to register the securities with the SEC. Rule 501 of Reg D contains definitions that apply to the rest of Reg D. Rule 502 contains the general conditions that must be met to take advantage of the exemptions under Regulation D. Generally speaking, these conditions are (1) that all sales within a certain time period that are part of the same Reg D offering must be "integrated", meaning they must be treated as one offering, (2) information and disclosures must be provided, (3) there must be no "general solicitation", and (4) that the securities being sold contain restrictions on their resale.

Reseller

A reseller is a company or individual that purchases goods or services with the intention of reselling them rather than consuming or using them. This is usually done for profit (but could be resold at a loss.) One example can be found in the industry of telecommunications, where companies buy excess amounts of transmission capacity or call time from other carriers and resell it to smaller carriers.

Private placement

In the United States, a private placement is an offering of securities that are not registered with the Securities and Exchange Commission (SEC.) Such offerings exploit an exemption offered by the Securities Act of 1933 that comes with several restrictions, including a prohibition against general solicitation. This exemption allows companies to avoid quarterly reporting requirements and many of the legal liabilities associated with the Sarbanes-Oxley Act.

Stock Certificate

In corporate law, a Stock certificate is a legal document that certifies ownership of a specific number of stock shares in a corporation. In large corporations, buying shares does not always lead to a Stock certificate

In at least one unspecified country, usually only shareholders with Stock certificate s can vote in a shareholders" general meeting.

Private Securities Litigation Reform Act

The United States Private Securities Litigation Reform Act of 1995, Pub. L. 104-67, 109 Stat. 737 (codified as amended in scattered sections of 15 U.S.C.) ("Private Securities Litigation Reform Act") implemented several substantive changes affecting certain cases brought under the federal securities laws, including changes related to pleading, discovery, liability, class representation, and awards fees and expenses.

Securities Litigation Uniform Standards Act

The Securities Litigation Uniform Standards Act of 1998 is a federal legislative act in the United States regarding private class action lawsuits for securities fraud. Securities Litigation Uniform Standards Act amended portions of the Securities Act of 1933 and the Securities Exchange Act of 1934 to preempt certain class actions that alleged fraud under state law "in connection with the purchase or sale" of securities. Such lawsuits cannot be filed in state or federal court.

Misappropriation

In law, Misappropriation is the intentional, illegal use of the property or funds of another person for one"s own use or other unauthorized purpose, particularly by a public official, a trustee of a trust, an executor or administrator of a dead person"s estate or by any person with a responsibility to care for and protect another"s assets (a fiduciary duty). It is a felony, a crime punishable by a prison sentence.

Misappropriation does not occur in instances where the capital was obtained for a service rendered.

Profit

A profit , in the law of real property, is a nonpossessory interest in land similar to the better-known easement, which gives the holder the right to take natural resources such as petroleum, minerals, timber, and wild game from the land of another. Indeed, because of the necessity of allowing access to the land so that resources may be gathered, every profit contains an implied easement for the owner of the profit to enter the other party"s land for the purpose of collecting the resources permitted by the profit.

Like an easement, profits can be created expressly by an agreement between the property owner and the owner of the profit, or by prescription, where the owner of the profit has made "open and notorious" use of the land for a continuous and uninterrupted statutory period.

Chief brand officer

A Chief brand officer is a relatively new executive level position at a corporation, company, organization typically reporting directly to the CEO or board of directors. The Chief brand officer is responsible for a brand"s image, experience, and promise, and propagating it throughout all aspects of the company. The brand officer oversees marketing, advertising, design, public relations and customer service departments.

Rescission

In contract law, rescission has been defined as the unmaking of a contract between parties. rescission is the unwinding of a transaction. This is done to bring the parties, as far as possible, back to the position in which they were before they entered into a contract (the "status quo ante".)

Contract

Agreement is said to be reached when an offer capable of immediate acceptance is met with a "mirror image" acceptance (ie, an unqualified acceptance). The parties must have the necessary capacity to Contract and the Contract must not be either trifling, indeterminate, impossible or illegal. Contract law is based on the principle expressed in the Latin phrase pacta sunt servanda .

Corporate governance

Corporate governance is the set of processes, customs, policies, laws, and institutions affecting the way a corporation (or company) is directed, administered or controlled. Corporate governance also includes the relationships among the many stakeholders involved and the goals for which the corporation is governed. The principal stakeholders are the shareholders/members, management, and the board of directors.

Shareholder

A mutual shareholder or stockholder is an individual or company (including a corporation) that legally owns one or more shares of stock in a joint stock company. A company"s shareholder s collectively own that company. Thus, the typical goal of such companies is to enhance shareholder value.

Option

In finance, an option is a contract between a buyer and a seller that gives the buyer the right--but not the obligation--to buy or to sell a particular asset (the underlying asset) at a later day at an agreed price. In return for granting the option, the seller collects a payment (the premium) from the buyer. A call option gives the buyer the right to buy the underlying asset; a put option gives the buyer of the option the right to sell the underlying asset.

Options backdating

Options backdating is the practice of granting an employee stock option that is dated prior to the date that the company actually granted the option. This practice raises a number of legal and accounting issues. The practice of backdating itself is not illegal, nor is granting of discounted stock options.

Audit committee	In a publicly-held company, an Audit committee is an operating committee of the Board of Directors, typically charged with oversight of financial reporting and disclosure. Committee members are drawn from members of the Company"s board of directors, with a Chairperson selected from among the members. An Audit committee of a publicly-traded company in the United States is composed of independent and outside directors referred to as non-executive directors, at least one of which is typically a financial expert.
Misrepresentation	Misrepresentation is a contract law concept. It means a false statement of fact made by one party to another party, which has the effect of inducing that party into the contract. For example, under certain circumstances, false statements or promises made by a seller of goods regarding the quality or nature of the product that the seller has may constitute Misrepresentation.
Uniform Securities Act	The Uniform Securities Act is a model statute designed to guide each state in drafting its state securities law. It was created by the National Conference of Commissioners on Uniform State Laws (NCCUSL.) The purpose of the Uniform Securities Act is to provide model legislation that can be adopted by a state to deal with securities fraud at the state level, supplementing enforcement and regulation efforts of the U.S. Securities and Exchange Commission (SEC.)
Room	A Room, in architecture, is any distinguishable space within a structure. Most typically a Room is separated by interior walls from other spaces or passageways; moreover, it is separated by an exterior wall from outdoor areas, sometimes with a door. Historically the use of Rooms dates at least to early Minoan cultures about 2200 BC, where excavations on Santorini, Greece at Akrotiri reveal clearly defined Rooms within structures.
Securities Fraud	Securities fraud is a practice in which investors make purchase or sale decisions on the basis of false information, frequently resulting in losses, in violation of the securities laws. Generally speaking, Securities fraud consists of deceptive practices in the stock and commodity markets, and occurs when investors are enticed to part with their money based on untrue statements. Securities fraud includes outright theft from investors and misstatements on a public company"s financial reports.

Business

There are many ways in which a business may be owned under the legal system of England and Wales. Different types of ownership are suitable for organisations depending on the degree of control the owners wish to have over the business. The choice of ownership methor also relates to the organisations ability to raise funds for the business activities.

United States

· History of competition law
· Monopoly

· Coercive monopoly
· Natural monopoly
· Barriers to entry
· Market power
· SSNIP test
· Relevant market
· Merger control

Anti-competitive practices

· Monopolization
· Collusion

· Formation of cartels
· Price fixing
· Bid rigging
· Product bundling and tying
· Refusal to deal

· Group boycott
· Exclusive dealing
· Dividing territories
· Conscious parallelism
· Predatory pricing
· Misuse of patents and copyrights

Laws and doctrines

United States

· Sherman Antitrust Act
· Clayton Antitrust Act
· Robinson-Patman Act
· FTC Act
· Hart-Scott-Rodino Act
· Merger guidelines
· Essential facilities doctrine
· Noerr-Pennington doctrine
· Parker immunity doctrine
· Rule of reason

Europe

· UK competition law
· Irish competition law

Australia

· Trade Practices Act 1974

Enforcement authorities and organizations

Competition law history refers to attempts by governments to regulate competitive markets for goods and services, leading up to the modern competition or antitrust laws around the world today. The earliest records traces back to the efforts of Roman legislators to control price fluctuations and unfair trade practices. Through the Middle Ages in Europe, Kings and Queens repeatedly cracked down on monopolies, including those created through state legislation.

· International Competition Network
· List of competition regulators

Limited liability — Limited liability is a concept whereby a person"s financial liability is limited to a fixed sum, most commonly the value of a person"s investment in a company or partnership with Limited liability. In other words, if a company with Limited liability is sued, then the plaintiffs are suing the company, not its owners or investors. A shareholder in a limited company is not personally liable for any of the debts of the company, other than for the value of his investment in that company.

Partnership — A Partnership is a type of business entity in which partners (owners) share with each other the profits or losses of the business. Partnership s are often favored over corporations for taxation purposes, as the Partnership structure does not generally incur a tax on profits before it is distributed to the partners (i.e. there is no dividend tax levied.) However, depending on the Partnership structure and the jurisdiction in which it operates, owners of a Partnership may be exposed to greater personal liability than they would as shareholders of a corporation.

Duty — Duty (from "due," that which is owing, O. Fr. deu, did, past participle of devoir; Lat. debere, debitum; cf.

Obligation

An obligation is a requirement to take some course of action, whether legal or moral. There are also obligation s in other normative contexts, such as obligation s of etiquette, social obligation s, and possibly in terms of politics, where obligation s are requirements which must be fulfilled. These are generally legal obligation s, which can incur a penalty for unfulfilment, although certain people are obliged to carry out certain actions for other reasons as well, whether as a tradition or for social reasons.

S corporation

An S corporation for United States federal income tax purposes, is a corporation that makes a valid election to be taxed under Subchapter S of Chapter 1 of the Internal Revenue Code.

In general, S corporation s do not pay any income taxes. Instead, the corporation"s income or losses are divided among and passed through to its shareholders.

Consideration

Consideration is the legal concept of value in connection with contracts. It is anything of value in the common sense, promised to another when making a contract. It can take the form of money, physical objects, services, promised actions, or even abstinence from a future action.

Franchise Tax

Franchise tax is a tax charged by some US states to corporations formed in those states based on the number of shares they issue or, in some cases, the amount of their assets. The purpose of the tax is to raise revenue for the state. The State of Delaware has a significant Franchise tax, while other states, such as Nevada, have none at all or a smaller one.

Trademark

A trademark or trade mark is a distinctive sign or indicator used by an individual, business organization and to distinguish its products or services from those of other entities.

A trademark is designated by the following symbols:

· â„¢ (for an unregistered trademark that is, a mark used to promote or brand goods);
· â„ (for an unregistered service mark, that is, a mark used to promote or brand services); and
· Â® (for a registered trademark)

A trademark is a type of intellectual property, and typically a name, word, phrase, logo, symbol, design, image, or a combination of these elements. There is also a range of non-conventional trademark s comprising marks which do not fall into these standard categories.

The owner of a registered trademark may commence legal proceedings for trademark infringement to prevent unauthorized use of that trademark

Contract

Agreement is said to be reached when an offer capable of immediate acceptance is met with a "mirror image" acceptance (ie, an unqualified acceptance). The parties must have the necessary capacity to Contract and the Contract must not be either trifling, indeterminate, impossible or illegal. Contract law is based on the principle expressed in the Latin phrase pacta sunt servanda .

Limited liability company	A Limited liability company in the law of the vast majority of United States jurisdictions is a legal form of business company that provides limited liability to its owners. Often incorrectly called a "limited liability corporation" (instead of company), it is a hybrid business entity having certain characteristics of both a corporation and a partnership or sole proprietorship (depending on how many owners there are). An Limited liability company, although a business entity, is a type of unincorporated association and is not a corporation.
Numerary	Numerary is a civil designation for persons who are incorporated in a fixed or permanent way to a society or group: regular member of the working staff, permanent staff distinguished from a super Numerary . The term Numerary and its counterpart, "super Numerary ," originated in Spanish and Latin American academy and government; it is now also used in countries all over the world, such as France, the U.S., England, Italy, etc. There are Numerary members of surgical organizations, of universities, of gastronomical associations, etc.
Chief brand officer	A Chief brand officer is a relatively new executive level position at a corporation, company, organization typically reporting directly to the CEO or board of directors. The Chief brand officer is responsible for a brand"s image, experience, and promise, and propagating it throughout all aspects of the company. The brand officer oversees marketing, advertising, design, public relations and customer service departments.
Operating Agreement	An operating agreement is an agreement among limited liability company ("LLC") Members governing the LLC"s business, and Member"s financial and managerial rights and duties. Many states require an LLC to have an operating agreement. LLCs operating without an operating agreement are governed by the State"s default rules contained in the relevant statute and developed through state court decisions.
Business judgment rule	The Business judgment rule is an American case law-derived concept in corporations law whereby the "directors of a corporation .
Board of directors	A Board of directors is a body of elected or appointed members who jointly oversee the activities of a company or organization. The body sometimes has a different name, such as board of trustees, board of governors, board of managers, or executive board. It is often simply referred to as "the board." A board"s activities are determined by the powers, duties, and responsibilities delegated to it or conferred on it by an authority outside itself.
Patent	A patent is a set of exclusive rights granted by a state to an inventor or his assignee for a limited period of time in exchange for a disclosure of an invention. The procedure for granting patent s, the requirements placed on the patent ee and the extent of the exclusive rights vary widely between countries according to national laws and international agreements. Typically, however, a patent application must include one or more claims defining the invention which must be new, inventive, and useful or industrially applicable.

Trade secret	A trade secret is a formula, practice, process, design, instrument, pattern by which a business can obtain an economic advantage over competitors or customers. In some jurisdictions, such secrets are referred to as "confidential information" or "classified information". The precise language by which a trade secret is defined varies by jurisdiction (as do the particular types of information that are subject to trade secret protection.)
United States Patent and Trademark Office	The United States Patent and Trademark Office is an agency in the United States Department of Commerce that issues patents to inventors and businesses for their inventions, and trademark registration for product and intellectual property identification. The USPTO is currently based in Alexandria, Virginia, after a 2006 move from the Crystal City area of Arlington, Virginia. The offices under Patents and the Chief Information Officer that remained just outside the southern end of Crystal City completed moving to Randolph Square, a brand new building in Shirlington Village, on 27 April 2009.
Employment	Employment is a contract between two parties, one being the employer and the other being the employee. An employee may be defined as: "A person in the service of another under any contract of hire, express or implied, oral or written, where the employer has the power or right to control and direct the employee in the material details of how the work is to be performed." Black"s Law Dictionary page 471 (5th ed. 1979).
Lease	A Lease is a contract conferring a right on one person to possess property belonging to another person (called a landlord or lessor) to the exclusion of the owner landlord, and all others except with the invitation of the tenant. It is a rental agreement between landlord and tenant. The relationship between the tenant and the landlord is called a tenancy, and the right to possession by the tenant is sometimes called a Leasehold interest.
Buy-sell Agreement	A Buy-sell agreement may be thought of as a sort of "premarital agreement" between business partners/shareholders. It is sometimes called a "business will". An insured Buy-sell agreement (agreement funded with life insurance on the participating owner"s lives) is often recommended by business succession specialists and financial planners to ensure the buy-sell arrangement is well-funded and also to guarantee there will be money when the buy-sell event is triggered.
United Nations Convention on Contracts for the International Sale of Goods	The United Nations Convention on Contracts for the International Sale of Goods is a treaty offering a uniform international sales law that, as of July 2008, had been ratified by 71 countries that account for a significant proportion of world trade, making it one of the most successful international uniform laws. Japan is the most recent State to have ratified the Convention. It allows exporters to avoid choice of law issues as it offers "accepted substantive rules on which contracting parties, courts, and arbitrators may rely".
Negotiable instrument	A Negotiable instrument is a specialized type of "contract" for the payment of money that is unconditional and capable of transfer by negotiation. Common examples include cheques, banknotes (paper money), and commercial paper.

A Negotiable instrument is not a contract, as contract formation requires an offer, acceptance, and consideration, none of which is an element of a Negotiable instrument.

Refusal to deal

Refusal to deal is one of several anti-competitive practices forbidden in countries which have restricted market economies. For example, in Australia:

· Agreements involving competitors that involve restricting the supply of goods are prohibited if they have the purpose or effect of substantially lessening competition in a market in which the businesses operate. "Refusal to deal" Reference: The Competition Act, 2002 (India) S4-d."Refusal to deal" includes any agreement which restricts, or is likely to restrict, by any method the persons or classes of persons to whom goods are sold or from whom goods are bought

Statute

A statute is a formal written enactment of a legislative authority that governs a country, state, city, or county. Typically, statute s command or prohibit something, or declare policy. The word is often used to distinguish law made by legislative bodies from case law and the regulations issued by Government agencies.

Statute of Frauds

The Statute of Frauds refers to the requirement that certain kinds of contracts be made in writing and signed.

Traditionally, the Statute of Frauds requires a writing signed by the defendant in the following circumstances:

· Contracts in consideration of marriage.
· Contracts which cannot be performed within one year.
· Contracts for the transfer of an interest in land.
· Contracts by the executor of a will to pay a debt of the estate with their own money.
· Contracts for the sale of goods above a certain value.
· Contracts in which one party becomes a surety (acts as guarantor) for another party"s debt or other obligation.

This can be remembered by the mnemonic "MY LEGS": Marriage, one year, land, executor, goods, surety.

The term Statute of Frauds comes from an English Act of Parliament passed in 1677 (authored by Sir Leoline Jenkins and passed by the Cavalier Parliament), and more properly called An Act for Prevention of Frauds and Perjuries. Many common law jurisdictions have made similar statutory provisions, while a number of civil law jurisdictions have equivalent legislation incorporated into their civil codes.

Shareholder

A mutual shareholder or stockholder is an individual or company (including a corporation) that legally owns one or more shares of stock in a joint stock company. A company"s shareholder s collectively own that company. Thus, the typical goal of such companies is to enhance shareholder value.

Employment discrimination

Employment discrimination (or workplace discrimination) is discrimination in hiring, promotion, job assignment, termination, and compensation. It includes various types of harassment.

Many jurisdictions prohibit some types of Employment discrimination, often by forbidding discrimination based on certain traits ("protected categories").

Occupational Safety and Health Administration: The United States Occupational Safety and Health Administration is an agency of the United States Department of Labor. It was created by Congress under the Occupational Safety and Health Act, signed by President Richard M. Nixon, on December 29, 1970. Its mission is to prevent work-related injuries, illnesses, and deaths by issuing and enforcing rules (called standards) for workplace safety and health.

Bankruptcy: Bankruptcy is a legally declared inability or impairment of ability of an individual or organization to pay its creditors. Creditors may file a Bankruptcy petition against a debtor ("involuntary Bankruptcy") in an effort to recoup a portion of what they are owed or initiate a restructuring. In the majority of cases, however, Bankruptcy is initiated by the debtor (a "voluntary Bankruptcy" that is filed by the insolvent individual or organization).

Firing: Firing is the act by an employer of terminating employment. Though such a decision can be made by an employer for a variety of reasons, ranging from an economic downturn to performance-related problems on the part of the employee, being fired has a strong stigma in many cultures. To be fired, as opposed to quitting voluntarily (or being laid off), is often perceived as being the employee"s fault, and is therefore considered to be disgraceful and a sign of failure.

Unemployment: Unemployment occurs when a person is available to work and seeking work but currently without work. The prevalence of Unemployment is usually measured using the Unemployment rate, which is defined as the percentage of those in the labor force who are unemployed. The Unemployment rate is also used in economic studies and economic indexes such as the United States" Conference Board"s Index of Leading Indicators as a measure of the state of the macroeconomics.

Unemployment Compensation: Unemployment compensation is money received by an unemployed worker from the United States or a state. In the United States, this compensation is classified as a type of social welfare benefit. According to the Internal Revenue Code, these types of benefits are to be included in a taxpayer"s gross income.

Independent contractor: An Independent contractor is a natural person, business, or corporation which provides goods or services to another entity under terms specified in a contract or within a verbal agreement. Unlike an employee, an Independent contractor does not work regularly for an employer but works as and when required, during which time she or he may be subject to the Law of Agency. Independent contractors are usually paid on a freelance basis.

Corporate governance: Corporate governance is the set of processes, customs, policies, laws, and institutions affecting the way a corporation (or company) is directed, administered or controlled. Corporate governance also includes the relationships among the many stakeholders involved and the goals for which the corporation is governed. The principal stakeholders are the shareholders/members, management, and the board of directors.

Sarbanes-Oxley Act

The Sarbanes-Oxley Act of 2002 (Pub.L. 107-204, 116 Stat. 745, enacted July 30, 2002), also known as the Public Company Accounting Reform and Investor Protection Act of 2002 and commonly called Sarbanes-Oxley, Sarbox or SOX, is a United States federal law enacted on July 30, 2002, as a reaction to a number of major corporate and accounting scandals including those affecting Enron, Tyco International, Adelphia, Peregrine Systems and WorldCom.

Securities and Exchange Commission

The U.S. Securities and Exchange Commission is an independent agency of the United States government which holds primary responsibility for enforcing the federal securities laws and regulating the securities industry, the nation"s stock and options exchanges, and other electronic securities markets. The SEC was created by section 4 of the Securities Exchange Act of 1934 (now codified as 15 U.S.C. Â§ 78d and commonly referred to as the 1934 Act.)

Tyco International

Tyco International Ltd. NYSE: TYC is a highly diversified global manufacturing company incorporated in Switzerland, with United States operational headquarters in Princeton, New Jersey (Tyco International (US) Inc).. Tyco International is composed of five major business segments: ADT Worldwide, Fire Protection Services, Safety Products, Flow Control and Electrical and Metal Products.

Insolvency

Insolvency means the inability to pay one"s debts as they fall due. Usually used in Business terms, Insolvency refers to the inability for a company to pay off its debts.

Business Insolvency is defined in two different ways:

Cash flow Insolvency

Unable to pay debts as they fall due.

Misrepresentation

Misrepresentation is a contract law concept. It means a false statement of fact made by one party to another party, which has the effect of inducing that party into the contract. For example, under certain circumstances, false statements or promises made by a seller of goods regarding the quality or nature of the product that the seller has may constitute Misrepresentation.

Sentencing guidelines

The Federal Sentencing guidelines are rules that set out a uniform sentencing policy for convicted felons in the United States federal courts system.

The Guidelines are the product of the United States Sentencing Commission and are part of an overall federal sentencing reform package that took effect in the mid-1960s. The implementation of this reform package was the result of bipartisan cooperation, led chiefly by Senator Edward Kennedy, as Chair of the Senate Judiciary Committee, and Attorney General Edwin Meese.

United States Sentencing Commission

The United States Sentencing Commission is an independent agency of the judicial branch of the federal government of the United States. It is responsible for articulating the sentencing guidelines for the United States federal courts. The Commission promulgates the Federal Sentencing Guidelines, which replaced the prior system of indeterminate sentencing that allowed trial judges to give sentences ranging from probation to the maximum statutory punishment for the offense.

Room

A Room, in architecture, is any distinguishable space within a structure. Most typically a Room is separated by interior walls from other spaces or passageways; moreover, it is separated by an exterior wall from outdoor areas, sometimes with a door. Historically the use of Rooms dates at least to early Minoan cultures about 2200 BC, where excavations on Santorini, Greece at Akrotiri reveal clearly defined Rooms within structures.

Securities Fraud

Securities fraud is a practice in which investors make purchase or sale decisions on the basis of false information, frequently resulting in losses, in violation of the securities laws.

Generally speaking, Securities fraud consists of deceptive practices in the stock and commodity markets, and occurs when investors are enticed to part with their money based on untrue statements.

Securities fraud includes outright theft from investors and misstatements on a public company"s financial reports.

White-collar

The term white-collar worker refers to a salaried professional or an educated worker who performs semi-professional office, administrative, and sales coordination tasks, as opposed to a blue-collar worker, whose job requires manual labor. "white-collar work" is an informal term, defined in contrast to "blue-collar work".

The term "white collar" was first used by Upton Sinclair in relation to modern clerical, administrative and management workers during the 1930s.

White-collar Crime

Within the field of criminology, White-collar crime has been defined by Edwin Sutherland as "a crime committed by a person of respectability and high social status in the course of his occupation" (1949.) Sutherland was a proponent of Symbolic Interactionism, and believed that criminal behavior was learned from interpersonal interaction with others. White-collar crime therefore overlaps with corporate crime because the opportunity for fraud, bribery, insider trading, embezzlement, computer crime, and forgery is more available to white-collar employees.

Wire Fraud

Wire fraud is a legal concept in the United States Code which provides for enhanced penalty of any criminally fraudulent activity if it is determined that the activity involved electronic communications of any kind, at any phase of the event. As in the case of mail fraud, this statute is often used as a basis for a separate federal prosecution of what would otherwise have been only a violation of a state law.

The crime of Wire fraud is codified in Title 18 of the United States Code at 18 U.S.C.

Chief brand officer	A Chief brand officer is a relatively new executive level position at a corporation, company, organization typically reporting directly to the CEO or board of directors. The Chief brand officer is responsible for a brand"s image, experience, and promise, and propagating it throughout all aspects of the company. The brand officer oversees marketing, advertising, design, public relations and customer service departments.
Employment	Employment is a contract between two parties, one being the employer and the other being the employee. An employee may be defined as: "A person in the service of another under any contract of hire, express or implied, oral or written, where the employer has the power or right to control and direct the employee in the material details of how the work is to be performed." Black"s Law Dictionary page 471 (5th ed. 1979).
Federal Trade Commission	The Federal Trade Commission is an independent agency of the United States government, established in 1914 by the Federal Trade Commission Act. Its principal mission is the promotion of "consumer protection" and the elimination and prevention of what regulators perceive to be harmfully "anti-competitive" business practices, such as coercive monopoly. The Federal Trade Commission Act was one of President Wilson"s major acts against trusts.
Occupational Safety and Health Administration	The United States Occupational Safety and Health Administration is an agency of the United States Department of Labor. It was created by Congress under the Occupational Safety and Health Act, signed by President Richard M. Nixon, on December 29, 1970. Its mission is to prevent work-related injuries, illnesses, and deaths by issuing and enforcing rules (called standards) for workplace safety and health.
Securities and Exchange Commission	The U.S. Securities and Exchange Commission is an independent agency of the United States government which holds primary responsibility for enforcing the federal securities laws and regulating the securities industry, the nation"s stock and options exchanges, and other electronic securities markets. The SEC was created by section 4 of the Securities Exchange Act of 1934 (now codified as 15 U.S.C. Â§ 78d and commonly referred to as the 1934 Act.)
Business	There are many ways in which a business may be owned under the legal system of England and Wales. Different types of ownership are suitable for organisations depending on the degree of control the owners wish to have over the business. The choice of ownership methor also relates to the organisations ability to raise funds for the business activities.
Job description	A Job description is a list of the general tasks and responsibilities of a position. Typically, it also includes to whom the position reports, specifications such as the qualifications needed by the person in the job, salary range for the position, etc. A Job description is usually developed by conducting a job analysis, which includes examining the tasks and sequences of tasks necessary to perform the job.

Regulatory

Regulation refers to "controlling human or societal behaviour by rules or restrictions." Regulation can take many forms: legal restrictions promulgated by a government authority, self-regulation, social regulation (e.g. norms), co-regulation and market regulation. One can consider regulation as actions of conduct imposing sanctions (such as a fine.) This action of administrative law, or implementing regulatory law, may be contrasted with statutory or case law.

Rulemaking

In administrative law, Rulemaking refers to the process that executive and independent agencies use to create regulations. In general, legislatures first set broad policy mandates by passing laws, then agencies create more detailed regulations through Rulemaking.

By bringing detailed scientific and other types of expertise to bear on policy, the Rulemaking process has been the means by which some of the most far-reaching government regulations of the 20th century have been created.

United States

- History of competition law
- Monopoly
  - Coercive monopoly
  - Natural monopoly
  - Barriers to entry
  - Market power
  - SSNIP test
  - Relevant market
  - Merger control

Anti-competitive practices

- Monopolization
- Collusion

- Formation of cartels
- Price fixing
- Bid rigging
- Product bundling and tying
- Refusal to deal
  - Group boycott
  - Exclusive dealing
  - Dividing territories
  - Conscious parallelism
  - Predatory pricing
  - Misuse of patents and copyrights

Laws and doctrines

United States

- Sherman Antitrust Act
- Clayton Antitrust Act
- Robinson-Patman Act
- FTC Act
- Hart-Scott-Rodino Act
- Merger guidelines
- Essential facilities doctrine
- Noerr-Pennington doctrine
- Parker immunity doctrine
- Rule of reason

Europe

- UK competition law
- Irish competition law

Australia

- Trade Practices Act 1974

Enforcement authorities and organizations

Competition law history refers to attempts by governments to regulate competitive markets for goods and services, leading up to the modern competition or antitrust laws around the world today. The earliest records traces back to the efforts of Roman legislators to control price fluctuations and unfair trade practices. Through the Middle Ages in Europe, Kings and Queens repeatedly cracked down on monopolies, including those created through state legislation.

- International Competition Network
- List of competition regulators

United States Department of Justice: The United States Department of Justice is a Cabinet department in the United States government designed to enforce the law and defend the interests of the United States according to the law and to ensure fair and impartial administration of justice for all Americans The DOJ is administered by the United States Attorney General (see 28 U.S.C.

United States Department of Transportation: The United States Department of Transportation is a federal Cabinet department of the United States government concerned with transportation. It was established by an act of Congress on October 15, 1966 and began operation on April 1, 1967. It is administered by the United States Secretary of Transportation.

United States Department of the Interior: The United States Department of the Interior is the United States federal executive department of the U.S. government responsible for the management and conservation of most federal land and the administration of programs relating to Native Americans, Alaska Natives, and Native Hawaiians, and to insular areas of the United States.

The Department is administered by the United States Secretary of the Interior, who is a member of the Cabinet of the President. The current Secretary is Ken Salazar of Colorado.

Subpoena

A Subpoena is commonly defined as a written command to a person to testify before a court or be punished.
More accurately, a Subpoena is the conditional threat of punishment made by a governmental authority. It is attached to a command, so that if the recipient does not do as commanded then he may be punished.

Constitution

· Apostolic Constitution (a class of Roman Catholic Church documents)
· Constitution of the Roman Republic
· Constitutional court
· Constitutionalism
· Corporate Constitution
· Judicial activism
· Judicial restraint
· Judicial review

Judicial philosophies of Constitutional interpretation (note: generally specific to United States Constitutional law)

· List of national Constitutions
· Originalism
· Strict constructionism
· Textualism
· Proposed European Union Constitution

· Treaty of Lisbon (adopts same changes, but without Constitutional name)
· United Nations Charter

Trade secret

A trade secret is a formula, practice, process, design, instrument, pattern by which a business can obtain an economic advantage over competitors or customers. In some jurisdictions, such secrets are referred to as "confidential information" or "classified information".
The precise language by which a trade secret is defined varies by jurisdiction (as do the particular types of information that are subject to trade secret protection.)

Sunshine Act

The Government in the Sunshine Act is a US law passed in 1976. It is one of a number of so-called sunshine laws, intended to create greater openness in government.
"The Sunshine Act provides, with ten specified exemptions, that "every portion of every meeting of an agency shall be open to public observation." 5 U.S.C.

Federal Trade Commission	The Federal Trade Commission is an independent agency of the United States government, established in 1914 by the Federal Trade Commission Act. Its principal mission is the promotion of "consumer protection" and the elimination and prevention of what regulators perceive to be harmfully "anti-competitive" business practices, such as coercive monopoly. The Federal Trade Commission Act was one of President Wilson"s major acts against trusts.
Statute	A statute is a formal written enactment of a legislative authority that governs a country, state, city, or county. Typically, statute s command or prohibit something, or declare policy. The word is often used to distinguish law made by legislative bodies from case law and the regulations issued by Government agencies.
Restitution	The law of restitution is the law of gains-based recovery. It is to be contrasted with the law of compensation, which is the law of loss-based recovery. Obligations to make restitution and obligations to pay compensation are each a type of legal response to events in the real world.
Consumer Protection	Consumer protection laws are designed to ensure fair competition and the free flow of truthful information in the marketplace. The laws are designed to prevent businesses that engage in fraud or specified unfair practices from gaining an advantage over competitors and may provide additional protection for the weak and those unable to take care of themselves. Consumer protection laws are a form of government regulation which protects the interests of consumers.
Damages	Damages for breach of contract is a common law remedy, available as of right. It is designed to compensate the victim for their actual loss as a result of the wrongdoer"s breach rather than to punish the wrongdoer. If no loss has been occasioned by the plaintiff, only nominal Damages will be awarded.
Telemarketing	Telemarketing is a method of direct marketing in which a salesperson solicits to prospective customers to buy products or services, either over the phone or through a subsequent face to face or Web conferencing appointment scheduled during the call. telemarketing can also include recorded sales pitches programmed to be played over the phone via automatic dialing. telemarketing has come under fire in recent years, being viewed as an annoyance by many.
Treble Damages	Treble damages, in law, is a term that indicates that a statute permits a court to triple the amount of the actual/compensatory damages to be awarded to a prevailing plaintiff, generally in order to punish the losing party for willful conduct. Treble damages are a multiple of, and not an addition to, actual damages. Thus, where a person received an award of $100 for an injury, a court applying Treble damages would raise the award to $300.
United Nations Convention on Contracts for the International Sale of Goods	The United Nations Convention on Contracts for the International Sale of Goods is a treaty offering a uniform international sales law that, as of July 2008, had been ratified by 71 countries that account for a significant proportion of world trade, making it one of the most successful international uniform laws. Japan is the most recent State to have ratified the Convention.

It allows exporters to avoid choice of law issues as it offers "accepted substantive rules on which contracting parties, courts, and arbitrators may rely".

United States

- History of competition law
- Monopoly
  - Coercive monopoly
  - Natural monopoly
  - Barriers to entry
  - Market power
  - SSNIP test
  - Relevant market
  - Merger control

Anti-competitive practices

- Monopolization
- Collusion
- Formation of cartels
- Price fixing
- Bid rigging
- Product bundling and tying
- Refusal to deal
  - Group boycott
  - Exclusive dealing
  - Dividing territories
  - Conscious parallelism
  - Predatory pricing
  - Misuse of patents and copyrights

Laws and doctrines

United States

- Sherman Antitrust Act
- Clayton Antitrust Act
- Robinson-Patman Act
- FTC Act
- Hart-Scott-Rodino Act
- Merger guidelines
- Essential facilities doctrine
- Noerr-Pennington doctrine
- Parker immunity doctrine
- Rule of reason

Europe

· UK competition law
· Irish competition law

Australia

· Trade Practices Act 1974

Enforcement authorities and organizations

Competition law history refers to attempts by governments to regulate competitive markets for goods and services, leading up to the modern competition or antitrust laws around the world today. The earliest records traces back to the efforts of Roman legislators to control price fluctuations and unfair trade practices. Through the Middle Ages in Europe, Kings and Queens repeatedly cracked down on monopolies, including those created through state legislation.

· International Competition Network
· List of competition regulators

Warning label	A warning label is a label attached to an item warning the user about risks associated with the use of the item as intended by the manufacturer or seller. Most of them are intended to limit civil liability in lawsuits against the item''s manufacturer or seller. That sometimes results in labels which for some people seem to state the obvious.
Postal Reorganization Act	The Postal Reorganization Act of 1970 abolished the United States Post Office Department, a part of the cabinet, and created the United States Postal Service, a corporation-like independent agency with an official monopoly on the delivery of mail in the United States. Pub.L. 91-375 was signed by President Richard Nixon on August 12, 1970.
Rescission	In contract law, rescission has been defined as the unmaking of a contract between parties. rescission is the unwinding of a transaction. This is done to bring the parties, as far as possible, back to the position in which they were before they entered into a contract (the "status quo ante".)
Contract	Agreement is said to be reached when an offer capable of immediate acceptance is met with a "mirror image" acceptance (ie, an unqualified acceptance). The parties must have the necessary capacity to Contract and the Contract must not be either trifling, indeterminate, impossible or illegal. Contract law is based on the principle expressed in the Latin phrase pacta sunt servanda .
Risk of loss	Risk of loss is a term used in the law of contracts to determine which party should bear the burden of risk for damage occurring to goods after the sale has been completed, but before delivery has occurred. Such considerations generally come into play after the contract is formed but before buyer receives goods, something bad happens.

There are four risk of loss rules, in order of application:

· Agreement - the agreement of the parties controls
· Breach - the breaching party is liable for any uninsured loss even though breach is unrelated to the problem. Hence, if the breach is the time of delivery, and the goods show up broken, then the breaching rule applies risk of loss on the seller.
· Delivery by common carrier other than by seller.

· risk of loss shifts from seller to buyer at the time that seller completes its delivery obligations
· If it is a destination contract (FOB (buyer"s city)), then risk of loss is on the seller.
· If it is a delivery contract (standard, or FOB (seller"s city)), then the risk of loss is on the buyer.

· If the seller is a merchant, then the risk of loss shifts to the buyer upon buyer"s "receipt" of the goods. If the buyer never takes possession, then the seller still has the risk of loss.

Leasing

· A definite term (whether fixed or periodic)
· At a rent
· confer exclusive possession

An owner can allow another the use of a vehicle (such as vehicle Leasing of a car, a truck or an airliner) or a computer either for a fixed period of time or at will. This can be a simple Leasing transaction, or it can be a transaction intended to allow the user the right to buy the item at some future time.

· In a simple lease (rental) of a car, P pays O a rental for the use of the car during the agreed period which may be a few days (e.g. for a holiday trip) or longer where it is more economic to pay for use rather than pay for the ownership of an asset of depreciating value.

Chief brand officer

A Chief brand officer is a relatively new executive level position at a corporation, company, organization typically reporting directly to the CEO or board of directors. The Chief brand officer is responsible for a brand"s image, experience, and promise, and propagating it throughout all aspects of the company. The brand officer oversees marketing, advertising, design, public relations and customer service departments.

Consideration

Consideration is the legal concept of value in connection with contracts. It is anything of value in the common sense, promised to another when making a contract. It can take the form of money, physical objects, services, promised actions, or even abstinence from a future action.

Punitive Damages

Punitive Damages are damages not awarded in order to compensate the plaintiff, but in order to reform or deter the defendant and similar persons from pursuing a course of action such as that which damaged the plaintiff.

punitive Damages are often awarded where compensatory damages are deemed an inadequate remedy. The court may impose them to prevent under-compensation of plaintiffs, to allow redress for undetectable torts and taking some strain away from the criminal justice system.

Fair Debt Collection	Fair debt collection broadly refers to regulation of the debt collection industry at both the U.S. Federal and state levels of government. At the Federal level, it is primarily governed by the Fair debt collection Practices Act ("Fair debt collectionPA"). In addition, many U.S. States also have debt collection laws that regulate the credit and collection industry and give consumer debtors protection from abusive and deceptive practices.
Statute of limitations	A statute of limitations is a statute in a common law legal system that sets forth the maximum period of time, after certain events, that legal proceedings based on those events may be initiated. In civil law systems, similar provisions are usually part of the civil code or criminal code and are often known collectively as "periods of prescription" or "prescriptive periods." A common law legal system might have a statute limiting the time for prosecution of crimes called misdemeanors to two years after the offense occurred. In that statute, if a person is discovered to have committed a misdemeanor three years ago, the time has expired for the prosecution of the misdemeanor.
Garnishment	A Garnishment is a means of collecting a monetary judgment against a defendant by ordering a third party (the garnishee) to pay money, otherwise owed to the defendant, directly to the plaintiff. In the case of collecting for taxes, the law of a jurisdiction may allow for collection without a judgment or other court order. Wage Garnishment, the most common type of Garnishment, is the process of deducting money from an employee"s monetary compensation (including salary), sometimes as a result of a court order.
Duty	Duty (from "due," that which is owing, O. Fr. deu, did, past participle of devoir; Lat. debere, debitum; cf.
Guarantee	The act of becoming a surety is also called a Guarantee. Traditionally a Guarantee was distinguished from a surety in that the surety"s liability was joint and primary with the principal, whereas the guaranty"s liability was ancillary and derivative, but many jurisdictions have abolished this distinction
Consumer Product Safety Act	The Consumer Product Safety Act was enacted in 1972 by the United States Congress. It established the United States Consumer Product Safety Commission as an independent agency of the United States federal government and defined its basic authority. The act gives CPSC the power to develop safety standards and pursue recalls for products that present unreasonable or substantial risks of injury or death to consumers.
Consumer Product Safety Commission	The United States Consumer Product Safety Commission is an independent agency of the United States government created in 1972 through the Consumer Product Safety Act to protect "against unreasonable risks of injuries associated with consumer products." As of 2006 its acting chairman is Nancy Nord, a Republican. The other commissioner is Thomas Hill Moore, a Democrat. Normally the board has three commissioners.

Strict liability

Strict liability makes a person responsible for the damage and loss caused by his/her acts and omissions regardless of culpability .) Strict liability is important in torts (especially product liability), corporations law, and criminal law. For analysis of the pros and cons of Strict liability as applied to product liability, the most important Strict liability regime, see product liability.

Contract

Agreement is said to be reached when an offer capable of immediate acceptance is met with a "mirror image" acceptance (ie, an unqualified acceptance). The parties must have the necessary capacity to Contract and the Contract must not be either trifling, indeterminate, impossible or illegal. Contract law is based on the principle expressed in the Latin phrase pacta sunt servanda .

Pollution

Pollution is the introduction of contaminants into an environment that causes instability, disorder, harm or discomfort to the ecosystem i.e. physical systems or living organisms . Pollution can take the form of chemical substances, or energy, such as noise, heat, or light energy. Pollutants, the elements of Pollution, can be foreign substances or energies, or naturally occurring; when naturally occurring, they are considered contaminants when they exceed natural levels.

Chief brand officer

A Chief brand officer is a relatively new executive level position at a corporation, company, organization typically reporting directly to the CEO or board of directors. The Chief brand officer is responsible for a brand''s image, experience, and promise, and propagating it throughout all aspects of the company. The brand officer oversees marketing, advertising, design, public relations and customer service departments.

Regulatory

Regulation refers to "controlling human or societal behaviour by rules or restrictions." Regulation can take many forms: legal restrictions promulgated by a government authority, self-regulation, social regulation (e.g. norms), co-regulation and market regulation. One can consider regulation as actions of conduct imposing sanctions (such as a fine.) This action of administrative law, or implementing regulatory law, may be contrasted with statutory or case law.

Tort

Tort law is a body of law that addresses, and provides remedies for, civil wrongs not arising out of contractual obligations. A person who suffers legal damages may be able to use Tort law to receive compensation from someone who is legally responsible, or "liable," for those injuries. Generally speaking, Tort law defines what constitutes a legal injury and establishes the circumstances under which one person may be held liable for another''s injury.

United States

- History of competition law
- Monopoly
  - Coercive monopoly
  - Natural monopoly
  - Barriers to entry
  - Market power
  - SSNIP test
  - Relevant market
  - Merger control

Anti-competitive practices

- Monopolization
- Collusion

- Formation of cartels
- Price fixing
- Bid rigging
- Product bundling and tying
- Refusal to deal

- Group boycott
- Exclusive dealing
- Dividing territories
- Conscious parallelism
- Predatory pricing
- Misuse of patents and copyrights

Laws and doctrines

United States

- Sherman Antitrust Act
- Clayton Antitrust Act
- Robinson-Patman Act
- FTC Act
- Hart-Scott-Rodino Act
- Merger guidelines
- Essential facilities doctrine
- Noerr-Pennington doctrine
- Parker immunity doctrine
- Rule of reason

Europe

- UK competition law
- Irish competition law

Australia

- Trade Practices Act 1974

Enforcement authorities and organizations

Competition law history refers to attempts by governments to regulate competitive markets for goods and services, leading up to the modern competition or antitrust laws around the world today. The earliest records traces back to the efforts of Roman legislators to control price fluctuations and unfair trade practices. Through the Middle Ages in Europe, Kings and Queens repeatedly cracked down on monopolies, including those created through state legislation.

· International Competition Network
· List of competition regulators

United States Department of Justice	The United States Department of Justice is a Cabinet department in the United States government designed to enforce the law and defend the interests of the United States according to the law and to ensure fair and impartial administration of justice for all Americans The DOJ is administered by the United States Attorney General (see 28 U.S.C.
United States Department of the Interior	The United States Department of the Interior is the United States federal executive department of the U.S. government responsible for the management and conservation of most federal land and the administration of programs relating to Native Americans, Alaska Natives, and Native Hawaiians, and to insular areas of the United States. The Department is administered by the United States Secretary of the Interior, who is a member of the Cabinet of the President. The current Secretary is Ken Salazar of Colorado.
Personal property	Personal property is a type of property. In the common law systems Personal property may also be called chattels or personalty. It is distinguished from real property, or real estate. Personal property may be classified in a variety of ways. Tangible Personal property refers to any type of property that can generally be moved (i.e., it is not attached to real property or land), touched or felt. These generally include items such as furniture, clothing, jewelry, art, writings, or household goods. In some cases, there can be formal title documents that show the ownership and transfer rights of that property after a person"s death (for example, motor vehicles, boats, etc.) In many cases, however, tangible Personal property will not be "titled" in an owner"s name and is presumed to be whatever property he or she was in possession of at the time of his or her death. Intangible Personal property or "intangibles" refers to Personal property that cannot actually be moved, touched or felt, but instead represents something of value such as negotiable instruments, securities, goods, and intangible assets including chose in action.
Ocean dumping	Deliberate disposal of wastes at sea is called Ocean dumping. Some forms of marine debris, such as driftwood, occur naturally, and human activities have been discharging similar material into the oceans for thousands of years. Recently however, with the increasing use of plastic, human influence has become an issue as many types of plastics do not biodegrade.
Oil Pollution Act	The Oil Pollution Act was passed by the United States Congress to prevent further oil spills from occurring in the United States. It was made after the Exxon Valdez oil spill.

Toxic Substances Control Act	The Toxic Substances Control Act is a United States law, passed by the United States Congress in 1976, that regulates the introduction of new or already existing chemicals. It grandfathered most existing chemicals, in contrast to the Registration, Evaluation and Authorization of Chemicals (REACH) legislation of the European Union. However, as explained below, the Toxic Substances Control Act specifically regulates polychlorinated biphenyl (PCB) products.
Duty	Duty (from "due," that which is owing, O. Fr. deu, did, past participle of devoir; Lat. debere, debitum; cf.
Obligation	An obligation is a requirement to take some course of action, whether legal or moral. There are also obligation s in other normative contexts, such as obligation s of etiquette, social obligation s, and possibly in terms of politics, where obligation s are requirements which must be fulfilled. These are generally legal obligation s, which can incur a penalty for unfulfilment, although certain people are obliged to carry out certain actions for other reasons as well, whether as a tradition or for social reasons.
Superfund	Superfund is the common name for the Comprehensive Environmental Response, Compensation, and Liability Act (CERCLA), a United States federal law designed to clean up abandoned hazardous waste sites. Superfund provides broad federal authority to clean up releases or threatened releases of hazardous substances that may endanger public health or the environment. The law authorized the Environmental Protection Agency (EPA) to identify parties responsible for contamination of sites and compel the parties to clean up the sites.
Several Liability	Several liability is where the parties are liable for only their respective obligations. A common example of Several liability is in syndicated loan agreements, which will normally provide that each bank is severally liable for its own part of the loan. If one bank fails to advance its agreed part of the loan to the borrower, then the borrower can only sue that bank, and the other banks in the syndicate have no liability.

Business	There are many ways in which a business may be owned under the legal system of England and Wales. Different types of ownership are suitable for organisations depending on the degree of control the owners wish to have over the business. The choice of ownership methor also relates to the organisations ability to raise funds for the business activities.
The Commerce Clause	The Commerce Clause is an enumerated power listed in the United States Constitution (Article 1, Section 8, Clause 3.) The clause states that Congress has the power to regulate commerce with foreign nations, among the states, and with the Native American tribes. Courts and commentators have tended to discuss each of these three areas of commerce as a separate power granted to the Congress of the United States.
Sherman Antitrust Act	The Sherman Antitrust Act was the first United States Federal statute to limit cartels and monopolies. It falls under antitrust law.
Trust	In common law legal systems, a trust is an arrangement whereby property (including real, tangible and intangible) is managed by one person (or persons, or organizations) for the benefit of another. A trust is created by a settlor, who entrusts some or all of his or her property to people of his choice (the trustees.) The trustees hold legal title to the trust property (or trust corpus), but they are obliged to hold the property for the benefit of one or more individuals or organizations (the beneficiary, a.k.a. cestui que use or cestui que trust), usually specified by the settlor, who hold equitable title.
Power of attorney	A power of attorney or letter of attorney in common law systems or mandate in civil law systems is an authorization to act on someone else"s behalf in a legal or business matter. The person authorizing the other to act is the principal, granter or donor (of the power), and the one authorized to act is the agent, the attorney-in-fact, or in many Common Law jurisdictions, simply the attorney. The term attorney-in-fact is commonly used in the United States, to make a distinction from the term Attorney at law.
Per se	Per se: · A Latin phrase used in English arguments for "by itself" or "by themselves" It also is used in law: · Illegal per se, the legal usage of "per se" in criminal and anti-trust law · Negligence per se, legal use in tort law Other uses: · per se (restaurant), a New York City restaurant run by Thomas Keller "Gun ownership in Japan is not, per se, illegal; however, the restrictions are such that one could easily arrive at that conclusion." "Data trustworthiness should be attributed primarily to data per se, rather than being merely a reï¬,ection of the trust attributed to data-reporting entities."

Rule of reason

The Rule of reason is a doctrine developed by the United States Supreme Court in its interpretation of the Sherman Antitrust Act. The rule, stated and applied in the case of Standard Oil Co. of New Jersey v. United States, 221 U.S. 1 (1911), is that only combinations and contracts unreasonably restraining trade are subject to actions under the anti-trust laws and that size and possession of monopoly power are not illegal.

Contract

Agreement is said to be reached when an offer capable of immediate acceptance is met with a "mirror image" acceptance (ie, an unqualified acceptance). The parties must have the necessary capacity to Contract and the Contract must not be either trifling, indeterminate, impossible or illegal. Contract law is based on the principle expressed in the Latin phrase pacta sunt servanda .

Freedom of contract

Freedom of contract or contractualism is the freedom of individuals to bargain among themselves the terms of their own contracts, without government interference. Anything more than minimal regulations and taxes may be seen as infringements. It is the underpinning of the theory of laissez-faire economics.

Joint venture

A Joint venture is an entity formed between two or more parties to undertake economic activity together. The parties agree to create a new entity by both contributing equity, and they then share in the revenues, expenses, and control of the enterprise. The venture can be for one specific project only, or a continuing business relationship such as the Fuji Xerox Joint venture.

Misrepresentation

Misrepresentation is a contract law concept. It means a false statement of fact made by one party to another party, which has the effect of inducing that party into the contract. For example, under certain circumstances, false statements or promises made by a seller of goods regarding the quality or nature of the product that the seller has may constitute Misrepresentation.

Refusal to deal

Refusal to deal is one of several anti-competitive practices forbidden in countries which have restricted market economies. For example, in Australia:

· Agreements involving competitors that involve restricting the supply of goods are prohibited if they have the purpose or effect of substantially lessening competition in a market in which the businesses operate. "Refusal to deal" Reference: The Competition Act, 2002 (India) S4-d."Refusal to deal" includes any agreement which restricts, or is likely to restrict, by any method the persons or classes of persons to whom goods are sold or from whom goods are bought

Chief brand officer

A Chief brand officer is a relatively new executive level position at a corporation, company, organization typically reporting directly to the CEO or board of directors. The Chief brand officer is responsible for a brand"s image, experience, and promise, and propagating it throughout all aspects of the company. The brand officer oversees marketing, advertising, design, public relations and customer service departments.

Price-fixing

Price fixing is an agreement between business competitors to sell the same product or service at the same price. In general, it is an agreement intended to ultimately push the price of a product as high as possible, leading to profits for all the sellers. price-fixing can also involve any agreement to fix, peg, discount or stabilize prices.

Job interview

A Job interview is a process in which a potential employee is evaluated by an employer for prospective employment in their company, organization and was established in the late 16th century.

A Job interview typically precedes the hiring decision, and is used to evaluate the candidate. The interview is usually preceded by the evaluation of submitted résumés from interested candidates, then selecting a small number of candidates for interviews.

Reseller

A reseller is a company or individual that purchases goods or services with the intention of reselling them rather than consuming or using them. This is usually done for profit (but could be resold at a loss.) One example can be found in the industry of telecommunications, where companies buy excess amounts of transmission capacity or call time from other carriers and resell it to smaller carriers.

Federal Trade Commission

The Federal Trade Commission is an independent agency of the United States government, established in 1914 by the Federal Trade Commission Act. Its principal mission is the promotion of "consumer protection" and the elimination and prevention of what regulators perceive to be harmfully "anti-competitive" business practices, such as coercive monopoly.

The Federal Trade Commission Act was one of President Wilson"s major acts against trusts.

Monopolization

- History of competition law
- Monopoly
  - Coercive monopoly
  - Natural monopoly
  - Barriers to entry
  - Market power
  - SSNIP test
  - Relevant market
  - Merger control

Anti-competitive practices

- Monopolization
- Collusion
  - Formation of cartels
  - Price fixing
  - Bid rigging
  - Product bundling and tying
  - Refusal to deal

- Group boycott
- Exclusive dealing
- Dividing territories
- Conscious parallelism
- Predatory pricing
- Misuse of patents and copyrights

Laws and doctrines

United States

- Sherman Antitrust Act
- Clayton Antitrust Act
- Robinson-Patman Act
- FTC Act
- Hart-Scott-Rodino Act
- Merger guidelines
- Essential facilities doctrine
- Noerr-Pennington doctrine
- Parker immunity doctrine
- Rule of reason

Europe

- UK competition law
- Irish competition law

Australia

- Trade Practices Act 1974

Enforcement authorities and organizations

- International Competition Network
- List of competition regulators

The term Monopolization refers to an offense under Section 2 of the American Sherman Antitrust Act, passed in 1890. Section 2 states that any person "who shall monopolize .

Predatory pricing

Predatory pricing is the practice of selling a product or service at a very low price, intending to drive competitors out of the market, or create barriers to entry for potential new competitors. If competitors or potential competitors cannot sustain equal or lower prices without losing money, they go out of business or choose not to enter the business. The predatory merchant then has fewer competitors or is even a de facto monopoly, and can then raise prices above what the market would otherwise bear.

Relevant market

In competition law the Relevant market defines the market in which one or more goods compete. Therefore, the Relevant market defines whether two or more products can be considered substitute goods and whether they constitute a particular and separate market for competition analysis.

	The Relevant market combines the product market and the geographic market, defined as follows: · A relevant product market comprises all those products and/or services which are regarded as interchangeable or substitutable by the consumer by reason of the products" characteristics, their prices and their intended use; · A relevant geographic market comprises the area in which the firms concerned are involved in the supply of products or services and in which the conditions of competition are sufficiently homogeneous. The notion of Relevant market is used in order to identify the products and undertakings which are directly competing in a business. Therefore, the Relevant market is the market where the competition takes place.
Robinson-Patman Act	The Robinson-Patman Act of 1936 (or Anti-Price Discrimination Act, 15 U.S.C. Â§ 13) is a United States federal law that prohibits what were considered, at the time of passage, to be anticompetitive practices by producers, specifically price discrimination. It grew out of practices in which chain stores were allowed to purchase goods at lower prices than other retailers.
Price Discrimination	Price discrimination exists when sales of identical goods or services are transacted at different prices from the same provider. In a theoretical market with perfect information, no transaction costs or prohibition on secondary exchange (or re-selling) to prevent arbitrage, Price discrimination can only be a feature of monopoly and oligopoly markets, where market power can be exercised. Otherwise, the moment the seller tries to sell the same good at different prices, the buyer at the lower price can arbitrage by selling to the consumer buying at the higher price but with a tiny discount.
Parol evidence	The Parol evidence rule is the legal application of a rule of substantive law in contract cases that prevents a party to a written contract from contradicting (or sometimes adding to) the terms of the contract by seeking the admission of evidence "extrinsic" (outside) to the contract. For example, Carl agrees in writing to sell Betty a car for $1,000. Betty argues that Carl told her that she would only need to pay Carl $800.
Parol evidence rule	The Parol evidence rule is the legal application of a rule of substantive law in contract cases that prevents a party to a written contract from contradicting (or sometimes adding to) the terms of the contract by seeking the admission of evidence "extrinsic" (outside) to the contract. For example, Carl agrees in writing to sell Betty a car for $1,000. Betty argues that Carl told her that she would only need to pay Carl $800.
Statute	A statute is a formal written enactment of a legislative authority that governs a country, state, city, or county. Typically, statute s command or prohibit something, or declare policy. The word is often used to distinguish law made by legislative bodies from case law and the regulations issued by Government agencies.
Statute of Frauds	The Statute of Frauds refers to the requirement that certain kinds of contracts be made in writing and signed.

Traditionally, the Statute of Frauds requires a writing signed by the defendant in the following circumstances:

· Contracts in consideration of marriage.
· Contracts which cannot be performed within one year.
· Contracts for the transfer of an interest in land.
· Contracts by the executor of a will to pay a debt of the estate with their own money.
· Contracts for the sale of goods above a certain value.
· Contracts in which one party becomes a surety (acts as guarantor) for another party"s debt or other obligation.

This can be remembered by the mnemonic "MY LEGS": Marriage, one year, land, executor, goods, surety.

The term Statute of Frauds comes from an English Act of Parliament passed in 1677 (authored by Sir Leoline Jenkins and passed by the Cavalier Parliament), and more properly called An Act for Prevention of Frauds and Perjuries. Many common law jurisdictions have made similar statutory provisions, while a number of civil law jurisdictions have equivalent legislation incorporated into their civil codes.

Consideration

Consideration is the legal concept of value in connection with contracts. It is anything of value in the common sense, promised to another when making a contract. It can take the form of money, physical objects, services, promised actions, or even abstinence from a future action.

Foreclosure

Foreclosure is the legal and professional proceeding in which a mortgagee usually a lender, obtains a court ordered termination of a mortgagor"s equitable right of redemption. Usually a lender obtains a security interest from a borrower who mortgages or pledges an asset like a house to secure the loan. If the borrower defaults and the lender tries to repossess the property, courts of equity can grant the borrower the equitable right of redemption if the borrower repays the debt.

Interlocking directorate

Interlocking directorate refers to the practice of members of corporate board of directors serving on the boards of multiple corporations. This practice, although widespread and lawful, raises questions about the quality and independence of board decisions.

The average board of directors has nine members, and the total population of board members of public companies traded on the NYSE, NASDAQ and AMEX stock exchanges is about 53,000.

Lien

In law, a Lien is a form of security interest granted over an item of property to secure the payment of a debt or performance of some other obligation. The owner of the property, who grants the Lien, is referred to as the Lienor and the person who has the benefit of the Lien is referred to as the Lienee.

The etymological root is Anglo-French Lien, loyen bond, restraint, from Latin ligamen, from ligare to bind.

Damages

Damages for breach of contract is a common law remedy, available as of right. It is designed to compensate the victim for their actual loss as a result of the wrongdoer"s breach rather than to punish the wrongdoer. If no loss has been occasioned by the plaintiff, only nominal Damages will be awarded.

Duty

Duty (from "due," that which is owing, O. Fr. deu, did, past participle of devoir; Lat. debere, debitum; cf.

Negotiable instrument

A Negotiable instrument is a specialized type of "contract" for the payment of money that is unconditional and capable of transfer by negotiation. Common examples include cheques, banknotes (paper money), and commercial paper.

A Negotiable instrument is not a contract, as contract formation requires an offer, acceptance, and consideration, none of which is an element of a Negotiable instrument.

Obligation

An obligation is a requirement to take some course of action, whether legal or moral. There are also obligation s in other normative contexts, such as obligation s of etiquette, social obligation s, and possibly in terms of politics, where obligation s are requirements which must be fulfilled. These are generally legal obligation s, which can incur a penalty for unfulfilment, although certain people are obliged to carry out certain actions for other reasons as well, whether as a tradition or for social reasons.

Several Liability

Several liability is where the parties are liable for only their respective obligations. A common example of Several liability is in syndicated loan agreements, which will normally provide that each bank is severally liable for its own part of the loan. If one bank fails to advance its agreed part of the loan to the borrower, then the borrower can only sue that bank, and the other banks in the syndicate have no liability.

Treble Damages

Treble damages, in law, is a term that indicates that a statute permits a court to triple the amount of the actual/compensatory damages to be awarded to a prevailing plaintiff, generally in order to punish the losing party for willful conduct. Treble damages are a multiple of, and not an addition to, actual damages. Thus, where a person received an award of $100 for an injury, a court applying Treble damages would raise the award to $300.

Noerr-Pennington doctrine

Under the Noerr-Pennington doctrine, private entities are immune from liability under the antitrust laws for attempts to influence the passage or enforcement of laws, even if the laws they advocate for would have anticompetitive effects. Eastern Railroad Presidents Conference v. Noerr Motor Freight, Inc., 365 U.S. 127, 135 (1961); United Mine Workers v. Pennington, 381 U.S. 657, 670 (1965). The doctrine is grounded in the First Amendment protection of political speech, and "upon a recognition that the antitrust laws, "tailored as they are for the business world, are not at all appropriate for application in the political arena." " City of Columbia v. Omni Outdoor Advertising, Inc., 499 U.S. 365, 380 (1991) (quoting Noerr, 365 U.S. 127, 141 (1961).

Small Business Act

The Small Business Administration is a United States government agency that provides support to small businesses.

The mission of the Small Business Administration is "to maintain and strengthen the nation"s economy by enabling the establishment and viability of small businesses and by assisting in the economic recovery of communities after disasters."

The Small Business Act makes loans directly to businesses and acts as a guarantor on bank loans. In some circumstances it also makes loans to victims of natural disasters, works to get government procurement contracts for small businesses, and assists businesses with management, technical and training issues.

Personal property

Personal property is a type of property. In the common law systems Personal property may also be called chattels or personalty. It is distinguished from real property, or real estate.

Personal property may be classified in a variety of ways. Tangible Personal property refers to any type of property that can generally be moved (i.e., it is not attached to real property or land), touched or felt. These generally include items such as furniture, clothing, jewelry, art, writings, or household goods. In some cases, there can be formal title documents that show the ownership and transfer rights of that property after a person''s death (for example, motor vehicles, boats, etc.) In many cases, however, tangible Personal property will not be "titled" in an owner''s name and is presumed to be whatever property he or she was in possession of at the time of his or her death.

Intangible Personal property or "intangibles" refers to Personal property that cannot actually be moved, touched or felt, but instead represents something of value such as negotiable instruments, securities, goods, and intangible assets including chose in action.

Warranty

In commercial and consumer transactions, a warranty is an obligation or guarantee that an article or service sold is as factually stated or legally implied by the seller, and that often provides for a specific remedy such as repair or replacement in the event the article or service fails to meet the warranty. A breach of warranty occurs when the promise is broken, i.e., a product is defective or not as should be expected by a reasonable buyer.

In business and legal transactions, a warranty is an assurance by one party to the other party that certain facts or conditions are true or will happen; the other party is permitted to rely on that assurance and seek some type of remedy if it is not true or followed.

Merger guidelines

The Merger guidelines are a set of internal rules promulgated by the Antitrust Division of the United States Department of Justice (DOJ) in conjunction with the Federal Trade Commission (FTC). These rules, which have been revised a number of times in the past four decades, govern the extent to which these two regulatory bodies will scrutinize and/or challenge a potential merger on grounds of market concentration or threat to competition within a relevant market.

The Merger guidelines have sections governing both horizontal integration and vertical integration.

Consumer protection

Consumer protection laws are designed to ensure fair competition and the free flow of truthful information in the marketplace. The laws are designed to prevent businesses that engage in fraud or specified unfair practices from gaining an advantage over competitors and may provide additional protection for the weak and those unable to take care of themselves. Consumer protection laws are a form of government regulation which protects the interests of consumers.

Pollution	Pollution is the introduction of contaminants into an environment that causes instability, disorder, harm or discomfort to the ecosystem i.e. physical systems or living organisms . Pollution can take the form of chemical substances, or energy, such as noise, heat, or light energy. Pollutants, the elements of Pollution, can be foreign substances or energies, or naturally occurring; when naturally occurring, they are considered contaminants when they exceed natural levels.

Patent	A patent is a set of exclusive rights granted by a state to an inventor or his assignee for a limited period of time in exchange for a disclosure of an invention. The procedure for granting patent s, the requirements placed on the patent ee and the extent of the exclusive rights vary widely between countries according to national laws and international agreements. Typically, however, a patent application must include one or more claims defining the invention which must be new, inventive, and useful or industrially applicable.

Chapter 47. Personal Property and Bailments

Personalty

Personal property is a type of property. In the common law systems personal property may also be called chattels or Personalty. It is distinguished from real property, or real estate.

Share

In business and finance, a share of stock (also referred to as equity share) means a share of ownership in a corporation (company.) In the plural, stocks is often used as a synonym for shares especially in the United States, but it is less commonly used that way outside of North America.

In the United Kingdom, South Africa, and Australia, stock can also refer to completely different financial instruments such as government bonds or, less commonly, to all kinds of marketable securities.

Trademark

A trademark or trade mark is a distinctive sign or indicator used by an individual, business organization and to distinguish its products or services from those of other entities.

A trademark is designated by the following symbols:

· â„¢ (for an unregistered trademark that is, a mark used to promote or brand goods);
· â„ (for an unregistered service mark, that is, a mark used to promote or brand services); and
· Â® (for a registered trademark)

A trademark is a type of intellectual property, and typically a name, word, phrase, logo, symbol, design, image, or a combination of these elements. There is also a range of non-conventional trademark s comprising marks which do not fall into these standard categories.

The owner of a registered trademark may commence legal proceedings for trademark infringement to prevent unauthorized use of that trademark

Personal property

Personal property is a type of property. In the common law systems Personal property may also be called chattels or personalty. It is distinguished from real property, or real estate.

Personal property may be classified in a variety of ways. Tangible Personal property refers to any type of property that can generally be moved (i.e., it is not attached to real property or land), touched or felt. These generally include items such as furniture, clothing, jewelry, art, writings, or household goods. In some cases, there can be formal title documents that show the ownership and transfer rights of that property after a person''s death (for example, motor vehicles, boats, etc.) In many cases, however, tangible Personal property will not be "titled" in an owner''s name and is presumed to be whatever property he or she was in possession of at the time of his or her death.

Intangible Personal property or "intangibles" refers to Personal property that cannot actually be moved, touched or felt, but instead represents something of value such as negotiable instruments, securities, goods, and intangible assets including chose in action.

Tangible

In law, tangibility is the attribute of being detectable with the senses.

In criminal law, one of the elements of an offense of larceny is that the stolen property must be tangible.

In the context of intellectual property, expression in tangible form is one of the requirements for copyright protection.

Real property

In the common law, real property refers to one of the three main classes of property, the other two classes being personal property and intellectual property. real property generally encompasses land, land improvements resulting from human effort including buildings and machinery sited on land, and various property rights over the preceding.

	The concept is variously named and defined in other jurisdictions: heritable property in Scotland, immobilier in France, and immovable property in Canada, United States, India, Pakistan, Bangladesh, Malta, Cyprus, and in countries where civil law systems prevail, including most of Europe, Russia, and South America.
Revocation	Revocation is the act of recall or annulment. It is the reversal of an act, the recalling of a grant, or the making void of some deed previously existing. In the law of contracts, revocation is a type of remedy for buyers when the buyer accepts a nonconforming good from the seller.
Chief brand officer	A Chief brand officer is a relatively new executive level position at a corporation, company, organization typically reporting directly to the CEO or board of directors. The Chief brand officer is responsible for a brand''s image, experience, and promise, and propagating it throughout all aspects of the company. The brand officer oversees marketing, advertising, design, public relations and customer service departments.
Statute	A statute is a formal written enactment of a legislative authority that governs a country, state, city, or county. Typically, statute s command or prohibit something, or declare policy. The word is often used to distinguish law made by legislative bodies from case law and the regulations issued by Government agencies.
Arbitration	Arbitration, a form of alternative dispute resolution (ADR), is a legal technique for the resolution of disputes outside the courts, wherein the parties to a dispute refer it to one or more persons (the "arbitrators", "arbiters" or "arbitral tribunal"), by whose decision (the "award") they agree to be bound. It is a settlement technique in which a third party reviews the case and imposes a decision that is legally binding for both sides. Other forms of ADR include mediation (a form of settlement negotiation facilitated by a neutral third party) and non-binding resolution by experts.
Contract	Agreement is said to be reached when an offer capable of immediate acceptance is met with a "mirror image" acceptance (ie, an unqualified acceptance). The parties must have the necessary capacity to Contract and the Contract must not be either trifling, indeterminate, impossible or illegal. Contract law is based on the principle expressed in the Latin phrase pacta sunt servanda .
Writ	In law, a writ is a formal writ ten order issued by a body with administrative or judicial jurisdiction; in modern usage, this public body is generally a court. Warrants, prerogative writ s and subpoenas are types of writ s; there are many others. Originally, a writ was a letter or command from the Sovereign, or from some person with appropriate jurisdiction.
Writ of attachment	A Writ of attachment is a court order to "attach" or seize an asset. It is issued by a court to a law enforcement officer or sheriff. The Writ of attachment is issued in order to satisfy a judgment issued by the court.

Proprietorship	A sole Proprietorship). All assets of the business are owned by the proprietor and all debts of the business are his debts and he must pay them from his personal resources.
Lien	In law, a Lien is a form of security interest granted over an item of property to secure the payment of a debt or performance of some other obligation. The owner of the property, who grants the Lien, is referred to as the Lienor and the person who has the benefit of the Lien is referred to as the Lienee. The etymological root is Anglo-French Lien, loyen bond, restraint, from Latin ligamen, from ligare to bind.
Duty	Duty (from "due," that which is owing, O. Fr. deu, did, past participle of devoir; Lat. debere, debitum; cf.
Obligation	An obligation is a requirement to take some course of action, whether legal or moral. There are also obligation s in other normative contexts, such as obligation s of etiquette, social obligation s, and possibly in terms of politics, where obligation s are requirements which must be fulfilled. These are generally legal obligation s, which can incur a penalty for unfulfilment, although certain people are obliged to carry out certain actions for other reasons as well, whether as a tradition or for social reasons.
Parol evidence	The Parol evidence rule is the legal application of a rule of substantive law in contract cases that prevents a party to a written contract from contradicting (or sometimes adding to) the terms of the contract by seeking the admission of evidence "extrinsic" (outside) to the contract. For example, Carl agrees in writing to sell Betty a car for $1,000. Betty argues that Carl told her that she would only need to pay Carl $800.
Parol evidence rule	The Parol evidence rule is the legal application of a rule of substantive law in contract cases that prevents a party to a written contract from contradicting (or sometimes adding to) the terms of the contract by seeking the admission of evidence "extrinsic" (outside) to the contract. For example, Carl agrees in writing to sell Betty a car for $1,000. Betty argues that Carl told her that she would only need to pay Carl $800.
Statute of Frauds	The Statute of Frauds refers to the requirement that certain kinds of contracts be made in writing and signed. Traditionally, the Statute of Frauds requires a writing signed by the defendant in the following circumstances: · Contracts in consideration of marriage. · Contracts which cannot be performed within one year. · Contracts for the transfer of an interest in land. · Contracts by the executor of a will to pay a debt of the estate with their own money. · Contracts for the sale of goods above a certain value. · Contracts in which one party becomes a surety (acts as guarantor) for another party"s debt or other obligation. This can be remembered by the mnemonic "MY LEGS": Marriage, one year, land, executor, goods, surety.

	The term Statute of Frauds comes from an English Act of Parliament passed in 1677 (authored by Sir Leoline Jenkins and passed by the Cavalier Parliament), and more properly called An Act for Prevention of Frauds and Perjuries. Many common law jurisdictions have made similar statutory provisions, while a number of civil law jurisdictions have equivalent legislation incorporated into their civil codes.
Consideration	Consideration is the legal concept of value in connection with contracts. It is anything of value in the common sense, promised to another when making a contract. It can take the form of money, physical objects, services, promised actions, or even abstinence from a future action.
Implied warranty	In common law jurisdictions, an Implied warranty is a contract law term for certain assurances that are presumed to be made in the sale of products or real property, due to the circumstances of the sale. These assurances are characterized as warranties irrespective of whether the seller has expressly promised them orally or in writing. They include an Implied warranty of fitness for a particular purpose, an Implied warranty of merchantability for products, Implied warranty of workmanlike quality for services, and an Implied warranty of habitability for a home.
Strict liability	Strict liability makes a person responsible for the damage and loss caused by his/her acts and omissions regardless of culpability .) Strict liability is important in torts (especially product liability), corporations law, and criminal law. For analysis of the pros and cons of Strict liability as applied to product liability, the most important Strict liability regime, see product liability.
Warranty of merchantability	The Warranty of merchantability is implied, unless expressly disclaimed by name the goods must reasonably conform to an ordinary buyer"s expectations, i.e., they are what they say they are. For example, a fruit that looks and smells good but has hidden defects would violate the implied Warranty of merchantability if its quality does not meet the standards for such fruit "as passes ordinarily in the trade". In Massachusetts consumer protection law, it is illegal to disclaim this warranty on household goods sold to consumers etc.

Real property

In the common law, real property refers to one of the three main classes of property, the other two classes being personal property and intellectual property. real property generally encompasses land, land improvements resulting from human effort including buildings and machinery sited on land, and various property rights over the preceding.

The concept is variously named and defined in other jurisdictions: heritable property in Scotland, immobilier in France, and immovable property in Canada, United States, India, Pakistan, Bangladesh, Malta, Cyprus, and in countries where civil law systems prevail, including most of Europe, Russia, and South America.

Personal property

Personal property is a type of property. In the common law systems Personal property may also be called chattels or personalty. It is distinguished from real property, or real estate.

Personal property may be classified in a variety of ways. Tangible Personal property refers to any type of property that can generally be moved (i.e., it is not attached to real property or land), touched or felt. These generally include items such as furniture, clothing, jewelry, art, writings, or household goods. In some cases, there can be formal title documents that show the ownership and transfer rights of that property after a person"s death (for example, motor vehicles, boats, etc.) In many cases, however, tangible Personal property will not be "titled" in an owner"s name and is presumed to be whatever property he or she was in possession of at the time of his or her death.

Intangible Personal property or "intangibles" refers to Personal property that cannot actually be moved, touched or felt, but instead represents something of value such as negotiable instruments, securities, goods, and intangible assets including chose in action.

Tenancy

Leasehold is a form of property tenure where one party buys the right to occupy land or a building for a given length of time. As lease is a legal estate, leasehold estate can be bought and sold on the open market. A leasehold thus differs from a freehold where the ownership of a property is purchased outright and thereafter held for an indeterminate length of time, and also differs from a tenancy where a property is let on a periodic basis such as weekly or monthly.

Profit

A profit , in the law of real property, is a nonpossessory interest in land similar to the better-known easement, which gives the holder the right to take natural resources such as petroleum, minerals, timber, and wild game from the land of another. Indeed, because of the necessity of allowing access to the land so that resources may be gathered, every profit contains an implied easement for the owner of the profit to enter the other party"s land for the purpose of collecting the resources permitted by the profit.

Like an easement, profits can be created expressly by an agreement between the property owner and the owner of the profit, or by prescription, where the owner of the profit has made "open and notorious" use of the land for a continuous and uninterrupted statutory period.

Pollution

Pollution is the introduction of contaminants into an environment that causes instability, disorder, harm or discomfort to the ecosystem i.e. physical systems or living organisms . Pollution can take the form of chemical substances, or energy, such as noise, heat, or light energy. Pollutants, the elements of Pollution, can be foreign substances or energies, or naturally occurring; when naturally occurring, they are considered contaminants when they exceed natural levels.

Contract	Agreement is said to be reached when an offer capable of immediate acceptance is met with a "mirror image" acceptance (ie, an unqualified acceptance). The parties must have the necessary capacity to Contract and the Contract must not be either trifling, indeterminate, impossible or illegal. Contract law is based on the principle expressed in the Latin phrase pacta sunt servanda .
License	The verb License or grant License means to give permission. The noun License refers to that permission as well as to the document memorializing that permission. License may be granted by a party to another party as an element of an agreement between those parties.
Chief brand officer	A Chief brand officer is a relatively new executive level position at a corporation, company, organization typically reporting directly to the CEO or board of directors. The Chief brand officer is responsible for a brand"s image, experience, and promise, and propagating it throughout all aspects of the company. The brand officer oversees marketing, advertising, design, public relations and customer service departments.
Lease	A Lease is a contract conferring a right on one person to possess property belonging to another person (called a landlord or lessor) to the exclusion of the owner landlord, and all others except with the invitation of the tenant. It is a rental agreement between landlord and tenant. The relationship between the tenant and the landlord is called a tenancy, and the right to possession by the tenant is sometimes called a Leasehold interest.
Habitability	Habitability is the conformance of a residence or abode to the implied warranty of Habitability. A residence that complies is said to be "habitable". It is an implied warranty or contract, meaning it does not have to be an express contract, covenant, or provision of a contract.
Implied warranty	In common law jurisdictions, an Implied warranty is a contract law term for certain assurances that are presumed to be made in the sale of products or real property, due to the circumstances of the sale. These assurances are characterized as warranties irrespective of whether the seller has expressly promised them orally or in writing. They include an Implied warranty of fitness for a particular purpose, an Implied warranty of merchantability for products, Implied warranty of workmanlike quality for services, and an Implied warranty of habitability for a home.
Mortgage loan	A Mortgage loan is a loan secured by real property through the use of a document which evidences the existence of the loan and the encumbrance of that realty through the granting of a mortgage which secures the loan. However, the word mortgage alone, in everyday usage, is most often used to mean Mortgage loan. A home buyer or builder can obtain financing (a loan) either to purchase or secure against the property from a financial institution, such as a bank, either directly or indirectly through intermediaries.
Duty	Duty (from "due," that which is owing, O. Fr. deu, did, past participle of devoir; Lat. debere, debitum; cf.

Quitclaim deed

A Quitclaim deed is a term used to describe a document by which a person (the "grantor") disclaims any interest the grantor may have in a piece of real property and passes that claim to another person (the grantee.) A Quitclaim deed neither warrants nor professes that the grantor"s claim is valid. By contrast, the deeds normally used for real estate sales (called grant deeds or warranty deeds, depending on the jurisdiction) contain guarantees from the grantor to the grantee that the title is clear.

Statute

A statute is a formal written enactment of a legislative authority that governs a country, state, city, or county. Typically, statute s command or prohibit something, or declare policy. The word is often used to distinguish law made by legislative bodies from case law and the regulations issued by Government agencies.

Warranty

In commercial and consumer transactions, a warranty is an obligation or guarantee that an article or service sold is as factually stated or legally implied by the seller, and that often provides for a specific remedy such as repair or replacement in the event the article or service fails to meet the warranty. A breach of warranty occurs when the promise is broken, i.e., a product is defective or not as should be expected by a reasonable buyer.

In business and legal transactions, a warranty is an assurance by one party to the other party that certain facts or conditions are true or will happen; the other party is permitted to rely on that assurance and seek some type of remedy if it is not true or followed.

Warranty deed

A general Warranty deed is a type of deed where the grantor (seller) guarantees that he or she holds clear title to a piece of real estate and has a right to sell it to the grantee (buyer.) The guarantee is not limited to the time the grantor owned the property--it extends back to the property"s origins. A General Warranty deed includes six traditional forms of Covenants for Title.

Arbitration

Arbitration, a form of alternative dispute resolution (ADR), is a legal technique for the resolution of disputes outside the courts, wherein the parties to a dispute refer it to one or more persons (the "arbitrators", "arbiters" or "arbitral tribunal"), by whose decision (the "award") they agree to be bound. It is a settlement technique in which a third party reviews the case and imposes a decision that is legally binding for both sides. Other forms of ADR include mediation (a form of settlement negotiation facilitated by a neutral third party) and non-binding resolution by experts.

Quiet enjoyment

Under the common law, persons in possession of real property (either land owners or tenants) are entitled to the quiet enjoyment of their lands. If a neighbour interferes with that quiet enjoyment, either by creating smells, sounds, pollution or any other hazard that extends past the boundaries of the property, the affected party may make a claim in nuisance.

Legally, the term "nuisance" is traditionally used in three ways:

· 1) to describe an activity or condition that is harmful or annoying to others (e.g., indecent conduct, a rubbish heap or a smoking chimney)
· 2) to describe the harm caused by the before-mentioned activity or condition (e.g., loud noises or objectionable odors)
· 3) to describe a legal liability that arises from the combination of the two. However, the "interference" was not the result of a neighbor stealing land or trespassing on the land. Instead, it arose from activities taking place on another person"s land that affected the enjoyment of that land.

The law of nuisance was created to stop such bothersome activities or conduct when they unreasonably interfered either with the rights of other private landowners (i.e., private nuisance) or with the rights of the general public (i.e., public nuisance)

A public nuisance is an unreasonable interference with the public''s right to property. It includes conduct that interferes with public health, safety, peace or convenience.

Negotiable instrument

A Negotiable instrument is a specialized type of "contract" for the payment of money that is unconditional and capable of transfer by negotiation. Common examples include cheques, banknotes (paper money), and commercial paper.

A Negotiable instrument is not a contract, as contract formation requires an offer, acceptance, and consideration, none of which is an element of a Negotiable instrument.

Constitution

· Apostolic Constitution (a class of Roman Catholic Church documents)
· Constitution of the Roman Republic
· Constitutional court
· Constitutionalism
· Corporate Constitution
· Judicial activism
· Judicial restraint
· Judicial review

Judicial philosophies of Constitutional interpretation (note: generally specific to United States Constitutional law)

· List of national Constitutions
· Originalism
· Strict constructionism
· Textualism
· Proposed European Union Constitution

· Treaty of Lisbon (adopts same changes, but without Constitutional name)
· United Nations Charter

United States

· History of competition law
· Monopoly

· Coercive monopoly
· Natural monopoly
· Barriers to entry
· Market power
· SSNIP test
· Relevant market
· Merger control

Anti-competitive practices

· Monopolization
· Collusion

· Formation of cartels
· Price fixing
· Bid rigging
· Product bundling and tying
· Refusal to deal

· Group boycott
· Exclusive dealing
· Dividing territories
· Conscious parallelism
· Predatory pricing
· Misuse of patents and copyrights

Laws and doctrines

United States

· Sherman Antitrust Act
· Clayton Antitrust Act
· Robinson-Patman Act
· FTC Act
· Hart-Scott-Rodino Act
· Merger guidelines
· Essential facilities doctrine
· Noerr-Pennington doctrine
· Parker immunity doctrine
· Rule of reason

Europe

· UK competition law
· Irish competition law

Australia

· Trade Practices Act 1974

Enforcement authorities and organizations

Competition law history refers to attempts by governments to regulate competitive markets for goods and services, leading up to the modern competition or antitrust laws around the world today. The earliest records traces back to the efforts of Roman legislators to control price fluctuations and unfair trade practices. Through the Middle Ages in Europe, Kings and Queens repeatedly cracked down on monopolies, including those created through state legislation.

- International Competition Network
- List of competition regulators

Business

There are many ways in which a business may be owned under the legal system of England and Wales. Different types of ownership are suitable for organisations depending on the degree of control the owners wish to have over the business. The choice of ownership methor also relates to the organisations ability to raise funds for the business activities.

Cash

Two primary accounting methods, cash and accrual basis, are used to calculate taxable income for U.S. federal income taxes. According to the Internal Revenue Code, a taxpayer may compute taxable income by:

- the cash receipts and disbursements method;
- an accrual method;
- any other method permitted by the chapter; or
- any combination of the foregoing methods permitted under regulations prescribed by the Secretary.

As a general rule, a taxpayer must compute taxable income using the same accounting method he uses to compute income in keeping his books.

Damages

Damages for breach of contract is a common law remedy, available as of right. It is designed to compensate the victim for their actual loss as a result of the wrongdoer"s breach rather than to punish the wrongdoer. If no loss has been occasioned by the plaintiff, only nominal Damages will be awarded.

Risk of loss

Risk of loss is a term used in the law of contracts to determine which party should bear the burden of risk for damage occurring to goods after the sale has been completed, but before delivery has occurred. Such considerations generally come into play after the contract is formed but before buyer receives goods, something bad happens.

There are four risk of loss rules, in order of application:

- Agreement - the agreement of the parties controls
- Breach - the breaching party is liable for any uninsured loss even though breach is unrelated to the problem. Hence, if the breach is the time of delivery, and the goods show up broken, then the breaching rule applies risk of loss on the seller.
- Delivery by common carrier other than by seller.
    - risk of loss shifts from seller to buyer at the time that seller completes its delivery obligations
    - If it is a destination contract (FOB (buyer"s city)), then risk of loss is on the seller.
    - If it is a delivery contract (standard, or FOB (seller"s city)), then the risk of loss is on the buyer.
- If the seller is a merchant, then the risk of loss shifts to the buyer upon buyer"s "receipt" of the goods. If the buyer never takes possession, then the seller still has the risk of loss.

Sublease

In real estate law, Sublease is the name given to an arrangement in which the lessee in a lease assigns the lease to a third party, thereby making the old lessee the sublessor, and the new lessee the sublessee, or subtenant. This means you are renting and renting out the same property at the same time. For example, the owner of an office building may lease the whole building to a management company.

Obligation

An obligation is a requirement to take some course of action, whether legal or moral. There are also obligation s in other normative contexts, such as obligation s of etiquette, social obligation s, and possibly in terms of politics, where obligation s are requirements which must be fulfilled. These are generally legal obligation s, which can incur a penalty for unfulfilment, although certain people are obliged to carry out certain actions for other reasons as well, whether as a tradition or for social reasons.

Parol evidence

The Parol evidence rule is the legal application of a rule of substantive law in contract cases that prevents a party to a written contract from contradicting (or sometimes adding to) the terms of the contract by seeking the admission of evidence "extrinsic" (outside) to the contract. For example, Carl agrees in writing to sell Betty a car for $1,000. Betty argues that Carl told her that she would only need to pay Carl $800.

Parol evidence rule

The Parol evidence rule is the legal application of a rule of substantive law in contract cases that prevents a party to a written contract from contradicting (or sometimes adding to) the terms of the contract by seeking the admission of evidence "extrinsic" (outside) to the contract. For example, Carl agrees in writing to sell Betty a car for $1,000. Betty argues that Carl told her that she would only need to pay Carl $800.

Statute of Frauds	The Statute of Frauds refers to the requirement that certain kinds of contracts be made in writing and signed. Traditionally, the Statute of Frauds requires a writing signed by the defendant in the following circumstances: · Contracts in consideration of marriage. · Contracts which cannot be performed within one year. · Contracts for the transfer of an interest in land. · Contracts by the executor of a will to pay a debt of the estate with their own money. · Contracts for the sale of goods above a certain value. · Contracts in which one party becomes a surety (acts as guarantor) for another party"s debt or other obligation. This can be remembered by the mnemonic "MY LEGS": Marriage, one year, land, executor, goods, surety. The term Statute of Frauds comes from an English Act of Parliament passed in 1677 (authored by Sir Leoline Jenkins and passed by the Cavalier Parliament), and more properly called An Act for Prevention of Frauds and Perjuries. Many common law jurisdictions have made similar statutory provisions, while a number of civil law jurisdictions have equivalent legislation incorporated into their civil codes.
Consideration	Consideration is the legal concept of value in connection with contracts. It is anything of value in the common sense, promised to another when making a contract. It can take the form of money, physical objects, services, promised actions, or even abstinence from a future action.
Proprietorship	A sole Proprietorship). All assets of the business are owned by the proprietor and all debts of the business are his debts and he must pay them from his personal resources.
Freedom of contract	Freedom of contract or contractualism is the freedom of individuals to bargain among themselves the terms of their own contracts, without government interference. Anything more than minimal regulations and taxes may be seen as infringements. It is the underpinning of the theory of laissez-faire economics.
Misrepresentation	Misrepresentation is a contract law concept. It means a false statement of fact made by one party to another party, which has the effect of inducing that party into the contract. For example, under certain circumstances, false statements or promises made by a seller of goods regarding the quality or nature of the product that the seller has may constitute Misrepresentation.
Unconscionability	Unconscionability is a term used in contract law to describe a defense against the enforcement of a contract based on the presence of terms unfair to one party. Typically, such a contract is held to be unenforceable because the consideration offered is lacking or is so obviously inadequate that to enforce the contract would be unfair to the party seeking to escape the contract. In and of itself, inadequate consideration is likely not enough to make a contract unenforceable.

Employment	Employment is a contract between two parties, one being the employer and the other being the employee. An employee may be defined as: "A person in the service of another under any contract of hire, express or implied, oral or written, where the employer has the power or right to control and direct the employee in the material details of how the work is to be performed." Black"s Law Dictionary page 471 (5th ed. 1979).
Employment Discrimination	Employment discrimination (or workplace discrimination) is discrimination in hiring, promotion, job assignment, termination, and compensation. It includes various types of harassment. Many jurisdictions prohibit some types of Employment discrimination, often by forbidding discrimination based on certain traits ("protected categories").

Negotiable instrument	A Negotiable instrument is a specialized type of "contract" for the payment of money that is unconditional and capable of transfer by negotiation. Common examples include cheques, banknotes (paper money), and commercial paper. A Negotiable instrument is not a contract, as contract formation requires an offer, acceptance, and consideration, none of which is an element of a Negotiable instrument.
Bankruptcy	Bankruptcy is a legally declared inability or impairment of ability of an individual or organization to pay its creditors. Creditors may file a Bankruptcy petition against a debtor ("involuntary Bankruptcy") in an effort to recoup a portion of what they are owed or initiate a restructuring. In the majority of cases, however, Bankruptcy is initiated by the debtor (a "voluntary Bankruptcy" that is filed by the insolvent individual or organization).
Contract	Agreement is said to be reached when an offer capable of immediate acceptance is met with a "mirror image" acceptance (ie, an unqualified acceptance). The parties must have the necessary capacity to Contract and the Contract must not be either trifling, indeterminate, impossible or illegal. Contract law is based on the principle expressed in the Latin phrase pacta sunt servanda .
Lease	A Lease is a contract conferring a right on one person to possess property belonging to another person (called a landlord or lessor) to the exclusion of the owner landlord, and all others except with the invitation of the tenant. It is a rental agreement between landlord and tenant. The relationship between the tenant and the landlord is called a tenancy, and the right to possession by the tenant is sometimes called a Leasehold interest.
Arbitration	Arbitration, a form of alternative dispute resolution (ADR), is a legal technique for the resolution of disputes outside the courts, wherein the parties to a dispute refer it to one or more persons (the "arbitrators", "arbiters" or "arbitral tribunal"), by whose decision (the "award") they agree to be bound. It is a settlement technique in which a third party reviews the case and imposes a decision that is legally binding for both sides. Other forms of ADR include mediation (a form of settlement negotiation facilitated by a neutral third party) and non-binding resolution by experts.
Arbitration clause	An Arbitration clause is a commonly used clause in a contract that requires the parties to resolve their disputes through an arbitration process. Although such a clause may or may not specify that arbitration occur within a specific jurisdiction, it always binds the parties to a type of resolution outside of the courts, and is therefore considered a kind of forum selection clause. In the United States, the federal government has expressed a policy of support of Arbitration clauses, because they reduce the burden on court systems to resolve disputes.
Cash	Two primary accounting methods, cash and accrual basis, are used to calculate taxable income for U.S. federal income taxes. According to the Internal Revenue Code, a taxpayer may compute taxable income by: · the cash receipts and disbursements method; · an accrual method; · any other method permitted by the chapter; or · any combination of the foregoing methods permitted under regulations prescribed by the Secretary.

	As a general rule, a taxpayer must compute taxable income using the same accounting method he uses to compute income in keeping his books.
Rescission	In contract law, rescission has been defined as the unmaking of a contract between parties. rescission is the unwinding of a transaction. This is done to bring the parties, as far as possible, back to the position in which they were before they entered into a contract (the "status quo ante".)
Damages	Damages for breach of contract is a common law remedy, available as of right. It is designed to compensate the victim for their actual loss as a result of the wrongdoer"s breach rather than to punish the wrongdoer. If no loss has been occasioned by the plaintiff, only nominal Damages will be awarded.
Punitive Damages	Punitive Damages are damages not awarded in order to compensate the plaintiff, but in order to reform or deter the defendant and similar persons from pursuing a course of action such as that which damaged the plaintiff. punitive Damages are often awarded where compensatory damages are deemed an inadequate remedy. The court may impose them to prevent under-compensation of plaintiffs, to allow redress for undetectable torts and taking some strain away from the criminal justice system.
Vesting	In law, Vesting is to give an immediately secured right of present or future enjoyment. One has a vested right to an asset that cannot be taken away by any third party, even though one may not yet possess the asset. When the right, interest or title to the present or future possession of a legal estate can be transferred to any other party, it is termed a vested interest.
Pollution	Pollution is the introduction of contaminants into an environment that causes instability, disorder, harm or discomfort to the ecosystem i.e. physical systems or living organisms . Pollution can take the form of chemical substances, or energy, such as noise, heat, or light energy. Pollutants, the elements of Pollution, can be foreign substances or energies, or naturally occurring; when naturally occurring, they are considered contaminants when they exceed natural levels.
Omnibus clause	An Omnibus clause is a clause that provides that liability insurance for the designated automobile applies to the named insured, any member of the insured"s household, and to any person using the automobile with the insured"s permission, provided the use was within the scope of permission.
Product liability	Product liability is the area of law in which manufacturers, distributors, suppliers, retailers, and others who make products available to the public are held responsible for the injuries those products cause. In the United States, the claims most commonly associated with Product liability are negligence, strict liability, breach of warranty, and various consumer protection claims. The majority of Product liability laws are determined at the state level and vary widely from state to state.
Business	There are many ways in which a business may be owned under the legal system of England and Wales.

Different types of ownership are suitable for organisations depending on the degree of control the owners wish to have over the business. The choice of ownership methor also relates to the organisations ability to raise funds for the business activities.

Prenuptial	A prenuptial agreement, antenuptial agreement commonly abbreviated to prenup or prenupt, is a contract entered into prior to marriage or civil union by the people intending to marry. The content of a prenuptial agreement can vary widely, but commonly includes provisions for division of property and spousal support in the event of divorce or breakup of marriage. Many countries, including Canada, France, Italy, and Germany, have matrimonial regimes, in addition to in lieu of prenuptial agreements.
Probate	Probate is the legal process of administering the estate of a deceased person by resolving all claims and distributing the deceased person"s property under the valid will. A surrogate court decides the validity of a testator"s will. A probate interprets the instructions of the deceased, decides the executor as the personal representative of the estate, and adjudicates the interests of heirs and other parties who may have claims against the estate.
Settlor	In law a Settlor is a person who settles property on express trust for the benefit of beneficiaries. In some legal systems, a Settlor is also referred to as a trustor, or occasionally, a grantor or donor. Where the trust is a testamentary trust, the Settlor is usually referred to as the testator.
Statute	A statute is a formal written enactment of a legislative authority that governs a country, state, city, or county. Typically, statute s command or prohibit something, or declare policy. The word is often used to distinguish law made by legislative bodies from case law and the regulations issued by Government agencies.
Testate	Intestacy is the condition of the estate of a person who dies owning property greater than the sum of his or her enforceable debts and funeral expenses without having made a valid will or other binding declaration; alternatively where such a will or declaration has been made, but only applies to part of the estate, the remaining estate forms the "In Testate Estate". Intestacy law, also referred to as the law of descent and distribution or in Testate succession statutes, refers to the body of law that determines who is entitled to the property from the estate under the rules of inheritance. Intestacy has a limited application in those jurisdictions that follow civil law or Roman law because the concept of a will is itself less important; the doctrine of legitime automatically gives a deceased person"s relatives title to all or a large part of the estate"s property by operation of law, beyond the power of the deceased person to alter by legacy.
Testator	A Testator is a person who has written and executed a last will and testament that is in effect at the time of his/her death. It is any "person who makes a will." · A female Testator is sometimes referred to as a testatrix, particularly in older cases)

· A will is also known as a Last will and testament.
· Testacy means the status of being testate, that is, having executed a will. The property of such a person goes through the probate process.
· Intestacy means the status of not having made a will, or to have died without a valid will. The estate of a person who dies intestate, undergoes administration, rather than probate.
· The Attestation clause of a will is where the witnesses to a will attest to certain facts concerning the making of the will by the Testator, and where they sign their names as witnesses. .

Trust

In common law legal systems, a trust is an arrangement whereby property (including real, tangible and intangible) is managed by one person (or persons, or organizations) for the benefit of another. A trust is created by a settlor, who entrusts some or all of his or her property to people of his choice (the trustees.) The trustees hold legal title to the trust property (or trust corpus), but they are obliged to hold the property for the benefit of one or more individuals or organizations (the beneficiary, a.k.a. cestui que use or cestui que trust), usually specified by the settlor, who hold equitable title.

Uniform Probate Code

The Uniform Probate Code is a uniform act drafted by National Conference of Commissioners on Uniform State Laws (NCCUSL) governing inheritance and the decedents" estates in the USA. The primary purposes of the act were to streamline the probate process and to standardize and modernize the various state laws governing wills, trusts, and intestacy.
Drafting of the Uniform Probate Code began in 1964.

Testamentary Capacity

In the common law tradition, Testamentary capacity is the legal term of art used to describe a person"s legal and mental ability to make a valid will. This concept has also been called sound mind and memory or disposing mind and memory.
Adults are presumed to have the ability to make a will.

Valid

The term valid ity in logic applies to arguments or statements.
An argument is valid if and only if the truth of its premises entails the truth of its conclusion, it would be self-contradictory to affirm the premises and deny the conclusion. The corresponding conditional of a valid argument is a logical truth and the negation of its corresponding conditional is a contradiction.

Revocation

Revocation is the act of recall or annulment. It is the reversal of an act, the recalling of a grant, or the making void of some deed previously existing.
In the law of contracts, revocation is a type of remedy for buyers when the buyer accepts a nonconforming good from the seller.

Writ

In law, a writ is a formal writ ten order issued by a body with administrative or judicial jurisdiction; in modern usage, this public body is generally a court. Warrants, prerogative writ s and subpoenas are types of writ s; there are many others.
Originally, a writ was a letter or command from the Sovereign, or from some person with appropriate jurisdiction.

Writ of attachment	A Writ of attachment is a court order to "attach" or seize an asset. It is issued by a court to a law enforcement officer or sheriff. The Writ of attachment is issued in order to satisfy a judgment issued by the court.
Operation of law	The phrase "by Operation of law" is a legal term that indicates that a right or liability has been created for a party, irrespective of the intent of that party, because it is dictated by existing legal principles. For example, if a person dies without a will, his heirs are determined by Operation of law. Similarly, if a person marries or has a child after his or her will has been executed, the law writes this pretermitted spouse or pretermitted heir into the will if no provision for this situation was specifically included.
Chief brand officer	A Chief brand officer is a relatively new executive level position at a corporation, company, organization typically reporting directly to the CEO or board of directors. The Chief brand officer is responsible for a brand"s image, experience, and promise, and propagating it throughout all aspects of the company. The brand officer oversees marketing, advertising, design, public relations and customer service departments.
Contract	Agreement is said to be reached when an offer capable of immediate acceptance is met with a "mirror image" acceptance (ie, an unqualified acceptance). The parties must have the necessary capacity to Contract and the Contract must not be either trifling, indeterminate, impossible or illegal. Contract law is based on the principle expressed in the Latin phrase pacta sunt servanda .
Probate Court	A surrogate court, sometimes referred to as probate Court, is a specialized court which deals with matters of probate and the administration of estates. It adjudicates in cases to do with the distribution of deceased persons" estates. The surrogate court issues the grant of probate or, if a person dies intestate, a grant of administration, thereby giving judicial approval to the personal representative to administer matters of the estate.
Retirement	Retirement is the point where a person stops employment completely. A person may also semi-retire and keep some sort of Retirement job, out of choice rather than necessity. This usually happens upon reaching a determined age, when physical conditions don"t allow the person to work any more (by illness or accident), or even for personal choice (usually in the presence of an adequate pension or personal savings.)
Tenancy	Leasehold is a form of property tenure where one party buys the right to occupy land or a building for a given length of time. As lease is a legal estate, leasehold estate can be bought and sold on the open market. A leasehold thus differs from a freehold where the ownership of a property is purchased outright and thereafter held for an indeterminate length of time, and also differs from a tenancy where a property is let on a periodic basis such as weekly or monthly.
Child labour	Child labour refers to the employment of children at regular and sustained labour. This practice is considered exploitative by many international organizations and is illegal in many countries. Child labour was utilized to varying extents through most of history, but entered public dispute with the advent of universal schooling, with changes in working conditions during the industrial revolution, and with the emergence of the concepts of workers" and children"s rights.

Trustee

Trustee is a legal term that refers to a holder of property on behalf of a beneficiary. A trust can be set up either to benefit particular persons, or for any charitable purposes (but not generally for non-charitable purposes): typical examples are a will trust for the testator"s children and family, a pension trust (to confer benefits on employees and their families), and a charitable trust. In all cases, the Trustee may be a person or company, whether or not they are a prospective beneficiary.

Bankruptcy

Bankruptcy is a legally declared inability or impairment of ability of an individual or organization to pay its creditors. Creditors may file a Bankruptcy petition against a debtor ("involuntary Bankruptcy") in an effort to recoup a portion of what they are owed or initiate a restructuring. In the majority of cases, however, Bankruptcy is initiated by the debtor (a "voluntary Bankruptcy" that is filed by the insolvent individual or organization).

Testamentary Trust

A Testamentary trust (sometimes referred to as a will trust) is a trust which arises upon the death of the testator, and which is specified in his will Testamentary trust literally means a trust in a will.) A will may contain more than one Testamentary trust and may address all or any portion of the estate.

Testamentary trust s are distinguished from inter vivos trusts, which are created during the settlor"s lifetime.

Spendthrift Trust

A Spendthrift trust is a trust that is created for the benefit of a person (often because he or she is unable to control spending) that gives an independent trustee full authority to make decisions as to how the trust funds may be spent for the benefit of the beneficiary. Creditors of the beneficiary generally cannot reach the funds in the trust, and the funds are not actually under the control of the beneficiary.

The creator of a trust (whether or not it is a Spendthrift trust) is sometimes called the "trustor," "grantor," or "settlor" of the trust.

Resulting Trust

A Resulting trust is the creation of an implied trust by operation of law, as where property gets transferred to one who pays nothing for it; and then is implied to have held the property for benefit of another person. The trust property is said to "result" back to the transferor . In this instance, the word "result" means "in the result, remains with", or something similar to "revert" except that in the result the beneficial interest is held on trust for the settlor.

Power of attorney

A power of attorney or letter of attorney in common law systems or mandate in civil law systems is an authorization to act on someone else"s behalf in a legal or business matter. The person authorizing the other to act is the principal, granter or donor (of the power), and the one authorized to act is the agent, the attorney-in-fact, or in many Common Law jurisdictions, simply the attorney.

The term attorney-in-fact is commonly used in the United States, to make a distinction from the term Attorney at law.

Arthur Andersen	Arthur Andersen LLP, based in Chicago, was once one of the "Big Five" accounting firms among PricewaterhouseCoopers, Deloitte Touche Tohmatsu, Ernst ' Young and KPMG, providing auditing, tax, and consulting services to large corporations. In 2002, the firm voluntarily surrendered its licenses to practice as Certified Public Accountants in the United States after being found guilty of criminal charges relating to the firm"s handling of the auditing of Enron, the energy corporation, resulting in the loss of 85,000 jobs. Although the verdict was subsequently overturned by the Supreme Court of the United States, it has not returned as a viable business.
Lease	A Lease is a contract conferring a right on one person to possess property belonging to another person (called a landlord or lessor) to the exclusion of the owner landlord, and all others except with the invitation of the tenant. It is a rental agreement between landlord and tenant. The relationship between the tenant and the landlord is called a tenancy, and the right to possession by the tenant is sometimes called a Leasehold interest.
Sarbanes-Oxley Act	The Sarbanes-Oxley Act of 2002 (Pub.L. 107-204, 116 Stat. 745, enacted July 30, 2002), also known as the Public Company Accounting Reform and Investor Protection Act of 2002 and commonly called Sarbanes-Oxley, Sarbox or SOX, is a United States federal law enacted on July 30, 2002, as a reaction to a number of major corporate and accounting scandals including those affecting Enron, Tyco International, Adelphia, Peregrine Systems and WorldCom.
Contract	Agreement is said to be reached when an offer capable of immediate acceptance is met with a "mirror image" acceptance (ie, an unqualified acceptance). The parties must have the necessary capacity to Contract and the Contract must not be either trifling, indeterminate, impossible or illegal. Contract law is based on the principle expressed in the Latin phrase pacta sunt servanda .
Duty	Duty (from "due," that which is owing, O. Fr. deu, did, past participle of devoir; Lat. debere, debitum; cf.
Terrorism	Terrorism is a policy or ideology of violence intended to intimidate or cause terror for the purpose of "exerting pressure on decision making by state bodies." The term "terror" is largely used to indicate clandestine, low-intensity violence that targets civilians and generates public fear. Thus "terror" is distinct from asymmetric warfare, and violates the concept of a common law of war in which civilian life is regarded. The term "-ism" is used to indicate an ideology --typically one that claims its attacks are in the domain of a "just war" concept, though most condemn such as crimes against humanity.
Embezzlement	Embezzlement is the act of dishonestly appropriating or secreting assets, usually financial in nature, by one or more individuals to whom such assets have been entrusted. It is a kind of financial fraud. For instance, a clerk or cashier handling large sums of money can embezzle cash from his or her employer, a lawyer can embezzle funds from clients" trust accounts, a financial advisor can embezzle funds from investors, or a spouse can embezzle funds from his or her partner.

Obligation

An obligation is a requirement to take some course of action, whether legal or moral. There are also obligation s in other normative contexts, such as obligation s of etiquette, social obligation s, and possibly in terms of politics, where obligation s are requirements which must be fulfilled. These are generally legal obligation s, which can incur a penalty for unfulfilment, although certain people are obliged to carry out certain actions for other reasons as well, whether as a tradition or for social reasons.

Prima facie

Prima facie is a Latin expression meaning on its first appearance, or by first instance; at first sight. The literal translation would be "from first face", prima first, facie face, both in the ablative case. It is used in modern legal English to signify that on first examination, a matter appears to be self-evident from the facts.

Damages

Damages for breach of contract is a common law remedy, available as of right. It is designed to compensate the victim for their actual loss as a result of the wrongdoer"s breach rather than to punish the wrongdoer. If no loss has been occasioned by the plaintiff, only nominal Damages will be awarded.

Limited liability

Limited liability is a concept whereby a person"s financial liability is limited to a fixed sum, most commonly the value of a person"s investment in a company or partnership with Limited liability. In other words, if a company with Limited liability is sued, then the plaintiffs are suing the company, not its owners or investors. A shareholder in a limited company is not personally liable for any of the debts of the company, other than for the value of his investment in that company.

Misrepresentation

Misrepresentation is a contract law concept. It means a false statement of fact made by one party to another party, which has the effect of inducing that party into the contract. For example, under certain circumstances, false statements or promises made by a seller of goods regarding the quality or nature of the product that the seller has may constitute Misrepresentation.

Privity

The doctrine of privity in contract law provides that a contract cannot confer rights or impose obligations arising under it on any person or agent except the parties to it.

The premise is that only parties to contracts should be able to sue to enforce their rights or claim damages as such. However, the doctrine has proven problematic due to its implications upon contracts made for the benefit of third parties who are unable to enforce the obligations of the contracting parties.

Statute

A statute is a formal written enactment of a legislative authority that governs a country, state, city, or county. Typically, statute s command or prohibit something, or declare policy. The word is often used to distinguish law made by legislative bodies from case law and the regulations issued by Government agencies.

Statute of Frauds

The Statute of Frauds refers to the requirement that certain kinds of contracts be made in writing and signed.

Traditionally, the Statute of Frauds requires a writing signed by the defendant in the following circumstances:

· Contracts in consideration of marriage.
· Contracts which cannot be performed within one year.
· Contracts for the transfer of an interest in land.
· Contracts by the executor of a will to pay a debt of the estate with their own money.
· Contracts for the sale of goods above a certain value.
· Contracts in which one party becomes a surety (acts as guarantor) for another party"s debt or other obligation.

This can be remembered by the mnemonic "MY LEGS": Marriage, one year, land, executor, goods, surety.

The term Statute of Frauds comes from an English Act of Parliament passed in 1677 (authored by Sir Leoline Jenkins and passed by the Cavalier Parliament), and more properly called An Act for Prevention of Frauds and Perjuries. Many common law jurisdictions have made similar statutory provisions, while a number of civil law jurisdictions have equivalent legislation incorporated into their civil codes.

Estoppel

Estoppel is a legal doctrine at common law, where a party is barred from claiming or denying an argument on an equitable ground. Estoppel complements the requirement of consideration in contract law. In general, Estoppel protects an aggrieved party, if the counter-party induced an expectation from the aggrieved party, and the aggrieved party reasonably relied on the expectation and would suffer detriment if the expectation is not met.

Partnership

A Partnership is a type of business entity in which partners (owners) share with each other the profits or losses of the business. Partnership s are often favored over corporations for taxation purposes, as the Partnership structure does not generally incur a tax on profits before it is distributed to the partners (i.e. there is no dividend tax levied.) However, depending on the Partnership structure and the jurisdiction in which it operates, owners of a Partnership may be exposed to greater personal liability than they would as shareholders of a corporation.

Due diligence

Due diligence is a term used for a number of concepts involving either the performance of an investigation of a business or person, or the performance of an act with a certain standard of care. It can be a legal obligation, but the term will more commonly apply to voluntary investigations. A common example of Due diligence in various industries is the process through which a potential acquirer evaluates a target company or its assets for acquisition.

Private Securities Litigation Reform Act

The United States Private Securities Litigation Reform Act of 1995, Pub. L. 104-67, 109 Stat. 737 (codified as amended in scattered sections of 15 U.S.C.) ("Private Securities Litigation Reform Act") implemented several substantive changes affecting certain cases brought under the federal securities laws, including changes related to pleading, discovery, liability, class representation, and awards fees and expenses.

Securities Act	Congress enacted the Securities Act of 1933 (the "1933 Act," the "Truth in Securities Act" or the "Federal Securities Act", 48 Stat. 74, enacted 1933-05-27, codified at 15 U.S.C. Â§ 77a et seq.), in the aftermath of the stock market crash of 1929 and during the ensuing Great Depression.
Securities and Exchange Commission	The U.S. Securities and Exchange Commission is an independent agency of the United States government which holds primary responsibility for enforcing the federal securities laws and regulating the securities industry, the nation"s stock and options exchanges, and other electronic securities markets. The SEC was created by section 4 of the Securities Exchange Act of 1934 (now codified as 15 U.S.C. Â§ 78d and commonly referred to as the 1934 Act.)

United Nations Convention on Contracts for the International Sale of Goods	The United Nations Convention on Contracts for the International Sale of Goods is a treaty offering a uniform international sales law that, as of July 2008, had been ratified by 71 countries that account for a significant proportion of world trade, making it one of the most successful international uniform laws. Japan is the most recent State to have ratified the Convention. It allows exporters to avoid choice of law issues as it offers "accepted substantive rules on which contracting parties, courts, and arbitrators may rely".
Constitution	· Apostolic Constitution (a class of Roman Catholic Church documents) · Constitution of the Roman Republic · Constitutional court · Constitutionalism · Corporate Constitution · Judicial activism · Judicial restraint · Judicial review Judicial philosophies of Constitutional interpretation (note: generally specific to United States Constitutional law) · List of national Constitutions · Originalism · Strict constructionism · Textualism · Proposed European Union Constitution · Treaty of Lisbon (adopts same changes, but without Constitutional name) · United Nations Charter
Contract	Agreement is said to be reached when an offer capable of immediate acceptance is met with a "mirror image" acceptance (ie, an unqualified acceptance). The parties must have the necessary capacity to Contract and the Contract must not be either trifling, indeterminate, impossible or illegal. Contract law is based on the principle expressed in the Latin phrase pacta sunt servanda .
Star	The STAR (Situation, Task, Action, Result) format is a job interview technique used by interviewers to gather all the relevant information about a specific capability that the job requires. This interview format is said to have a higher degree of predictability of future on-the-job performance than the traditional interview.

· Situation: The interviewer wants you to present a recent challenge and situation in which you found yourself.
· Task: What did you have to achieve? The interviewer will be looking to see what you were trying to achieve from the situation.
· Action: What did you do? The interviewer will be looking for information on what you did, why you did it and what were the alternatives.
· Results: What was the outcome of your actions? What did you achieve through your actions and did you meet your objectives. What did you learn from this experience and have you used this learning since? .

Stare decisis

Stare decisis is the legal principle under which judges are obligated to follow the precedents established in prior decisions.

In the United States, which uses a common law system in its federal courts and most of its state courts, the Ninth Circuit Court of Appeals has stated:

Stare decisis is the policy of the court to stand by precedent; the term is but an abbreviation of Stare decisis et quieta non movere -- "to stand by and adhere to decisions and not disturb what is settled." Consider the word "decisis." The word means, literally and legally, the decision. Nor is the doctrine stare dictis; it is not "to stand by or keep to what was said." Nor is the doctrine stare rationibus decidendi -- "to keep to the rationes decidendi of past cases." Rather, under the doctrine of Stare decisis a case is important only for what it decides -- for the "what," not for the "why," and not for the "how." Insofar as precedent is concerned, Stare decisis is important only for the decision, for the detailed legal consequence following a detailed set of facts.

Statute

A statute is a formal written enactment of a legislative authority that governs a country, state, city, or county. Typically, statute s command or prohibit something, or declare policy. The word is often used to distinguish law made by legislative bodies from case law and the regulations issued by Government agencies.

Uniform Commercial Code

The Uniform Commercial Code is one of a number of uniform acts that have been promulgated in conjunction with efforts to harmonize the law of sales and other commercial transactions in all 50 states within the United States of America. This objective is deemed important because of the prevalence today of commercial transactions that extend beyond one state (for example, where the goods are manufactured in state A, warehoused in state B, sold from state C and delivered in state D.) The Uniform Commercial Code deals primarily with transactions involving personal property (movable property), not real property (immovable property.)

United States

· History of competition law
· Monopoly

· Coercive monopoly
· Natural monopoly
· Barriers to entry
· Market power
· SSNIP test
· Relevant market
· Merger control

Anti-competitive practices

· Monopolization
· Collusion

· Formation of cartels
· Price fixing
· Bid rigging
· Product bundling and tying
· Refusal to deal

· Group boycott
· Exclusive dealing
· Dividing territories
· Conscious parallelism
· Predatory pricing
· Misuse of patents and copyrights

Laws and doctrines

United States

· Sherman Antitrust Act
· Clayton Antitrust Act
· Robinson-Patman Act
· FTC Act
· Hart-Scott-Rodino Act
· Merger guidelines
· Essential facilities doctrine
· Noerr-Pennington doctrine
· Parker immunity doctrine
· Rule of reason

Europe

· UK competition law
· Irish competition law

Australia

· Trade Practices Act 1974

Enforcement authorities and organizations

Competition law history refers to attempts by governments to regulate competitive markets for goods and services, leading up to the modern competition or antitrust laws around the world today. The earliest records traces back to the efforts of Roman legislators to control price fluctuations and unfair trade practices. Through the Middle Ages in Europe, Kings and Queens repeatedly cracked down on monopolies, including those created through state legislation.

· International Competition Network
· List of competition regulators

Chief brand officer

A Chief brand officer is a relatively new executive level position at a corporation, company, organization typically reporting directly to the CEO or board of directors. The Chief brand officer is responsible for a brand"s image, experience, and promise, and propagating it throughout all aspects of the company. The brand officer oversees marketing, advertising, design, public relations and customer service departments.

Business

There are many ways in which a business may be owned under the legal system of England and Wales. Different types of ownership are suitable for organisations depending on the degree of control the owners wish to have over the business. The choice of ownership methor also relates to the organisations ability to raise funds for the business activities.

Ratification

Ratification is the act of approving and paying for supplies or services provided to and accepted by the government as a result of an unauthorized commitment. It gives official sanction or approval to a formal document such as a treaty or constitution. It includes the process of adopting an international treaty by the legislature, a constitution, or another nationally binding document (such as an amendment to a constitution) by the agreement of multiple sub-national entities.

Service provider

A service provider is an entity that provides services to other entities. Usually this refers to a business that provides subscription or web service to other businesses or individuals. Examples of these services include Internet access, Mobile phone operator, and web application hosting.

Sovereign Immunity

Sovereign immunity is a type of immunity that in common law jurisdictions traces its origins from early English law. Generally speaking it is the doctrine that the sovereign or state cannot commit a legal wrong and is immune from civil suit or criminal prosecution; hence the saying, the king (or queen) can do no wrong. In many cases, governments have waived this immunity to allow for suits; in some cases, an individual may technically appear as defendant on the state"s behalf.

Joint venture	A Joint venture is an entity formed between two or more parties to undertake economic activity together. The parties agree to create a new entity by both contributing equity, and they then share in the revenues, expenses, and control of the enterprise. The venture can be for one specific project only, or a continuing business relationship such as the Fuji Xerox Joint venture.
License	The verb License or grant License means to give permission. The noun License refers to that permission as well as to the document memorializing that permission. License may be granted by a party to another party as an element of an agreement between those parties.
Patent	A patent is a set of exclusive rights granted by a state to an inventor or his assignee for a limited period of time in exchange for a disclosure of an invention. The procedure for granting patent s, the requirements placed on the patent ee and the extent of the exclusive rights vary widely between countries according to national laws and international agreements. Typically, however, a patent application must include one or more claims defining the invention which must be new, inventive, and useful or industrially applicable.
Trade secret	A trade secret is a formula, practice, process, design, instrument, pattern by which a business can obtain an economic advantage over competitors or customers. In some jurisdictions, such secrets are referred to as "confidential information" or "classified information". The precise language by which a trade secret is defined varies by jurisdiction (as do the particular types of information that are subject to trade secret protection.)
Trademark	A trademark or trade mark is a distinctive sign or indicator used by an individual, business organization and to distinguish its products or services from those of other entities. A trademark is designated by the following symbols: · â„¢ (for an unregistered trademark that is, a mark used to promote or brand goods); · â„ (for an unregistered service mark, that is, a mark used to promote or brand services); and · Â® (for a registered trademark) A trademark is a type of intellectual property, and typically a name, word, phrase, logo, symbol, design, image, or a combination of these elements. There is also a range of non-conventional trademark s comprising marks which do not fall into these standard categories. The owner of a registered trademark may commence legal proceedings for trademark infringement to prevent unauthorized use of that trademark
Trading with the Enemy Act	The Trading with the Enemy Act, sometimes abbreviated as TWEA, is a United States federal law, 12 U.S.C. Â§ 95a, enacted in 1917 to restrict trade with countries hostile to the United States. The law gives the President the power to oversee or restrict any and all trade between the U.S. and her enemies in times of war.

Tariff	A Tariff is a duty imposed on goods when they are moved across a political boundary. They are usually associated with protectionism, the economic policy of restraining trade between nations. For political reasons, Tariff s are usually imposed on imported goods, although they may also be imposed on exported goods.
Duty	Duty (from "due," that which is owing, O. Fr. deu, did, past participle of devoir; Lat. debere, debitum; cf.
Obligation	An obligation is a requirement to take some course of action, whether legal or moral. There are also obligation s in other normative contexts, such as obligation s of etiquette, social obligation s, and possibly in terms of politics, where obligation s are requirements which must be fulfilled. These are generally legal obligation s, which can incur a penalty for unfulfilment, although certain people are obliged to carry out certain actions for other reasons as well, whether as a tradition or for social reasons.
Sarbanes-Oxley Act	The Sarbanes-Oxley Act of 2002 (Pub.L. 107-204, 116 Stat. 745, enacted July 30, 2002), also known as the Public Company Accounting Reform and Investor Protection Act of 2002 and commonly called Sarbanes-Oxley, Sarbox or SOX, is a United States federal law enacted on July 30, 2002, as a reaction to a number of major corporate and accounting scandals including those affecting Enron, Tyco International, Adelphia, Peregrine Systems and WorldCom.
Age Discrimination in Employment Act	The Age Discrimination in Employment Act of 1967, Pub. L. No. 90-202, 81 Stat. 602 (Dec.
Employment	Employment is a contract between two parties, one being the employer and the other being the employee. An employee may be defined as: "A person in the service of another under any contract of hire, express or implied, oral or written, where the employer has the power or right to control and direct the employee in the material details of how the work is to be performed." Black"s Law Dictionary page 471 (5th ed. 1979).
Employment discrimination	Employment discrimination (or workplace discrimination) is discrimination in hiring, promotion, job assignment, termination, and compensation. It includes various types of harassment. Many jurisdictions prohibit some types of Employment discrimination, often by forbidding discrimination based on certain traits ("protected categories").
Sexual harassment	Sexual harassment is unwelcome harassment of a sexual nature, or based upon the receiving party"s sex or gender. In some contexts or circumstances, Sexual harassment may be illegal. It includes a range of behavior from seemingly mild transgressions and annoyances to actual sexual abuse or sexual assault.

Reasonable accommodation

Reasonable accommodation is a term used in Canada to refer to the theory that equality rights set out in section 15 of the Canadian Charter of Rights and Freedoms demand that accommodation be made to various ethnic minorities. The concept is especially applied with reference to the anti-discrimination laws in Québec"s Charter of Human Rights and Freedoms. (The origin of the term "Reasonable accommodation" is found in labour law jurisprudence, specifically Central Okanagan School District No.

Tort

Tort law is a body of law that addresses, and provides remedies for, civil wrongs not arising out of contractual obligations. A person who suffers legal damages may be able to use Tort law to receive compensation from someone who is legally responsible, or "liable," for those injuries. Generally speaking, Tort law defines what constitutes a legal injury and establishes the circumstances under which one person may be held liable for another"s injury.

Arbitration

Arbitration, a form of alternative dispute resolution (ADR), is a legal technique for the resolution of disputes outside the courts, wherein the parties to a dispute refer it to one or more persons (the "arbitrators", "arbiters" or "arbitral tribunal"), by whose decision (the "award") they agree to be bound. It is a settlement technique in which a third party reviews the case and imposes a decision that is legally binding for both sides. Other forms of ADR include mediation (a form of settlement negotiation facilitated by a neutral third party) and non-binding resolution by experts.

Child labour

Child labour refers to the employment of children at regular and sustained labour. This practice is considered exploitative by many international organizations and is illegal in many countries. Child labour was utilized to varying extents through most of history, but entered public dispute with the advent of universal schooling, with changes in working conditions during the industrial revolution, and with the emergence of the concepts of workers" and children"s rights.

Statute of Frauds

The Statute of Frauds refers to the requirement that certain kinds of contracts be made in writing and signed.

Traditionally, the Statute of Frauds requires a writing signed by the defendant in the following circumstances:

· Contracts in consideration of marriage.
· Contracts which cannot be performed within one year.
· Contracts for the transfer of an interest in land.
· Contracts by the executor of a will to pay a debt of the estate with their own money.
· Contracts for the sale of goods above a certain value.
· Contracts in which one party becomes a surety (acts as guarantor) for another party"s debt or other obligation.

This can be remembered by the mnemonic "MY LEGS": Marriage, one year, land, executor, goods, surety.

	The term Statute of Frauds comes from an English Act of Parliament passed in 1677 (authored by Sir Leoline Jenkins and passed by the Cavalier Parliament), and more properly called An Act for Prevention of Frauds and Perjuries. Many common law jurisdictions have made similar statutory provisions, while a number of civil law jurisdictions have equivalent legislation incorporated into their civil codes.
Consumer protection	Consumer protection laws are designed to ensure fair competition and the free flow of truthful information in the marketplace. The laws are designed to prevent businesses that engage in fraud or specified unfair practices from gaining an advantage over competitors and may provide additional protection for the weak and those unable to take care of themselves. Consumer protection laws are a form of government regulation which protects the interests of consumers.
Estoppel	Estoppel is a legal doctrine at common law, where a party is barred from claiming or denying an argument on an equitable ground. Estoppel complements the requirement of consideration in contract law. In general, Estoppel protects an aggrieved party, if the counter-party induced an expectation from the aggrieved party, and the aggrieved party reasonably relied on the expectation and would suffer detriment if the expectation is not met.
Breach of contract	Breach of contract is a legal concept in which a binding agreement or bargained-for exchange is not honored by one or more of the parties to the contract by non-performance or interference with the other party''s performance. A minor breach, a partial breach or an immaterial breach, occurs when the non-breaching party is unentitled to an order for performance of its obligations, but only to collect the actual amount of their damages. For example, suppose a homeowner hires a contractor to install new plumbing and insists that the pipes, which will ultimately be sealed behind the walls, be red.

LaVergne, TN USA
13 October 2010
200642LV00001B/13/P

9 781616 544188